AUTHOR	CLASS
PLOWRIGHT, A.	796.51/PLO.

TITLE	Plowright follows Wainwright

PLOWRIGHT FOLLOWS WAINWRIGHT

Alan Plowright

MICHAEL JOSEPH
LONDON

MICHAEL JOSEPH LTD

Published by the Penguin Group
27 Wrights Lane, London w8 5tz
Viking Penguin Inc., 375 Hudson Street, New York, New York 10014, usa
Penguin Books Australia Ltd, Ringwood, Victoria, Australia
Penguin Books Canada Ltd, 10 Alcorn Avenue, Toronto, Ontario, Canada m4v 3b2
Penguin Books (NZ) Ltd, 182–190 Wairau Road, Auckland 10, New Zealand

Penguin Books Ltd, Registered Offices: Harmondsworth, Middlesex, England

First published 1995

Copyright © Alan Plowright 1995

Filmset by Datix International Limited, Bungay, Suffolk
Printed in England by Clays Ltd, St Ives plc
Set in 10/13¼ pt Monophoto Garamond

A CIP catalogue record for this book is available from the British Library

isbn 07181 3942 9

Contents

Dedication

I would like to humbly dedicate this book to Alfred Wainwright who introduced me to so many beautiful places.

I would also like to dedicate it to all those who feature in the book, and to those who helped me compile it. Without them it could not have been written.

Introduction

This book is intended as a personal tribute to Alfred Wainwright, the best loved creator of walking guides. 'Wainwright', as he was and is affectionately known, sadly died in 1991 but he will live forever in the memory of all who care about the countryside and are enthusiastic walkers. The story will follow many of the famous guides that Wainwright lovingly created over a period of thirty-five years, and along the way I hope it will illustrate what your average long-distance walker might expect to find or experience on his travels.

After commencing with walks in the limestone country of the Yorkshire Dales, where I broke in my boots, the story moves on to cover the formidable challenge of the Pennine Way. Wainwright's beloved Lakeland could not be missed, and that chapter describes my first two (wet, extremely wet) visits. Finally comes an encounter with what is probably the finest route, the Coast to Coast path from St Bees in Cumbria to Robin Hood's Bay on the North Sea.

I have written about the walks included in this book in the form of a narrative which is not intended as a definite guide to their routes. I have made reference at appropriate points in the text to available material concerning each particular walk and this will provide up-to-date route information and, where appropriate, details about official and unofficial organisations and the all-important safety factors. For example, on the Pennine Way route changes are on-going due to the continual repair of the main path. It is essential in the case of this walk that you use the revised edition (1994) of Wainwright's *Pennine Way Companion*, and also obtain an update on the current route changes from the Countryside Commission. Similarly, there have been a number of important changes to the Coast to Coast Walk, and these are listed in both the revised edition (1994) of Wainwright's *Coast to Coast Walk*, as well as the Ordnance Survey maps. Full details of the material available is given in the Appendices at the back of the book.

While following in the footsteps of the unforgettable and inimitable Wainwright you will discover a world of agony, ecstasy, companionship and hard-won experience.

It is laid before you, blisters and all!

Alan Plowright, 1995.

CHAPTER ONE

The Awakening

'Please give a warm welcome to Mr Wainwright.' It is strange how often I have heard these words of introduction to my slide lectures on walking. I always show my appreciation for the unintentional compliment, but hasten to point out that although our names are similar I should not be mistaken for the master of walking guides.

It was this common error, however, that spawned the idea of writing this book. The title may appear pretentious because Alfred Wainwright is an impossible act to follow. My only claim to a common characteristic shared with the great man is the mop of auburn hair that we both sported in our younger days. AW's turned white in his later years, whereas mine is now tinged with grey. The wiry thatch did not diminish with age in either case. Alfred Wainwright is known as 'Wainwright' to the followers of his guide books, and as 'AW' to his friends. Although I never had the honour or pleasure of meeting him, I like to think of him as a friend and have therefore used AW through the book.

Although I now class myself as an enthusiastic and quite experienced walker, I could not aspire to filling the boots of the man who was an inspiration to millions. He expressed his love of the countryside through, first, his meticulous Pictorial Guides, then his books with accompanying photographs for armchair walkers, and finally the exciting television series. Thus his popularity has spread to a host of followers, ranging from avid long-distance walkers to those who have never set foot on the hills.

There is no shortage today of books of the genre, but Wainwright's will live in the memory as immaculate accounts of walking, route finding and sheer enjoyment of what initially started out for him as a hobby, something to do whilst on holiday. He virtually devoted his life to researching his walks, drawing his superb maps and detailing the comprehensive instructions that accompany them. Thousands of users of his guides have found that the need for Ordnance Survey maps hardly arises above the intake walls, although essential for public access on to the fells from the valleys or starting points. I have always liked the underlying humour of his sometimes quirky observations of people and places. 'The signpost at the Tan Hill junction that says Keld ¼ deserves an Oscar: this is the longest quarter of a mile in the North of England.' When I was walking his long-distance routes it was a pleasure each evening to relax and read his account of what was in store on the following day's walk. This is not to say that I necessarily agreed with every observation, or automatically disliked his pet hates, such as Black Hill on the Pennine Way. This, he says with great emphasis, is not a place to be enjoyed. Although its summit is certainly boggy and desolate, I cannot help but marvel at the skill and tenacity of the Royal Ordnance Corps who erected the triangulation point, known as the 'Soldier's Lump', in the middle of this seemingly impregnable quagmire. Also, to wonder how they got it to that spot and managed to stop it from sinking into the oozing peat.

I should say that until nine years ago I had never even heard of the man, let alone done any serious walking.

Thinking back to my earlier years, I suppose I must have nurtured a latent desire to walk the fells. I remember during a holiday with my family in North Wales, I felt the urge to climb the overgrown spoil heaps that towered over Penmaenmawr so, one evening, I and my two sons made the steep ascent and enjoyed a fine view of the sunset over the Menai Straits, a scene which has remained in my memory ever since.

The thought of walking as a hobby did not enter my head until the children had grown up and gone to university. Things started in a simple way by my crossing the road where I live and strolling around the edge of nearby Baildon Moor. The reason for this sudden exertion was twofold. First, the reason I gave to my friends: to get some fresh air. Second, the reason I whispered to myself: to keep the middle-aged spread at bay. We did not walk as a family; my wife had other interests and my children were busy with their studies.

I feel that a brief description of the local area is worthwhile, as it was a significant factor in awakening my interest in walking and the countryside. I found that Baildon Moor had much more to offer than had previously met my eye. I had played cricket on its grassy slopes with my children and had huddled around the crackling bonfires with family and neighbours each Plot night. We didn't have a dog ourselves but a number of friends did and they were able to tell me about some of the best places to walk.

I soon became familiar with the network of paths across the moor that had lain undiscovered by me for years. On its higher reaches I saw remains of former mine workings, with bell pits much in evidence. The moor had been inhabited since prehistoric times and its summit was used for ancient rites of worship, including, apparently, human sacrifices. Now the only landmark on the summit is the trig pillar set amongst the undulating moorland, and the view from this point is imposing, taking in most of the Leeds/Bradford conurbation towards the south-east. Nearer to hand, the Leeds and Liverpool Canal can be seen wending its way through the town of Shipley and the adjoining village of Saltaire. This is an area rich in industrial history and is well worth visiting. Further up the Aire valley, the river, canal and trunk road travel side by side through Bingley and Keighley, and above the town of Keighley stretches Haworth Moor which, of course, is in the middle of Brontë country. Venture on these moors at your peril for it is little wonder that the Brontë family was decimated by consumption. Some hardy souls do walk across them to the Brontë Falls and onwards to the ruined farmhouse perched high up at Top Withens. In inclement weather, this bleak and lonely spot is fit only for sheep, but the view from it is something to be admired.

The local sheep have to be very hardy but have learned to look after themselves. The remains of the farmhouse, supposedly the one depicted in *Wuthering Heights*, lie at the side of the Pennine Way footpath, and the wily sheep have twigged that numerous walkers passing along this boggy path often find the ruins a convenient place to take the weight off their blisters and have a well-earned snack. Immediately the sheep queue up to help them dispose of the food and seem to have no qualms about searching rucksacks for further supplies. I experienced exactly this when I was on my Pennine Way walk. Even though I was tired from having made the long pull up onto Haworth Moor from Walshaw Dean, it was very hard to begrudge those poor sheep a share of my sandwiches as I huddled beside the ruins trying to keep my circulation going.

Swinging roughly ninety degrees northwards from Brontë country, the brooding expanse of Ilkley Moor dominates the skyline. This moor, which is part of the larger Rombalds Moor, divides the Aire Valley from Wharfedale and moorland stretches nearly to the Lancashire border. Completing the landmarks on view from the vantage point on top of Baildon Moor is the warning beacon on Otley Chevin. Its distinctive red light alerts aircraft approaching the adjoining airport of the wooded slopes and rocky pinnacle on which it stands. The ancient rituals performed on the summit of the moor have been replaced by more up-to-date pastimes. Hang gliders perform their modern version of Icarus in flight. Model aircraft loop the loop whilst invading the silence with the 'putt-putt' of their engines.

I walked all over Baildon Moor until I knew the area pretty well. The most important thing was that I found I was enjoying myself. I was also pretty pleased with my reducing waistline – even my dog-walking friends were impressed. So I turned my sights towards Ilkley Moor. This, I decided, would be my next objective.

Twenty odd years ago, I ventured over Ilkley Moor with my eldest son on a late winter's day. It was fine when we set off, taking the popular route via the famous old inn known as 'Dick Hudson's'. The broad, well-trodden track was easy to follow which was just as well as it started to snow as we crossed the highest stretch of the moor. I remember ringing up my wife on our arrival in Ilkley to tell her, quite excitedly, that we had completed the seven-mile journey successfully. In those days, I would not have dreamed of walking back to Baildon. Merely getting to Ilkley was an achievement.

On my first solo walk across the moor I took the same route on a hot summer's afternoon and arrived in Ilkley in a state of sweaty elation. Having sought refreshment in a local café, I started a conversation with the person sharing my table. I proudly told him that I had walked all the way from Baildon but he seemed unimpressed. I caught the bus back to Baildon undeterred, and determined to find out what else the moor had to offer.

CHAPTER TWO

Discovering Wainwright

Ilkley Moor is considerably larger than Baildon Moor and therefore presents a tougher proposition. With this in mind I acquired a local map in order to do some route planning. I studied the intricate pattern of paths that traverse the moor and undertook a series of exploratory walks which enabled me to familiarise myself with some of them. In the course of these walks I covered longer and longer distances until I was undertaking walks of up to fifteen miles without undue difficulty.

It was at this point that I realised I was becoming addicted to my new pastime. No longer satisfied with walks in my immediate locality, I was yearning to attempt even greater distances. With this goal in mind I began to survey the area beyond Ilkley and the River Wharfe, both of which lie on the far side of Ilkley Moor from my home. This reconnaissance entailed walks of over twenty miles and, to my surprise, I found that despite feeling very tired at the end of them they provided a great deal of pleasure and, most importantly, a sense of achievement.

Over a period of several months I seemed to have come a long way since my first tentative stroll around the edge of Baildon Moor.

Wanting to broaden my horizons, in the walking sense, I turned my attention to the Yorkshire Dales. I accompanied a local group from the Ramblers' Association on one of their organised walks in Wharfedale. It was a lovely experience and I thoroughly enjoyed the company; the only drawback being the distance covered, which was considerably less than that to which I was becoming accustomed. I found myself straining at the leash, eager to stride out at my own pace. Rightly or wrongly, I made the decision to learn by my own initiative and mistakes, rather than be led on organised walks. Unfortunately, at that time I had no regular companion to share my outings. I now have a very understanding friend who accompanies me and does not mind my frequent stops to take photographs, which can be an irritant to others when walking in a group. It was while I was gathering information on that area that I encountered one of the works of Alfred Wainwright. It was entitled *Walks in Limestone Country* and it opened my eyes to the huge scope of those dales. A section of his book which particularly intrigued me was a walk around what are known as the Three Peaks.

My eldest son had done this walk a few years earlier when he was in the Venture Scouts, taking part in numerous outdoor activities. He curtailed these when he went to university and, having no further need of his equipment, he passed it all on to me. As we are roughly the same size and build, everything fitted me very well. Put it down to meanness or, I hope, common sense, but I saw no point in laying out large sums of money on gear before I was sure I would persevere with my new found hobby.

My son and I studied the Ordnance Survey map of the Three Peaks together and he pointed out where he and his party had experienced difficulty in finding their way along part of the walk but this did not dampen my enthusiasm. I was keen to tackle the twenty-four mile circuit round the northern end of Ribblesdale, linking the peaks of Penyghent, Whernside and Ingleborough. I was, however, extremely apprehensive as I was totally inexperienced in map and compass reading. My previous outings had followed fairly straightforward routes, without the need to deal with mountains or extensive bogs. I would have dearly liked my son to accompany me, but he was unable to do so. Until then I had walked on my own but I would have been very glad of his company on this venture. Keeping my doubts to myself I pored over Wainwright's maps of the Three Peaks area for hours thinking that if a Scout Leader trained in route-finding could get lost there was no hope for me. Armed with Wainwright's book with its meticulous drawings and instructions, I felt that I had a lifeline, as only an idiot could fail to follow them. Like many other things in life, the theory can differ greatly from the practice. As I discovered, things usually look quite different on the ground to those depicted in a map or drawing.

Studying AW's handiwork I became aware of his personal

observations and profound but often cryptic comments that are a hallmark of his writings. He uses such phrases as 'Walking is a pleasure to be enjoyed in comfort, keep going steadily. Don't rush and don't give up or you will give up at difficulties throughout life.'

He suggests that the Three Peaks Walk should only be attempted in clear and settled weather, and recommends that the walker should have some foreknowledge of the terrain – in other words, to have climbed the three peaks individually before attempting to climb them all in one day. It was to be all or nothing for me. I reckoned that the detailed instructions in his book would be quite sufficient to guide me.

The chosen day eventually dawned and I set out early on that Sunday morning bound for the starting point at Horton in Ribblesdale. Unfortunately, the normally pleasant drive was spoiled by poor weather. It rained continually and the clouds hung menacingly above me. I did not take AW's advice about walking only in good weather and I have to say that, now, I am not proud of that decision. It was foolhardy for anyone as inexperienced as myself even to contemplate the walk. But I was not alone. When I arrived at the car park in Horton around seven thirty, I was surprised to find it practically full. I have since learned that it always fills up quickly on Sunday mornings; most walkers are early risers.

After pulling on my boots, I followed the other walkers to the nearby Penyghent Café from where they operate an essential service for Three Peaks walkers.* By means of a clock card, you can leave particulars of your car registration and relevant telephone numbers, as well as your starting time. If you do not return to clock back within twelve hours, the proprietors notify the police and a search party may set out to look for you. How they know where to look intrigued me, as the unfortunate walker could be anywhere along the twenty-four mile route. My card suitably clocked, I felt more secure in the knowledge that some brave and selfless souls would save me from death by exposure.

Eager as I was to be on my way, I waited for a friend who had

* *See* Appendix 1, page 236.

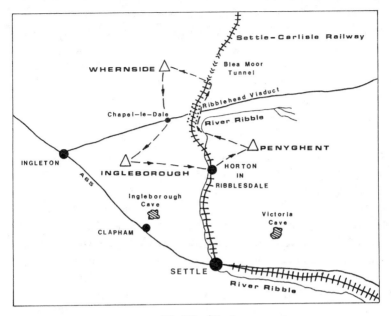

The Three Peaks

half-promised to accompany me on the first stretch of the walk. After half an hour I realised that he had more sense than to turn out on such a wretched morning. I could picture him enjoying a blissful lie-in, leaving fools like me to blunder up mist-shrouded hills.

Deciding that I could wait no longer, I gritted my teeth and set out to tackle the demanding first section of the course. This involved a stiff climb up the steep slopes of Penyghent. I was pleased to find that I was far from alone. The starting point resembled Blackpool beach on a sunny day. I was surrounded by people dressed in all kinds of attire, ranging from traditional cold-weather walking gear to sweatshirt, shorts and trainers. Some looked as if they were out for a Sunday stroll; this perplexed me for, although it was May, the weather seemed to have overlooked this fact and was behaving as though winter were still with us. I was wearing a cagoule, sweater and thick walking trousers which I thought suited the conditions.

A snake of humanity was crawling up the lower slopes of Penyghent from Brackenbottom. It stretched as far as the eye could see through the gloom. The path, obviously pounded into submission by thousands of feet, had spread itself like an open sore before us. I think now is the right time to add something important about the Three Peaks Walk and I quote from the most recent edition of Wainwright's book (1992) in which the following has been added: 'Due to the increasing popularity of this walk, some paths have been re-routed to avoid erosion. Therefore, you should check before starting out where the current diversions are.' The heavily eroded path to the summit of Penyghent meant there would be no need to refer to my map or book: a big advantage in the wet weather. On the minus side was the intermittent clamber over limestone outcrops, or the squelch through peat bogs. Wooden steps and duck boards had been laid over some of the worst bogs but it almost seemed like cheating to use them.

After about half an hour of sweat and toil, I reached a level stretch of ground and paused to rest and cool down. I was so inexperienced, I did not realise that clambering up fells soon warms you up. I was standing on a ridge where the Pennine Way joins the Three Peaks path. In normal weather conditions it would be seen winding its way up from Dale Head in lovely Silverdale. All I could see on this occasion were a few yards of it.

Looking optimistically upwards through the clammy, enveloping mist, I realised how futile it was to search for the summit. All I could see was a wide track ascending over scree and rock at an alarming angle. Following the line of fellow walkers I made laborious progress up this steep incline. It is funny how stupid thoughts enter the mind at such times, perhaps they help to numb the pain of tussling with gravity. In my mind's eye was the cartoon penned by AW of a line of little figures covering the Three Peaks. Had the weather been clearer, I may have been able to see more of his true to life chain of miniature walkers.

After an energy sapping struggle upwards, another barrier of rocks appeared out of the mist as if to test my resolve. A fair amount of scrambling was involved at this stage, until the final slope to the summit could be reached. Across the valley of Silverdale to my right lay, unbeknownst to me, Fountains Fell, with the Pennine Way footpath winding down its western slope. Thanks to the unrelenting mist I was not to have a view of it that day – and it would be many months before I did get to walk over it.

Leaving the rocks behind and with my breathing less laboured, I made for the summit. Again it was alternating bog and wide track with all the grass scoured from it. There were more duck boards along the worst section and I found myself gazing down into glutinous pools on either side. I had the feeling that if I fell in, the chances of re-appearing would be slim. The track expanded to the width of a road as I progressed upwards, my eyes straining for a sight of the trig point which marks the summit. After what seemed like an age it appeared out of the mist, surrounded by kindred souls.

I joined other walkers sheltering behind an adjacent stone wall, grateful for a moment's protection from the wind which was now at full strength. As I rested my complaining limbs, I gave due thanks to the stout-hearted wall-builders who had hauled stones up here in years past to provide the shelter. I also realised that I was now at the highest point I had ever climbed to in this country – 2273 feet – and, despite the conditions, I did feel a great sense of achievement. Incidentally, heights in this book will be given in feet and not metres in deference to AW's preference. I also pondered on the fact that I had seen nothing of the glories mentioned by AW such as magnificent views and exotic plants like purple saxifrage. How different was the actual from the imagined.

Listening to the conversation among my fellow walkers – at least, those who had the necessary energy – remarks of 'one down, two to go' were common. Although not in a very chatty mood myself, I did have time to commiserate with some of the unprepared souls who had obviously thought that they were out for a stroll. They huddled together in what little shelter was available, shivering in their lightweight clothes. One nearby group consisted of two young men and their female companion. She was obviously suffering badly, her attire being only a T-shirt, shorts and trainers. Looking back on the incident, if I had been anything like a gentleman I would have discarded my cagoule and thrown it around her trembling shoulders. Like a devout coward I kept it on and suggested to them that we quickly leave that wind-swept spot.

Still unable to see more than a few yards, we started a hesitant descent down the wide, rocky path that fell away quickly. A sign shortly appeared from the mist pointing towards Horton. After some deliberation we decided to give that path a miss, not wishing to end up where we had recently started. Our chosen path now narrowed considerably and it began to rain more heavily. Not having a clue where to go next, we saw a group veer off to the left of us down a treacherous, boggy slope. Having run out of path we followed, fighting to retain our balance. Halfway down I lost the battle and ended up, flat on my back, in the quagmire. I struggled to my feet, dripping wet and wondering what had possessed me to set out on such an expedition.

The four of us managed to progress for about half a mile without incident, only to be confronted by a wide, fast-flowing stream. We lost considerable time walking along its bank looking for a suitable crossing place but, unfortunately, most of the convenient rocks were now under the surface of this swollen barrier. There was only one thing to do so we tentatively hopped from stone to stone, getting our feet thoroughly wet in the process. We fared better than some poor souls, however, who ended up thigh-deep in the water. The memory of this incident makes me smile, for years later I was sitting on the other side of this stream – Hull Pot Beck – perfectly dry, right down to my socks. It was during one of my many subsequent trips around the Three Peaks. By then I was experienced enough to anticipate problem areas – to skirt the bogs and know the easiest crossing places. I watched some poor sodden walkers squelching out of the stream. One of them gazed in wonder at my dry state and asked how I had achieved it!

To return to my first attempt, we managed to cross the stream and follow the wide, boggy sore that passed for a path eventually crossing a track that came out of Horton – this is, in fact, the Pennine Way again. This was only reached after numerous 'bog-hopping' feats and immersion up to our thighs in the morass. A short time later we came to another track across our path, which we did not recognise. The rain was persisting and, like a fool, not wishing to get AW's precious guide wet, it stayed in my back-pack.

We searched around for someone to follow but our fellow walkers had disappeared, leaving us in eerie silence. Deciding that the wide track was the best route to follow, we turned onto it. I spent several uneasy minutes with the nagging feeling that we may have made the wrong choice. Eventually we came to a farm, which was at least some sort of landmark. Consulting my map I confirmed that my fears were justified, it was the farm at Old Ing and we were going in the wrong direction. Backtracking, we reached the point where we had left the path. Here we met a group from the Long-Distance Walkers Association who had been some way behind us. I was relieved to find that one of their number was acting as guide and had done the walk before. Here was an opportunity not to be missed. God in his wisdom had sent a lifeline. I asked if I could accompany their group for the rest of the walk and was given a friendly welcome – something that seems to be a hallmark of their association. For some reason, my three companions chose to make their own way although, by chance, we came across them later. As they disappeared into the mist, I felt concerned for the welfare of the girl in her far from suitable clothing.

My spirits lifted as I chatted to members of the group, secure in the knowledge that I was back on the correct route and unlikely to deviate again. The conditions underfoot also improved as we came onto a decent farm track and we were able to swing along at a good rate. I found that some of my companions were hardened walkers who had done the Yorkshire Dales Hundred the previous weekend. Figures of around thirty hours completion time were recorded for the hundred-mile challenge event. Such achievement seemed beyond my comprehension. I now belong to the Association (LDWA for short) and am familiar with their programme of challenge walks that are held throughout the year. I have taken part in several, one of which I will elaborate upon later. Numerous local groups organise their own additional programmes and on some occasions, such as the current walk, they combine with other groups under the guidance of a volunteer leader. It was from these good people that I learned about their magazine entitled *Strider* which is published quarterly, and is a fine advertisement for this enthusiastic organisation.

It was not long before we struck the road that winds from Horton to Ribblehead, our next destination. We had a mile or so of road walking which was accomplished at a fair rate of knots. I didn't have much breath for talking as I struggled to keep pace. Out of the mist loomed the bridge that carried the old turnpike road running from Lancaster to Richmond over the Batty Wife Beck. This is now a modern tarmac road linking Ingleton with Hawes. Whoever thought up that name for the beck obviously had a sense of humour, or marital problems.

To weary walkers, the sight of a refreshment van was hugely welcome and signified a rest for tired limbs and much needed succour. This point is at the heart of the Three Peaks area and all of them are visible on a good day. This was not one of those days. The thought did not trouble me, however, as I revived myself with hot tea.

We could not see the nearby massive viaduct with the long ridge of Whernside towering behind it. Ribblehead Viaduct, or to give it the correct title of Batty Moss Viaduct, is one of the vital sections of the Settle to Carlisle railway. Here the line is carried by twenty-four mighty arches over the Ribble valley on its way to Blea Moor and the tunnel.

The railway has been in the news often during recent years, as aficionados fought to keep it open. Without a doubt, it provides one of the country's most scenic railway journeys, but the high cost of maintenance was becoming a serious problem, and repairs to Ribblehead Viaduct were to cost £3,000,000 alone due to the crumbling limestone arches. Fortunately, money was forthcoming and the line has been saved. It would have been a tragedy if the one hundred and twenty year old railway had been abandoned. The mere feat of building it was a triumph for the Midland Railway who were determined to create their own line from Yorkshire to Scotland. They had to face the challenge of the high Pennines and during the line's construction thousands of navvies were employed and many shanty towns sprang up. One such town was Batty Green at Ribblehead where, during the 1870s, smallpox and frequent accidents involving falls from the viaduct took their toll. Two nearby churchyards overflowed so great was their business.

Suitably refreshed, but still wet through as the rain would not relent, we set off for the challenging ascent of Whernside – which I had to take on trust was there since we could not see even the fell's lowest slopes as we passed under the sombre, brooding arches of the viaduct. The route at that time was straight up the eastern face, but now a diversion is in operation which adds another two miles to the journey. It is for reasons such as this that it is essential that you should get details of any current changes to the route before setting out; AW's map in this respect is out of date. The Penyghent Café, which operates a Yorkshire Dales National Park Information Point, displays a description of this particular route revision. The diversion follows the railway line to Blea Moor signal box and onwards to the tunnel where the line passes under the moor to reappear in Dentdale. There follows a less severe climb onto the ridge of Whernside than the original route.

Of all the climbs on the Three Peaks, the original route up the east face was the most difficult. Ingleborough takes its toll but the ascent is not so steep for such a long distance. AW describes it as a 'steady and unremitting climb' and the most 'tedious and tiring section' of the walk. My memory of the climb that day – up the original route – is of struggling slowly up what seemed a near-vertical slope that went on forever. It was here that I learned the 'zigzag' technique of tackling steep ascents; it adds some distance to the climb but reduces the strain on your lungs and knees. I now swear by this technique and the length of the zigzags can be adjusted to suit the angle of gradient.

On the highest section of the climb, which was also the steepest, my lungs felt fit to burst and I spent most of the time scrambling on my hands and knees and, when possible, looking upwards in a vain search for release from the torture. All I could see was fellside disappearing inexorably into thick mist and this taught me another lesson. When attempting a difficult ascent, keep your head down and concentrate on each step at a time. Gazing upwards to find out how much farther there is to climb has a debilitating effect. Some years later I came upon an apt 'lesson according to Wainwright' featured in his Pictorial Guide, Book Six, describing Dale Head, which sums up this situation perfectly. 'The first lesson that every fellwalker learns and learns afresh every time he goes onto the hills, is that the summits are almost invariably more distant, a good deal higher, and require greater effort than expected. Fellwalking and wishful thinking have nothing in common.'

Eventually the slope began to flatten out and we came to an expansive and rutted track which crossed our path. Thinking that we were at the top, I relaxed but relief was short lived because Mark, the group's leader, turned right along this wide track. It took two further scrambles up rocky slopes and another few minutes of walking to reach the summit. At 2419 feet – another record for me – this was an anti-climax after that heart-stopping climb because the summit is barely discernible apart from the trig point that is partially obscured by the wall that runs along the ridge. We cowered behind the wall to escape from the ravages of the howling wind, huddled together in a soaking mass. I was reluctant to leave this sheltered spot but in what seemed no time at all Mark was spurring us into action. I think we would cheerfully have mutinied had we not been so weak. Cursing and groaning, we roused ourselves and prepared to play 'Follow my leader' again.

At this point I received something of a shock. The girl whom I had left earlier was slumped behind the wall, shivering violently and her teeth chattering like castanets. She managed to blurt out that her two companions had left her there as she was hampering their progress. She had been handed a map and compass, which she could not read, and left to fend for herself. Our group was appalled at such treatment for she would clearly soon succumb to exposure. Mark was a knight in shining armour as he produced a spare sweater and a survival bag to warm the girl. It meant we had to hang around a bit longer, but no one minded in the circumstances; we kept ourselves warm by expounding theories about what we would do to her companions were we to catch up with them. Those survival bags are miraculous things and the girl was soon warm enough to struggle to her feet and to join us on the descent down to Chapel-le-Dale where Mark suggested she would be able to take shelter in the Hill Inn.

Setting off, we retraced our steps to cross the path that we had clambered up earlier and then made steady progress along the ridge. I trusted Mark to know where we got down from it, but even he was peering into the mist for a sight of the steep path leading down towards the hamlet of Chapel-le-Dale. We eventually came to a path that veered off the ridge – and disappeared quickly into the mist. After some deliberation we started down it, struggling to keep our feet on the slippery surface; water was streaming off the fellside. When, in due course, we came to some steep wooden steps, they were more treacherous than the mud. Despite some pretty awful moments, we managed to reach the bottom with our limbs intact. It was easy going then along the lanes to the Hill Inn where we deposited the unfortunate girl. She insisted that she would be all right and would telephone home for assistance. (An important point to mention here: if you should ever do this walk and come to grief as that poor girl did, do please remember to ring the Penyghent Café, as well as your own personal rescue service, to tell them that you are abandoning the walk but are OK; otherwise, the emergency services will in due course be alerted by your non-arrival back at Horton. For this reason, don't forget to take telephone money with you.)

Chapel-le-Dale is normally a pleasant spot, nestling roughly halfway between Whernside and Ingleborough. The wide, eroded paths on each of the fells can be seen in decent weather. I had experienced enough of the route underfoot to realise the extent of its erosion. Much good work has been carried out since on sections of the path to overcome its ravages.

In 1987 the Yorkshire Dales National Park authority embarked on the 'Three Peaks Project', which has involved the rebuilding of existing footpaths utilising environmentally protective methods. The ancient principle of laying a 'raft' over the worst eroded stretches is employed. In many cases, this takes the form of an inert plastic mesh overlaid with stone chippings. New methods are also being pioneered to restore the natural plant cover over affected areas. Natural stone in the form of blocks or slabs is also used to assist ascent and descent of steep inclines.

We sat outside the inn, the rain still pouring down, trying to keep warm whilst having well-earned refreshment. Time was marching on, forcing us to be on our way once more. We now faced the long climb to the summit of Ingleborough, the most popular of the Three Peaks. Although the prospect was daunting and my body was loathe to stir itself, I was determined to succeed. Having come this far, the realisation that I was approaching the final hurdle spurred me on.

We set off at a good pace and after roughly a mile of reasonable walking on grassy, well-drained limestone, the going became tougher. Squelchy peat reappeared to hinder our progress and the gradient steepened. My breathing became laboured and conversation ceased as I pulled my boots through the clinging mud. I even mildly regretted the food and drink I had taken on board at the pub.

It was still raining steadily when suddenly, out of the mist loomed a rocky cleft in the fellside that appeared to soar vertically before us. The mist at least prevented us from seeing how far it extended. Ever thoughtful, Mark came back to where I was in the group to encourage me on and to try to ease my obvious dismay. I have always found fellwalkers to be friendly and helpful. This occasion was no exception. I am sure that I would not have completed my sodden way round that route if those kind people had not urged me on. I would have joined the girl on the 'not completed' list and, maybe, the experience would have put an end to my fellwalking days.

As instructed, I watched the person in front of me as we made our precarious way from one slippery rock to another. What I imagined to be a normally pleasant gurgling stream was now a rushing torrent surging down the cleft up which we were struggling. The drag up the boggy approach to this climb had been energy sapping but nothing compared to the current test. My first aim was to avoid being swept from the rocks by the swollen stream; the second was to summon up enough energy to keep going. My companions were offering encouragement as I placed water-logged boots on each succeeding treacherous rock and heaved myself upwards like a dead weight.

With lungs bursting and legs like jelly I made a supreme effort to conquer the climb as I detected the steep angle relent a little. The reassuring news from my colleagues was that we were nearing the top. Sure enough, after a few more hundred feet, with the struggle easing, we came to a fence where the rocks ended and a track crossed our path. Hanging onto the fence as though my life depended on it, I strained against the high wind that was blowing over the ridge where we were now standing. (Prospective

Three Peaks walkers will be pleased to know that stone steps have recently been provided to assist the climb up this formidable gully.)

My thought that we had all but gained the summit was a little premature. This took a further ten minutes to accomplish, including another scramble up a short, sharp series of gritstone rocks to reach the relatively flat 'sugar loaf' plateau. Leaning into the fierce wind and rain whilst approaching the highest point (2373 feet), I had the impression of walking on the moon's surface. I may just as well have been, for I did not know nor particularly care where we were. The ground had been scoured, as though by a giant rake; it was virtually devoid of vegetation and covered in rock fragments and stones.

How my spirits soared when a sombre, grey hulk loomed out of the encircling mist that refused to relent. The sound of voices, carried by the whining wind, drifted in our direction. The hulk began to take the shape of a four-pronged stone shelter. Viewed from the air it would look like a cross. Figures sat hunched on the stone seats in the sheltered sections. A few more steps and we were there, on top of mighty Ingleborough – with a view of nothing but the surrounding greyness. This did not trouble me, however, as I was able to shelter from the blast and wallow in the knowledge that the final climb was over. It was downhill from now on. Surely nothing could stop me reaching the walk's end. Holding my well-earned mug of coffee in cupped hands, I imagined myself safe and sound in Horton.

My thoughts were interrupted when I heard Mark discussing the correct path off the summit plateau with another walker. The wrong choice would evidently take us miles from our destination. This had a sobering effect on my reverie. How would a greenhorn like me find *any* path on this arid desert?

Once again I was to place my faith in the stalwart Mark who had not made a mistake yet. I had the uncomfortable feeling that AW would be disgusted at my failure to even try to follow his superb route instructions. Does he not state in them that his maps give all the necessary directions and should enable the walker to proceed without hesitation along the correct route? Without hesitation! Little did he know of wretches like me. To be fair, he does not take into account sogginess, which would surely have afflicted my edition. I was not yet to know that a waterproof map case could be carried to combat this.

These and many other thoughts invaded my mind as I sat chewing on my remaining sandwiches, now rubbery and mutilated. I overheard seasoned walkers discussing compass bearings, which meant that they must be just as anxious as our party to stride out in the right direction. In the deceptive mist I could not even have retraced my steps.

When everyone was fed and watered we prepared to start the last lap of our journey. Several parties left the comfort of the shelter simultaneously – all going in different directions. Trusting that Mark knew where he was going, I followed our particular human chain through the eerie, silent mist. Soon we were clambering down the rocks which even I knew signified the edge of the plateau. Mark was on the lookout for the path that forked away towards Horton and when we passed a small tarn on our left, he was reassured that we were on the correct route.

A tricky gradual descent followed through stones and mire, requiring all our concentration to stay on our feet. Unbeknownst to me, we were skirting the flank of Simon Fell which is sandwiched between Ingleborough and Park Fell. I have since learned that 'Simon' is quite a common name given to fells in Yorkshire and neighbouring Cumbria. The word 'Simon' is derived from Simon Magus who was a druid. Pagan worship took place here in early times, as it did on Simon's Seat, above Appletreewick. The name of the fell apparently relates to the early British and Roman occupation of Ingleborough and its adjacent fells. Our friends the Brigantes, who hated the might of Rome, camped on Ingleborough's lofty plateau during the Roman invasion. Very welcome they were to it, I say. They probably poured boiling oil onto the Romans and ruined their Three Peaks Walk!

None of this information would have been of interest to me at the time I was trying to get off Simon Fell with my limbs intact. The descent was broken by a stile over a boundary wall running down from the summit of the fell. Near the stile was a fenced portion of ground with various types of grass growing on it and a notice informed us that resurfacing trials were taking place with different types of grasses. The dilemma associated with reseeding any eroded footpath is, in my humble opinion, the time it needs to grow. The existing path has to be closed to prevent the young shoots from being trampled; this means that walkers have to skirt the original path – and erode another path alongside. It is a no-win situation.

I was not allowed to ponder over such thoughts as my friends had already climbed over the stile and were striding into the distance. Struggling to keep up, I was relieved to see that the mist was relenting at last and it had almost stopped raining. Better late than never. How strange it felt to be able to see for more than a few yards ahead, and I noticed a rather dilapidated stone building a hundred yards or so away. This turned out to be a shooting hut which marked the end of our descent. The path levelled out but, apart from not having to tangle with gravity, it was not a great improvement. It was deeply scoured and rutted and still boggy. Our problems were to ease somewhat, however, when we came to cross a wide layer of limestone. This section was a big improvement until we came to Sulber Nick, a narrow channel through wet limestone. Here we had to take extreme care not to slip on the treacherously greasy rocks. I was not seriously troubled by this as the thought of only being about two miles from the finish gave me added momentum.

As we left the limestone shelf, the terrain improved and was pleasantly grassy. A signpost showed that it was one and a half miles to Horton. It is an accepted fact amongst walkers that the last mile is also the longest, but the person who measured the one and a half miles in question must have had a particularly off day. Put it down to weariness or eagerness to finish, but it seemed twice that distance. My feet were finding the hard going very tiring.

After half an hour of anticipating that Horton was over the next brow or round the next bend, it did finally make an appearance. The excitement was slightly tempered by the view of a gash in the hillside to our right; this is Horton Quarry and deserves the title of the Tom Sharpe novel *Blot on the Landscape*. I accept that stone must be quarried, but this open sore dominates an otherwise superb view of the hills around Horton. The pool of vivid turquoise water at the base of the quarry also gave me a feeling of unease.

Within minutes we were in Horton itself, having crossed the

railway line that cuts through the village on its way to Ribblehead. This is the line running to the viaduct that we had trudged under some hours earlier. How much easier it would have been to have let the train take the strain and ridden back to Horton.

A short stretch of road runs from the railway station and, despite our aching and complaining limbs, we hurried along it to reach the small bridge over the River Ribble that heralds the side entrance to the car park that was our starting point and, now twenty-four miles later, was our journey's end.

The car park was still full of walkers discussing the day's events. Paying little heed to them, we almost ran to the Penyghent Café to clock in. The ring of the clocking-in machine was music to my ears as I checked my finishing time. It registered a period of nine hours which, Mark told me, was not bad for a beginner like myself. The time was not really important, the main thing was that I had achieved my objective. Despite many hours spent at home poring worriedly over maps, I had conquered the Three Peaks.

I doubt that AW would have been as proud of me as I was of myself because I had been led for most of the way, but maybe he would have given me a B for trying. I should say that I am now so familiar with this walk that I can do it without reference to a map – and whenever I can, I stop to help a walker needing assistance with the route. I hope that our brilliant leader Mark knew just how much I meant my effusive thanks.

The finale to this episode around the Three Peaks took place in the café. Sipping a mug of steaming hot tea that tasted like nectar was the ideal way to end the day. Apart from its invaluable monitoring service, it is a very friendly place and is perfect for swapping stories of your exploits with fellow walkers.

CHAPTER THREE

My First Fellsman

The title of this chapter may sound dubious, but I assure you that it is purely related to walking.

It is true that no one should rest on their laurels, for you either progress or retard. With this in mind I was soon looking for further challenges. AW's *Walks in Limestone Country* had spurred me on to discover more about Yorkshire's splendid fells and dales.

Despite the dreadful weather and strenuous nature of the Three Peaks Walk, I tried to recall only the pleasing and positive things I derived from it. As an 'off-comer' I could not claim that they were *my* Dales, I was born closer to the Derbyshire Dales than those of my adopted county. So I now set about looking for walks that encompassed as much of the Yorkshire Dales as possible, reasoning that this was the quickest way to learn about them.

Thus began several months of intensive activity; I became a regular in the local library and scoured many bookshops for useful information. AW's *Walks in Limestone Country* introduced me to the dramatic limestone areas around Malham, Settle and Austwick which were a revelation, and have remained favourite walking places ever since. I discovered some testing Open Challenge Walks and other long-distance walks in the Dales outlined in a very useful book entitled *Long Distance Walks – Volume 2 The Yorkshire Dales* by Tony Wimbush and Alan Gott. These Open Challenge Walks could be attempted by anyone at any time around a specified route and distance. Areas unbeknown to me at that time, such as Swaledale, Wensleydale and Wharfedale, were featured. I took the opportunity to explore them using this book and an Ordnance Survey map as a guide. I did not in all cases undertake the featured walks in their entirety as they covered distances of up to sixty-one miles and I did not consider myself to be in such a league. A section of the book relating to Ultra-Long Distance Challenges was quickly glossed over because I considered specified distances of up to 120 miles to be inconceivable as far as I was concerned. I did, however, note the inclusion of the Three Peaks Walks amongst the Open Challenge Walks, of which I could now claim a first-hand knowledge.

Interspersed among my walks taken with the aid of the above book were some of my own, devised solely with the use of Ordnance Survey maps. The Yorkshire Dales, I discovered, are very comprehensively covered by three maps within the 1:25000 Outdoor Leisure series. Like AW I derived immense pleasure from reading maps. He found them fascinating and magnificent. In fact, they were his favourite literature, he said he would rather study a map than read a book. AW considered the Ordnance Survey maps the best of all although he does warn that they are not always reliable in the matter of footpaths on the fells. He goes on to say that this matters little to an experienced walker who prefers, after his first few seasons, to find his own way across high country (thereby savouring the real joy of fellwalking) and depends less on his map.

I spent many hours devising circular walks with the aid of the large-scale maps of the Yorkshire Dales and subsequently following these routes of my own making. They provided an opportunity to practise map- and compass-reading. This was sorely needed following my Three Peaks débâcle. Although I never got completely lost I had some near misses. I was still far from being a star performer with the compass. I did find that, as AW indicated, a small percentage of paths shown on the map were non-existent or, in some instances, a path on the ground was not indicated on the map, but these minor occurrences did not seriously hamper my progress.

You may have noted my frequent references during this period to circular walks. These were the most convenient kind for me as they enabled me to drive to the starting point and return to the same spot to pick up my car. At that time I walked on my own and did not enjoy, until some years later, the luxury of being accompanied by friends and using two cars, which enabled us to do long linear walks.

I also joined the LDWA at this point, which I considered was the least that I could do to repay the kind people who had assisted me around the Three Peaks. Their quarterly issues of *Strider* were eagerly awaited and read from cover to cover.

In addition to my exploration of the Yorkshire Dales I joined a local night-school class where I began to learn about the history, geology and background of the area. The lecturer, Pat Dyson, had run the class for over twenty years and displayed extensive knowledge complimented by a very comprehensive collection of colour slides. It was his lectures that aroused my interest in photography which has given me so much pleasure in the succeeding years. His class also provided me with my introduction to the Fellsman Hike, the topic of which was casually raised in conversation with a fellow class member.

Apparently more entrants were required for this annual Challenge Event which her husband helped to organise. At the mention of a distance of sixty-one miles, I laughingly replied that I might manage thirty, but sixty was a bit over the top. I was assured that hundreds of masochists had already entered and that it was very well organised, with checkpoints every few miles. Most people completed it comfortably in twenty-four hours, she said – *twenty-four hours, sixty miles!!* – and were put into groups during the night section for safety. Despite my revelation that I could easily get lost in daylight and therefore stood no chance in the dark, I received no sympathy. I still said it wasn't for me. But the challenge began to nag at me and, finally, anxious not to appear completely spineless, I agreed to have a go, if only to swell the numbers.

A few days later the entry form duly arrived. It informed me that the hike would be held the following May and there was also an accompanying long list of rules, including kit and equipment to be carried. Thinking that hiking was for enjoyment, I queried if items such as bandages, whistles, emergency rations and survival bag were absolutely necessary. I was assured that every rule must be obeyed and any lapses would result in my disqualification. All kit would be checked prior to starting and also during the hike. My enthusiasm was on the wane and thoughts of sinking into a bog in pitch darkness entered my mind. I took the cowardly way out and said nothing. Looking back, I realise how completely naïve I was but we all have to learn.

The explanatory leaflet* showed a roughly horseshoe-shaped course that took in many of the fells mentioned in AW's book, *Walks in Limestone Country*. This fitted in nicely with my ambition to get to know the Dales better; the only problem was that I had not envisaged climbing quite so many in a single walk. There where eight peaks in all, including two which I had already climbed, Ingleborough and Whernside. The total height of ascent during the walk was eleven thousand feet. Hey ho . . .

As the hike was still a few months away, at least I had time to step up my peak-bagging; such practice was obviously required. Therefore, I did a series of walks involving as much fell climbing as possible. A few weeks before the dreaded date of the Fellsman, I even did another circuit of the Three Peaks. On this occasion, the weather was much improved and I managed to negotiate the walk without mishap.

During this period I received more detailed information from the Fellsman organisers concerning the sixty-one mile route. Map references were provided for strategic points such as checkpoints and fell summits. Immediately these references were pin-pointed on my Ordnance Survey map. The routes taken between the map references were left to the competitors' discretion, indicating that considerable expertise in map- and compass-reading would be required. (Gulp!)

I was also allocated an entry number which confirmed that there was now no possibility of escape. Secretly, I had hoped that the entries (limited to 450) would be over-subscribed and I would be unsuccessful in the resulting draw for places. What a wimp I was.

As dawn broke on the morning of the hike, I was wide awake. I looked apprehensively at the bedside clock, four-thirty, and since there was no further sign of sleep I got up, dressed and crept downstairs. I checked the bus timetables – I had checked them a hundred times the day before. I checked my kit – I had checked that too a dozen times over, fearful of being turned away from the starting point for not having the correct equipment. 'Anyone

* *See* Appendix 2, page 237.

checking in after ten thirty will be disqualified' were words etched in my mind. I wasn't looking forward to the journey of forty miles which I had to do by bus since competitors were advised not to drive immediately after the hike, for obvious reasons. With this in mind, I had cajoled my daughter to come and collect me.

A fragmented journey of walking, waiting at bus stations (where I took the opportunity of looking at the route on the maps – yet again) and several bus rides found me in Ingleton, the starting point – a mere three hours early! The walk began at twelve noon: perhaps not the ideal hour in warm weather but it did give people time to get to Ingleton on the Saturday and time to return home on the Sunday. Although the three hours I had to wait until noon seemed an eternity, I saw that I was far from the first there, and a crowd was already waiting for the official start time.

First came the kit inspection. Some tables were arranged in the form of a square, with half a dozen officials on the inside checking the kit of the hopeful entrants milling around the outside. 'Boots!' snapped the first official as I approached. I stuck my left boot on the table as I was already wearing them. He peered at the sole and prodded the uppers. 'Other one!' came the sharp command and the exercise was repeated. 'Pass along,' he said tersely. I moved to the next official who demanded to see my emergency rations and whistle. He rummaged through my chocolate bars and bags of nuts, weighed them and blew on my whistle. I stifled a laugh. Surely it wasn't to be taken this seriously? My next check proved it was, as every item in my first aid kit was counted, even four safety pins! As the last check was completed the official pointed to the nearby doorway with the command 'In there!'

As I approached the table in the next room, the official stuck out his hand and without looking up demanded my entry number. 'Four hundred and eleven,' I said, thinking that there must be at least four hundred and ten idiots like me. A plastic disc and a piece of string were then thrust into my hand, still without an official head being raised. 'Tally, don't lose it!' he spat out. I am not sure why the Fellsman Hike officials were so disgruntled; maybe they had all had too early a start, or were just very engrossed in their duties. But it certainly didn't fill me with much confidence.

I shuffled from the table, peering at my tally and wondering if the string was to hang myself with. A friendly voice behind me said, 'You have to get that clipped at each checkpoint,' I turned round to face a fellow sufferer who introduced himself as Geoff and had obviously been through this ritual before. We entrants apparently could not be trusted to stick to the official route. 'Your first time?' he enquired. Was it that obvious? 'I've done it once before,' said Geoff and introduced me to his two companions. Stuart, I discovered, was a first-timer like me and David was a veteran of twelve successful attempts.

The four of us spent the next two hours chatting and observing the antics of kindred souls making their preparations. The seasoned campaigners had not arrived in their hiking clothes, as I had done. They donned a varied selection of garbs including skintight trousers, shorts worn over tights and an assortment of training shoes. Such exotic clothing was unknown to a tenderfoot like me as I sat there in my regulation cagoule and walking trousers. These were certainly soon to be needed in the prevailing weather conditions. To relieve the monotony, we strolled to the local café, the centre of activity in the village. Around its walls were rows of posters imploring us to buy the latest revolution in hiking and pot-holing equipment, without which the self-respecting enthusiast could not function. Fellow entrants huddled around the tables sipping pints of tea and swapping boring tales.

I kept glancing at my watch, which seemed to be on a 'go slow'. Eventually the fateful hour of noon approached and we made our way to the nearby sports field for the starting ceremony. The weather? Yes, thank you: it was raining quite nicely, dampening everyone's clothes and spirits. Thoughts invaded the minds of the fainter hearted such as, what the hell am I doing here? A voice cracked over the loudspeaker, jerking everyone to life. 'Don't worry, the weather is poor at the moment but an improvement is forecast' it said reassuringly. How wrong he was! With best wishes and a quick count down to zero hour, we were sent on our way.

It was as if someone had pulled a giant plug. The field quickly emptied as over four hundred bodies spewed onto the road.

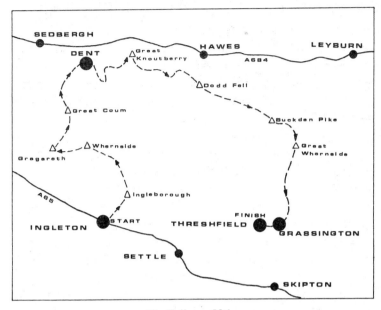

The Fellsman Hike

Ingleton was obviously prepared for this annual invasion as the whole of the local constabulary – two to be exact – had turned out to halt the traffic. As we jostled through the narrow streets, I fought the urge to wave to the onlookers. What must they think of this crazy mass of humanity rampaging through their village in the pouring rain? Eventually we left the road and began the climb towards Ingleborough. I was in the trailing group, on purpose as I was determined not to burn myself out after a few hours. Geoff and Stuart forged ahead whilst I kept a wary eye on David, also in the back group; I wanted to keep in touch with him and benefit from his experience.

Once out into the country the climb became steeper. The walkers ahead could be seen snaking up the hillside and the leading ones were already disappearing into a thick mist. The wind had freshened and the rain was now beating down. Just my luck that conditions could not be worse. Was I doomed to do all my long-distance walking in foul weather? Shortly David and I overtook Geoff who was already paying the price of his early onslaught. 'I feel sick,' he gasped, urging us to go on ahead and insisting that he would soon recover. David took him at his word and pressed on. Wishing Geoff the best of luck, I followed David and it wasn't long before we overtook Stuart who had also slowed considerably. After exchanging a few words of encouragement, David forged ahead. It seemed like every man for himself, so I too left the panting Stuart and tried to keep close to David as the mist began to envelop us.

Progress became harder as we clambered up the rocky approach to the summit (2373 feet). Puffing and panting, I reached the stone shelter on top and the nearby checkpoint which appeared out of the mist. 'Lovely weather for it,' came the cheery greeting from a chap holding a pair of clippers. Searching inside my sweater for my tally where I had hung it for safe-keeping, I hoped that it was still attached to the piece of string around my neck. As he clipped the first mark, I felt a warm glow. One down, only twenty-three to go! I studied the tally closely to ensure that it had been clipped correctly. (Were all beginners as over-keen?) Displayed on the tally were all the checkpoints in numerical order, their heights above sea level and the distance in miles to each of them from the starting point. It showed 3.8 miles completed and 2300 feet climbed, which was very little compared to the remaining 57.2 miles and 8700 feet.

As I looked up, David was already disappearing from view so I set off on the steep rocky descent. During the rest of the hike, I repeatedly felt for my tally, dreading that at one checkpoint I would find only an empty piece of string and be disqualified. The climb, although strenuous, had been accomplished without undue difficulty. My fitness must have improved since my first ascent of the Three Peaks, I thought to myself. Quite soon, I was at the top of the cleft in the rocks that I had struggled up during that first Three Peaks Walk. The memory of standing at the bottom gazing upwards was still vivid, but the view down from the top was even more daunting. The stream, acting true to form, was rushing over the rocks but thankfully was not so torrential on this occasion. Clinging on for dear life I teetered down the rocky cleft. The mist was beginning to clear but the rain had settled into a steady downpour. I was much relieved to reach the bottom without slipping.

Our next objective was the main road and the second checkpoint at Hill Inn and here we encountered luxury unlimited. After the ritual of tally clipping, we entered a large tent where hot tea and cold drinks were being served. There were to be many such checkpoints manned by an assortment of ministering angels. We did, however, encounter some deadpan servers of soup and also cruel cooks who prepared themselves a hearty meal as exhausted walkers chewing on their soup watched enviously. After a brief rest we set off on the assault of the next peak, Whernside. As we passed the inn, sounds of merriment issued from inside. I turned to David, his expression mirroring my thoughts that we needed our heads examining for being out in such weather.

As we progressed, I wondered how Geoff and Stuart were faring. I was very content to stick to David, like glue. We slogged our way up the steep fellside into the enveloping mist that had hung around at high level since we had started, and I began to strain my eyes for a glimpse of the checkpoint on the summit (2419 feet). Eventually, out of the gloom came the welcoming tent, and not wanting to linger a moment longer than necessary, we were soon retracing our steps down the slope which we had just struggled up. After a few minutes, we met Stuart plodding his way up. Geoff was nowhere to be seen and we assumed that he had fallen by the wayside. We discovered later that he had been forced to retire at one of the early checkpoints, an ankle injury causing him to limp badly. He had then been taken to the finishing point by the efficient motorised back-up service used for collecting such competitors from the checkpoints. One of the important rules of the hike stressed that retirement from the walk must be made at a checkpoint – apart from the direst emergencies. I was now beginning to see that what I initially thought were overbearing instructions by the organisers were in fact designed to ensure the absolute safety of walkers.

Branching off the main downward path we headed in the direction of Kingsdale. Our steps quickened as we descended out of the mist again to the welcoming sight of the Kingsdale Head checkpoint nestling in the valley below. We had been going for five hours and fatigue was creeping up on me as we reached the checkpoint. While we lay recovering, I surveyed the next stage of the route. David must have read my thoughts for he told me that the steep path leading up the fellside towards Gragareth was a 'pig of a climb'. I was reluctant to stir myself into action but I moved fast enough once David was on his way again; I didn't dare let him out of my sight.

He had not exaggerated about the climb and I was exhausted as we reached the summit plateau (2058 feet). Thankful to be on level ground again we made for the checkpoint, passing shadowy figures emerging from the mist. After checking in, we retraced our steps until we altered course for Great Coum (2250 feet), Flinter Gill and the descent into Dentdale. Having recovered a little of my strength and finding a second wind, this section was traversed without incident, and by seven-thirty p.m. we were dropping down Flinter Gill into the pleasant village of Dent. I had been looking forward to visiting the birthplace of Adam Sedgwick, one of the most famous Dalesmen, but the miserable weather spoilt its obvious attractiveness.

A spell of road walking then followed until we reached the checkpoint at Whernside Manor. From the conversation around us, it was evident that tiredness and perpetual wetness were beginning to take their toll. There was talk in some quarters of giving up; indeed, several were dropping out. The less faint-hearted reported to the grouping tent where we were herded into groups of five or more for the night section. We were instructed to remain in our groups until daybreak when we would be disbanded. A leader for our group was selected, someone who had exhaustively studied the route and I felt relieved that we had such a person at the helm. Unfortunately, due to tiredness, he was later to leave his map and his personal handwritten route details at Redshaw checkpoint, thus rendering himself helpless as a guide. David, a veteran of many Fellsman Hike completions, took over as leader.

We left Whernside Manor and climbed to Blea Moor. The rain had eased which made conditions a little more bearable. Dusk was gathering as we descended into the village of Stone House. We were passed by a mini-bus carrying its cargo of 'drop outs' back to base and we christened it the 'blunderbus'. The lighted tents of the next checkpoint beckoned through the gloom and we were greeted warmly by the pleasant team of helpers. I accepted the steaming hot mug of tea with anticipation as David had been singing the praises of 'Stone House tea' for the past hour. We were not disappointed in the brew or the accompanying soup.

Fortified, but still weary, we switched on our torches and set off up the track to Great Knoutberry. It was amusing to look ahead at the teams of walkers weaving up the fellside, easily identified by a series of bobbing torches. They looked like glow-worms. The highly organised had powerful lamps strapped to their heads, but novices like me had to make do with hand torches and hope that we did not fall into anything nasty. The track seemed interminable and after what seemed an eternity we reached a beacon that pointed the way to the top. After a struggle up the muddy fellside to Great Knoutberry's summit (2203 feet), we had to turn round and descend by the same route. On occasions like this one fervently wished one could miss out a trek up and return straight back, but the checkpoint at the top naturally ruled this out.

Crossing the track that we had recently left, we headed into the valley towards the welcoming lights of the Redshaw checkpoint. It was now approaching one o'clock in the morning and I have to admit that I was at a very low ebb. I slumped into a chair and did not stir for twenty minutes. Then, despite dog-tiredness and aching limbs I forced myself to my feet and the next section of the walk, across Redshaw Moss to Snaizeholme Fell, was completed more by will power than strength.

We then skirted the head of the Snaizeholme Beck which flows to join the Widdale Beck near Hawes in Wensleydale. In good weather it is one of the nicest spots in the Dales, a gentle saucer-shaped valley with its open end looking out onto Great Shunner Fell. We couldn't see a thing, obviously, because it was pitch black and, anyway, I was in no condition to appreciate anything except the necessity to put one foot in front of the other. A steep climb followed to the summit of Dodd Fell, a bleak and desolate place at any time (2189 feet). Perhaps I was experiencing the pain barrier or the reward for twenty-two hours without sleep, for I virtually crawled up the fellside on all fours, pulling myself up with the aid of clumps of grass. It was now two-thirty a.m. and I may well have dropped out at this point if it had not been for what happened next.

On reaching the summit plateau we found other teams of

walkers staggering hopelessly around searching for the check-point. Not having a clue where it was, we joined in the mêlée and spent a fruitless hour looking for the elusive tent. The night air was electric with oaths and expletives. Eventually our team decided that this ridiculous activity had gone on for long enough and that we may as well bed down and wait for the dawn. Now the importance of carrying the necessary kit became apparent as we clambered into our survival bags, still wearing boots, gaiters, jackets and all. Once again the forethought and planning of the organisers had come into its own. They obviously knew that idiots like me could blunder around fell tops in the darkness. My opinion of those seemingly gruff officials at the kit inspection had now turned into one of admiration. I then unwisely thought of AW. What would his reaction have been to my antics? Where was he when I needed him most? Pulling my bag around my neck I lay shivering for a few minutes before drowsiness overtook me and I fell into fitful sleep.

After an hour or so we were awakened by someone giving an army-type alarm call. Dawn was breaking, the mist had cleared – and I could see a small, dark tent no more than fifty yards away. It was the lost checkpoint which we must have circled endlessly in the darkness. The poor fellow in the tent who clipped our tallies suffered every kind of verbal abuse imaginable as he was con-verged upon from all sides by cross, dishevelled walkers; appar-ently the official's light had gone out in the early hours of darkness, just before we reached Dodd Fell's summit. We had lost two and a half hours due to our mishap, but the majority of our team decided that we may as well press on. One dissenter was to drop out at the next checkpoint. Luckily our team was disbanded there, otherwise, with one member short, the remainder would have been disqualified and forced to retire. Although no one feels at their best in the early hours of a bleak, chilly morning, some of my strength had returned and I felt better for the rest.

Down the fellside we tramped in search of the next landmark, the Roman road that runs from Ingleton to Bainbridge. This we found without difficulty and soon reached the checkpoint at Fleet Moss, high up on the road which leads to Langstrothdale. We were made welcome and revived with hot soup and tea, our first of the day. It was also a relief to discover that, despite our delay, we were still within the official time limit, which allowed us to continue. Any walkers who exceed this limit when checking in at a checkpoint are automatically retired. The conversation between walkers which had been substantial at the outset had, by this time, virtually dried up. Tiredness was gnawing at the mind with resulting lapses in concentration which were not conducive to friendly chatter. It was hardly the time of day for polite conversation. Our energies were concentrated on essentials: survival and finding the next checkpoint.

Feeling more like human beings again, we began the crossing of the notorious Fleet Moss, a desolate, boggy expanse of moorland that divides Wensleydale from Upper Wharfedale. One advantage of our lateness was to be able to cross this sea of peat in daylight. With only a boundary fence to guide us, we squelched and 'bog-hopped' our way to the Middle Tongue checkpoint hidden away amongst the peat hags. There are few less inviting spots that spring to mind but although anxious to be free of this morass, we found we had to plough through more clinging peat until we began the descent to Cray which nestles at the head of Wharfedale.

The going was firmer and we followed a network of stone walls which all looked identical, and I was glad of David's guidance. It was with relief that we descended the rough track to the checkpoint, but this was tempered with the prospect of Buckden Pike, our next objective across the valley. The weather had slightly improved overnight, allowing a glimpse of the forbidding fell with just its peak invisible. David and I couldn't decide whether it was better to have drier weather but be able to see the great climbs in front of us, or remain in blissful ignorance and get soaked by the mist. At Buckden Pike we seemed to be in a no-win situation since we could see the very steep climb quite clearly but the summit was obscured by mist. Pausing only for tally clipping at the checkpoint we made for the lower slopes of the Pike. An exhausting climb then brought us to more level ground which flattered only to deceive.

A familiar feeling on many fells is one of elation at reaching what you think is the top, only to find another slope looming above you. Here was no exception as the fellside rose in three tiers, an immensely frustrating experience for tired limbs. At last the flat boggy plateau that forms the summit (2302 feet) was reached. Another spell of 'bog-hopping' through the mist followed until we passed the memorial cross which marks the start of the descent. This was erected in memory of the Polish crew of an RAF plane which crashed on top of the Pike in 1942 during a blinding snowstorm. The sole survivor crawled out of the wreckage with his leg broken. Having no idea where he was, he happened to see a fox's paw prints in the snow. Reasoning that the fox would make its way down the fell in search of food, he dragged himself along the trail. His intuition proved correct and he managed to make his way to safety. So grateful was he for his deliverance that he had this memorial erected to his fellow crew members. He did not forget the fox, for set into the base of the cross is an ornamental fox's head, along with small fragments from the aircraft.

The comforting thought that only one further ascent remained spurred us on and we made good time to the checkpoint at Top Mere, high above Kettlewell. With soup and tea beckoning at our next checkpoint, we hurried onwards. Legs were moving mechanically now as willpower alone kept us going. Uncharacteristically, David was falling behind, so I slowed up and kept pace with him. He was obviously going through a bad patch which most long-distance walkers seem to experience. Mine caught up with me about two miles from the finish. David persevered and eventually got his second wind – or, more like it, his twenty-second – as we passed Cam Head. On a fine day, the view down the flat-bottomed Wharfe Valley can be enjoyed as it stretches down to Kilnsey and Grassington. We were not so lucky, so it provided no distraction. Park Rash checkpoint was imminent, but we could not help gazing into the distance at the steep western face of Great Whernside with snow still clinging to its upper reaches. *Snow in May* – no one had warned me about this! The fell was the last stiff challenge as once over the top it would be downhill to the finish.

At Park Rash, hot soup was thrust into our eager hands. As we chatted with our hosts, our capacity for conversation revived, we learned that because of the time lost on Dodd Fell we were amongst the back markers. At each checkpoint, the name and number of every walker is transmitted back to base as they check in. By this means, everyone's progress, or lack of it, can be monitored and their precise positions determined. Approximately half of the starters, we were told, had dropped out or been withdrawn by this stage so I was not dismayed by being in the trailing group. I counted myself lucky to be still walking. Stuart, we learned, was among the unfortunate half, suffering compulsory withdrawal for exceeding the time limit. It was with great reluctance that we dragged ourselves away from this comfortable respite to start the last climb up our eighth fell.

Twenty-three hours had now elapsed since the start and, probably due to fatigue, we had great difficulty finding the correct path onto its lower slopes. In fact, I became completely disorientated. Eventually we succeeded and after ten minutes of fairly easy walking we were reduced to *crawling* up the muddy path that went virtually straight up Great Whernside's steep face. At one point we had to circle a patch of deep snow and the footing was definitely treacherous. I clung on desperately, hoping that all I had achieved so far would not be ruined by my losing my grip. After frequent rests to catch our breath we reached the rocky summit (2310 feet). Once again we were denied a good view as it was shrouded in mist. Eight body-destroying climbs I had made – and not one solitary view had I had in return. Add to these my first Three Peaks Walk and I reckon it was a miracle that I ever continued to fellwalk!

After pausing to regain what little strength we had left we descended the southern slope and headed for the Capplestone Gate checkpoint. As we came out of the mist we passed several disused mine-workings, and I spared a sympathetic thought for the miners of a bygone era who had had to work under incredible hardship. My heart lightened when we found the checkpoint, merely a gate in one of the stone walls. Thanks to David's navigation we had only one more checkpoint to find. He pointed out that the presentations to the winners would already have taken place at Threshfield, our destination. They had been scheduled for 11 a.m., at which time we had been enjoying our soup and respite at Park Rash. The organisers had no consideration for slowcoaches like us. We laughingly agreed that they would have had to carry on without us. David had visibly improved now and was keen to be on the way again.

It was a downhill walk to the last checkpoint at Yarnbury and visibility was quite good. To our right, the ground fell away in a series of limestone steps and the village of Kilnsey, with its famous crag, could just be seen in the valley. Barely pausing to check in at Yarnbury, we set off on the last leg, which was to be all road walking, through Grassington and over the river Wharfe to Threshfield. The monotony of forcing one foot in front of the other had gone on for so long that it was difficult to imagine it ever ending. This was the point where my first blister developed and tiredness enveloped me like a blanket. I felt like the London Marathon runners look like at the end – zonked out. I had begun to limp, my whole body screamed in protest and every step required a supreme effort. Through a fog of fatigue came the frightening thought that I was going to fail short of the finish. Fighting the overpowering urge to lay down at the road-side and go to sleep, I staggered on as if in a dream. It was hurting; my God it was really hurting! Why had my boots become lead weights and my legs turned to jelly? The desire to stop and end this torture welled up inside me. It was only David's constant encouragement that kept me moving. As he urged me along he repeatedly told me that the end would soon be in sight.

How I ever completed those final two tortuous miles I will never know, but I will be forever grateful to David for his unstinting support at a time when he must have been suffering badly too. Staggering into the school that marked the finishing point at Threshfield I just managed to summon enough strength to hand over my tally for its final clipping. With encouraging calls of 'Well done' ringing in our ears, we collapsed in utter silence on a nearby bench. After a few minutes, David summoned enough energy to joke: 'Well, that was good. Feel like going round again?'

A hot shower revived us and David and I tucked into a hearty meal provided by the kind lady volunteers. It was an effort to stop myself from falling asleep and I was truly thankful that I had arranged a lift home. Throughout the meal I experienced a feeling of deep satisfaction and accomplishment. We learnt later that there were only three more finishers after us and that our time of twenty-seven hours and ten minutes was only just inside the official time limit. These facts mattered little to us, the main thing being that we had completed our objective, which over half of the entrants had failed to do.

My daughter picked us up in the car a short time later and was delighted – and quite surprised – to find that we had been successful. Her old dad went up in her estimation, I think. David and I struggled to keep our eyes open during the homeward journey. As we sat collapsed on the back seat our heads bobbed around like those imitation dogs which used to be seen in the rear windows of cars in years gone by. How wise had been the instruction not to drive after the event. When I got home I went straight to bed and slept for thirteen hours. Next morning I was told that I had tossed and turned all night, obviously reliving the anxieties of finding my way across sixty-one miles of unforgiving countryside. I had probably been looking for that small tent in the thick blackness of Dodd Fell!

A few weeks later a certificate arrived from the Keighley Scout Service Team, the hike organisers, congratulating me on my achievement. The certificate proclaimed 'Twas A Gradely Walk – Well Done'! People familiar with the Yorkshire dialect will know that it was certainly 'gradely'.

In spite of all that you have read, I foolishly agreed to go through it all again the following year!

CHAPTER FOUR

Pennine Way Practice

Realising that, although I would never be the world's fastest walker, I could walk a fair distance at a reasonable pace, my appetite was whetted for long-distance footpaths. Britain's most evocative footpath at that time, towards the end of the 1980s, was the Pennine Way. It was the one that most walkers wanted to attempt. AW's Coast to Coast route from St Bees in Cumbria to Robin Hood's Bay now appears to be overtaking it in popularity, thanks to its coverage in recent years by AW's television series.

It was back in 1935 that the idea for a footpath along the high Pennines was first put forward. The prime mover was Tom Stephenson, later to be Secretary of the Ramblers Association. Thirty years of struggle and hard work followed until the Pennine Way was officially opened. I can appreciate the effort that must have gone into its creation and to sustain the impetus for so long is remarkable; it is now in the capable care of the Countryside Commission. Knowing the opposition that exists to the acceptance of rights of way in many places, Tom Stephenson must have experienced years of argument, legal battles and downright obstruction. It all stemmed from a newspaper article submitted by him which could well have made no impact whatsoever. Fortunately it struck a chord with many walkers and led to a powerful demand for this suggested path, and was to be bolstered by the formation of the Pennine Way Association three years later. Following a period of research it was found that two-thirds of the proposed path followed presumed rights of way and the rest would need to be established.

Enthusiastic organisations put forward recommendations that this long-distance route should be set up as soon as practicable but it took until 1951 for the route to gain government approval, which initiated negotiations for creation of new rights of way.

After fourteen more years of fighting for recognition, the footpath was declared officially open. This feat of endurance was marked by a gathering on 24 April 1965 on Malham Moor of two thousand grateful walkers. By my reckoning, if a few stalwarts could spend thirty years struggling to create this path, then surely I could spend a little time out of my life walking it.

I decided, therefore, that the Pennine Way was to be my next challenge and set about researching the route. Once again, AW was the prime source with his *Pennine Way Companion*. I became aware of this guide when I noticed that it was listed in the preliminary information in *Walks in Limestone Country*. Trusting that it was as thorough as *Walks in Limestone Country*, I bought a copy and pored over it hungrily. I was not disappointed for the whole of the 270-mile journey is comprehensively covered in AW's own inimitable style. Fine, hand-drawn maps illustrate every stage from Edale, the starting point, to its end at Kirk Yetholm just over the Scottish Border.

The only problem I had initially with the book's continuous strip map of the route was that it is back to front, or so I thought. AW describes the route from north to south, starting at Kirk Yetholm. As I intended walking in the more usual direction of south to north it meant starting at the end of the book. Very Chinese, I thought, until a friend suggested that I should read the notes contained in the book's introductory section entitled 'Plan of the Guide' more carefully. So I did and I have to admit that AW's logic does make sense. AW reassures his readers that 'You don't have to stand on your head to use this guide and you don't have to walk backward.' Well, that was a relief, especially with a walk that long.

AW's introduction is, as usual, full of invaluable information on how to tackle the walk. He points out that the main difficulty is not the nature of the terrain, tough as it is, but following the approved route. The aim of the guide is to enable walkers to navigate the Way's entire length without putting a foot wrong. With my record that would be virtually impossible!

The preliminary groundwork for his guide book had been undertaken by four stalwart fellwalkers. This task had started in the same year that the footpath was officially opened. They were each allotted a section to explore, checking the approved route against maps and information from official sources. Compilation of the guide took three years of hard work and it was finally published in 1968. I found the dedication at the beginning of the guide intriguing. It reads; 'To the one who helped most of all.' This I assumed was his wife Betty who must have been a great support and source of inspiration to him.

True to form he voices his opinion regarding 'more haste less speed'. In his view, the Pennine Way is not intended to be a race against time. It is to be enjoyed, otherwise there is no point in attempting it. He does admit that there are times when the going becomes hard and you will feel like giving up. His antidote for this is the reminder that you may never pass that way again.

I noticed with dismay his comment that it is not an undertaking for the solitary walker, as I intended to walk it on my own. Unquestionably, early summer was, for me, the best time of year for doing the walk – I would need the maximum amount of daylight to allow for getting lost. I then stood a chance of not blundering around in the darkness, and of reaching my designated night's stop before all the supper was scoffed by other walkers. I chose early June of the following year for my attempt in order to give me plenty of time for training and preparation. This time I was determined to follow AW's advice that I had previously chosen to ignore when attempting my first Three Peaks Walk. You will recall that I referred earlier to his recommendation in *Walks in Limestone Country* that the walker should have some foreknowledge of the terrain before attempting such a walk. Being, I hope, a little wiser now, I decided that if such advice applied to the Three Peaks, it would certainly be useful when tackling my latest venture. With this in mind, and also to reduce the possibility of getting lost, I resolved to practice walking as much of the route as possible. For a 270-mile journey this would be some task.

The guide was a great help in selecting the sections to reconnoitre as AW had prepared a log of the journey showing the main landmarks on the route together with the distances between them. Another aid was that each section ends at a road, thus assisting transport to and from the walk. As his sequence of maps necessitates reading the book in reverse, I turned to the last chapter which is his log and worked backwards from there.

At the end of the guide, as with all his Pictorial Guides to the Lake District, is a section headed 'Some Personal Notes in Conclusion' and I found them to be a light relief from the serious business of route planning. It appeares that his early attempts to map out the route had ended in failure as he experienced seven days of continuous rain at the outset. Four of them at the Edale end and three at Kirk Yetholm after switching ends. He spent eighteen months in all walking the Pennine Way, mainly in the rain. At one stage, he met a walker who only experienced two hours of rain on the whole journey: would I be so fortunate, I wondered. Apparently conditions were so bad while AW was on Bleaklow, he began to lose the feeling in his legs and had to beat a hasty retreat. He underwent an unforgettable experience on Cam Fell above Hawes when a freezing wind 'shrivelled some of the body organs necessary for a full and enjoyable life'. What on earth was I letting myself in for, I thought, as my plans took shape. His final notes summed up his feelings about the route: 'You won't come across me anywhere along the Pennine Way. I've had enough of it.'

There are financial implications concerned with most ventures and I had to decide on the standard of accommodation for the duration of the walk. I sent for a copy of the YHA *Pennine Way Package** that I had heard about: this was launched in 1983 after an increasing number of walkers failed to complete the walk due to poor preparation and equipment. When the Package arrived, I found it full of helpful information and sensible instructions. It recommends a period of nineteen days for the walk and offers a booking service for each night at an appropriate Youth Hostel, bunkhouse or bed and breakfast, depending on availability. Within the nineteen days two rest days are advised, when only a few miles would be walked. With hindsight, I wish that I had ignored this advice as I found that it destroyed the rhythm of walking roughly fifteen miles per day. On the day after each rest day, I felt lethargic and really had to push myself to complete the necessary distance.

The booking service was operated at that time by Edgar Peel

---

* *see* Appendix 3, page 238.

who coincidentally lived in Baildon. As he was nearby, I called to see him regarding arrangements. He was a most pleasant and helpful person and, although getting on in years and unfortunately not able to be a distance walker himself, he took a great interest in his clients. All he required was the starting date of my walk and he would do the rest, thus relieving me of the burden of booking accommodation. It was not long before I received details of the bookings he had obtained at seventeen hostels, two bed and breakfasts and a bunkhouse. The list was long, impressive, and not without humour. Names of hostels such as 'Once Brewed' intrigued me and I found the note regarding Byrness very inviting: it stated that baths could be taken by arrangement with the lady warden ... This was more exciting than my days of hostelling during my teens!

In addition to the hostel information, the Package includes articles on the route itself, planning, safety and even body chemistry. The latter article was written by two scientists who had walked the Pennine Way in 1984. Their findings were somewhat daunting, with phrases such as: 'The first few days are a shock to the system.' That went without saying as far as I was concerned. The whole journey would be a shock to my system. Most of their article was above my head, particularly with comments such as 'The normal store of glycogen and free blood sugar is used up, giving rise to hypoglycaemia.' As I understood it, their advice was to take a supply of Vitamin B complex pills and Lecithin capsules. I was also advised to use plenty of salt on my food and to take a supply of ripe oranges or apples. Would there be room left in my rucksack for trivial things such as clothes and equipment? It was pleasing to note that if I made it as far as Malham, my body would have largely adapted to its tortuous regime and it should be plain sailing from then on.

When I did the walk I found considerable truth in this last statement. The general impression amongst fellow walkers/sufferers was that if you reached Malham the odds were with you to finish the whole distance. The closing note from the learned couple informed me that if I reached my objective I would be twice the man I was and if I gave up, I would be diminished. From this I gathered I would end up as either a schizophrenic or a dwarf!

At the risk of boring you with facts from this helpful booklet, I will mention that according to statistics there are two main reasons for dropping out, blisters and exhaustion. There is no indication whether these would occur simultaneously or one at a time.

Having read copiously about my impending challenge, the time had come to put down my books and get on with some serious action. I planned to start my preparation by tackling the section from Edale to the Snake Road, one of the main arteries over the Pennines, running between Manchester and Sheffield. My companion for this inaugural venture was Roy, an old school friend who enjoys walking as much as I. He was unable to join me on the actual walk as he could not take the required three weeks off work, but he had readily agreed to accompany me on this occasion. The distance was not far – 8½ miles – but involved the traverse of Kinder Plateau and the notorious Featherbed Moss.

We met on the appointed Sunday morning on the road above the Snake Pass: this may be a name familiar to many readers since it often crops up in road reports as the pass is notorious for being blocked with snow during bad winter weather. The weather on that autumn morning was standard for my outings, misty and wet. Leaving one car at the Snake Pass, we took the other to the start of the Pennine Way at Edale, thereby eliminating the need to walk the route in both directions. Full of anticipation and apprehension we pulled on our boots and joked about what we were letting ourselves in for. As we set off, the weather had improved not a jot.

According to AW the official start of the Pennine Way is at Grindsbrook Booth, a collection of cottages approximately one-third of a mile from the car park. What he does not make clear is that the nearby Old Nag's Head Inn is the starting point for most walkers. If the need arises, you can always call in to fortify yourself for the coming ordeal. It has been known for walkers to drop out at this point when they realise the enormity of their task and that good beer is going to waste!

(I should emphasise here that it is a number of years since I did this walk (1987) and the section which I am about to describe is not included in subsequent route revisions. The Countryside Commission, 'who now has a statutory responsibility for funding the maintenance of the path', has undertaken a huge programme of renovation in the interim period and several stretches of the route have been diverted in order 'to help conserve the landscape' on to ground 'that is far more resistant to erosion'.)*

Roy and I had our mind on other things as we walked past the inn, such as how we were going to find our way across the Kinder Plateau. I was charged with navigating, so the responsibility was mine. Spurning AW's alternative route via Jacob's Ladder, we set off on the ascent of Grindsbrook Clough that started as fairly easy walking and ended with a stiff scramble over gritstone boulders. As we clambered up onto the edge of the plateau we realised what lay before us. Over the few yards of visibility available, all we could make out was a sea of glutinous brown peat disappearing into nothingness. The rim on which we were standing was firm with weathered boulders lying on a bed of gravel. In that day's weather conditions it would probably have been wiser to stick to the rim and walk round the plateau, and I learned later that there is a recognised circuit of Kinder's edge, but the distance is considerable.

As we stood teetering on the brink, a line of AW's advice came into mind. 'The wisdom of leaving Edale on a wet morning should be debated earnestly. Better a postponement than a post mortem'! Never one to be hindered by prudence, I took a compass bearing for the direct route and we took our first step into the morass with much trepidation. The best way of describing the conditions underfoot would be mounds of clinging peat surrounded by water. To stop ourselves from becoming sub-merged required a minor miracle. The strain of extricating peat-laden boots and legs from the quagmire was tremendous. There was not a soul in sight and we were enveloped in an eerie silence that you could almost reach out and touch. The landmark of Crowden Head remained hidden in the mist. We were making for the head stream of the River Kinder – but were destined not to reach it that day.

As time dragged on and we became more and more tired, the

* I quote from the (typeset) introduction to the Revised edition of Wain-wright's *Pennine Way Companion*. Current information regarding the Pennine Way is shown in Appendix 3, page 238.

awful truth began to dawn that we had lost our way and were heading into the centre of the plateau. The hopping, or lurching, that was necessary from one peat hag to another had obviously taken us off course. AW describes the plateau as 'the difficult section'. He continues 'Rough walking, absence of views and loss of directional sense all contribute to the hazards of the plateau, even on a clear day.' How right he is! Unable to see for more than a few yards, there was no chance of taking further compass bearings to other landmarks. We were reduced to floundering around hoping for a miracle. What an ignominious start to walking the Pennine Way! A jumble of thoughts rushed through my mind. What must Roy be thinking? Fancy getting him lost three miles from the start. If this was the extent of my route-finding expertise, what chance had I of negotiating the remaining 267? I felt wretched and quite, quite helpless.

After what seemed an age of staggering aimlessly around, a landmark at last loomed out of the mist. It was a trig point that took us completely by surprise. As we struggled towards this lifeline amongst a sea of peat we could discern a man and a boy, whom we discovered later was his son, standing by it. Thankfully, the man knew the plateau very well. He told us that we were at Crowden Tower. On checking my map I found that we had wandered far from our intended north westerly route and were a long way from the River Kinder. The man knew the way down to Jacob's Ladder from where we were standing and offered to guide us. Roy accepted, a little too readily, I thought, although there was not much sense in those conditions in ploughing on to our original objective. A sense of failure permeated through me as we were led towards the rim of the plateau. We met some other walkers near Jacob's Ladder who joined us to return to Edale. On the way back I said very little, my confidence at a low ebb. Roy and our companions were chatting amiably for most of the way. They must have thought what miserable company I was.

We arrived back in the car park at Edale in the early afternoon, much sooner than we had anticipated ending the day's walk. This was just as well because we had to return to the Snake Road to pick up my car. We had deliberately driven down to Edale in Roy's car so that I could ferry him back there on completion of the walk and he would be pointing in the right direction for where he lived in Nottinghamshire. As it turned out, he had to drive me all the way back to my car at the Snake Pass and then make a longer journey home. He did not complain, but I was not surprised when he declined my invitation to try again the following weekend.

I set off back to Yorkshire, seething with frustration. Before I got home, however, I had made up my mind to have another crack on my own. I was determined not be beaten.

On the following Sunday morning I got up early and drove down to Edale for my second attempt. The visibility was poor and it was raining as usual, but I would not be diverted from my goal, despite AW's advice about postponement. I do not recommend that you do likewise, because I had already ignored it at my peril.

I made determined progress up Grindsbrook Clough to arrive at the ill-fated spot on which I had stood the previous week. Studying the map carefully and taking a compass bearing I headed north westwards across the plateau. Ignoring the steady rain and awful conditions I watched my compass continuously, concentrating on keeping as true a course as the mist and peat-hag-hopping would allow. Eventually I was rewarded with the delightful sight of the headstream of the River Kinder. The feeling of tension and frustration drained from me as I headed towards Kinder Downfall. My step was light as I progressed along the river's shingle edge. In what seemed no time at all I approached the Downfall to be greeted by a wall of spray caused by the wind rushing in from the west. I tentatively crept towards the edge of the craggy cleft to find that the water, instead of rushing over its edge, formed the spray that lashed onto the plateau with tremendous force. I was unable to appreciate the westerly view as it was obscured by the mist, but I was untroubled by this. I was not out to enjoy the scenery as there were more challenges to meet, like reaching the Snake Road and retracing my steps back to Edale.

With the comforting feeling that I had laid the bogey of Kinder Plateau, I strode along its edge upon which lie many large weathered gritstone boulders. The path suddenly fell away in front of me at a steep angle, eroded to the width of a motorway. A rough and tricky descent followed until the path levelled out, and the wind that had battered me for most of the way eased. Instead of improving, however, the terrain became treacherously boggy. I crossed an old trackway running up William Clough from Hayfield. It continued in a north-easterly direction down Ashop Clough to the Snake Inn. I made my way up a gradual incline towards a post that marks the summit of Mill Hill, which is merely a large, uninteresting hump, denoted by AW as 'no mill, not much hill'.

The remaining stretch to the Snake Road is mapped by AW into two sections. A line of nineteen posts mark the first section to another hump called Moss Castle. This was reasonable walking, but it deteriorated sharply on the second section across Featherbed Moss where progress was slowed by a series of peat groughs. As I staggered through these I noticed a runner finding better access a few hundred yards to my right. Assuming that this fellow knew what he was about, I clambered out of the soupy channel and headed towards him. Although he was moving much faster than I was, it was possible to discern the line of his route. This was across slightly higher ground than the Moss. Eventually I reached the route that he had taken and found it to be reasonably firm underfoot. Following it, I was able to reach the Snake Road without much difficulty and I made a mental note to follow this line when I made my attempt at the full distance.

It felt great to be on solid ground and a stop for rest and some food was called for. As I sat munching on my sandwiches, I was passed by several cars whose occupants stared through their windows at me. They were probably wondering who in their right mind would sit in that bleak, misty spot, thoroughly drenched by the persistent rain.

It was soon time to be back on my feet and start the return journey to Edale. This was accomplished without incident, including the re-crossing of Kinder Scout in the persistent mist. After a journey of 17-plus miles, a fair old distance in pretty atrocious weather, I felt well pleased. I paused only to send Roy a postcard, and then set off home with a light heart, knowing that I could cross Kinder Plateau in the worst of weather, and had cracked the intricacies of using a compass correctly.

What had at first seemed like an age to my starting date for the great adventure flew past. Before I knew it, there were only a few weeks to go and final preparations were underway. I had already been carrying my rucksack full of ballast on my training walks: I had walked several more sections of the Pennine Way in an effort to build up stamina. A detailed list of all the kit to be carried had been carefully drawn up. My daughter had bought me a copy of *The Walker's Handbook* by H.D. Westacott; this contains much useful information on clothing, equipment and the planning necessary for a long walk. Particularly useful are details of the sequence of packing a rucksack, and every item of kit required, together with their weights, is included.

Whilst on the subject of kit, I read somewhere an amusing tip on how to approach the intricate task of choosing what to carry. First, you should carefully lay out on the floor all the items that are considered absolutely necessary. You then discard half of them. This completed, you may now start packing your rucksack, confident in the knowledge that you will not suffer a double hernia on the first day of your walk.

I have always reckoned a total pack weight of around 26lbs, or 12kg in modern terminology, to be the optimum. Whilst walking the Pennine Way, I carried about 32lbs, which I put down to inexperience. This has gradually been reduced over the succeeding years. I must emphasise that these figures do not include a tent or cooking equipment, as the backpackers amongst you will obviously realise. However, on my one and only backpacking expedition, in the north-west of Scotland, I did manage to keep the weight down to 32lbs, a manageable level. On this occasion I backpacked from necessity as accommodation was very sparse in certain areas. I do recognise that many people enjoy backpacking and the freedom that it allows but it is not really for me.

My son's walking gear, which had proved adequate so far, was not suitable for a long-distance walk. Therefore a shopping trip was called for. I bought a Gore-Tex jacket and a pair of expensive boots. These, in my view, are the two most important items: a good jacket would prevent me from catching pneumonia, and a comfortable pair of well-fitting boots would not play havoc with my feet. The assistant in the shop where I purchased these items was most helpful. He took great pains to ensure that my boots fitted perfectly and for this care I was eternally grateful. They did not require any breaking in, which was a great help.

All too quickly the eve of my departure arrived and I went through the rucksack-filling performance, checking against my list that I was not leaving anything behind, particularly AW's *Pennine Way Companion* and the OS maps. I dreaded opening my rucksack and finding something vital missing.

Before long it was time for bed and a good night's sleep. Inevitably, I suppose, once in bed my mind raced round in circles. Had I packed everything? Would I catch the coach the following morning? What was I letting myself in for? Would I give up if the weather was its usual awful self? Had I packed that second pair of bootlaces? These thoughts and many more kept me tossing and turning for most of the night.

CHAPTER FIVE

Pennine Way Experiences

I awoke the next morning feeling exhausted. A fine start to my conquest of the Pennine Way, I thought. There I was, tired out and I had not done any walking yet. During the coach journey to Sheffield I half slept, but was frequently jerked back to consciousness by my apprehension. I was convinced that I was setting out on a foolish escapade and would never make it to the finish. I took a train from Sheffield to Edale and gazed at the dark and threatening clouds through the window. It looked as though I was to have my usual luck with the weather.

As I got off the train a voice behind me asked if I knew where Edale Youth Hostel was. I turned to see a fellow walker pulling a large rucksack through the carriage door. I said that I didn't know and suggested that we search for it together. On our way into the village, I learned that my new companion's name was Ben and that he lived in Harrogate which isn't that far from Baildon. He was also attempting the whole Pennine Way, was using the Pennine Way Package and by coincidence had chosen the same accommodation as myself. We struck up an immediate friendship and decided to join forces. It would be nice to have a companion to share the next two and a half weeks. Ben, I discovered, was a retired schoolteacher in his early sixties who had taken up walking rather late in life like me. It was also his first attempt and he appeared inexperienced like myself.

Day One: Edale–Crowden

We spent a comfortable night in the hostel, but I was awake early the next morning and lay wondering what fate had in store for us.

The supper provided by the hostel the evening before had been good, but breakfast was not a success. Being a sprog in walking terms and trying to follow every bit of advice from the experts, I avoided the traditional British breakfast and plumped for the high-protein content of baked beans on toast. What I actually got was an orange mound floating on an ebony raft. The beans were glutinous and the toast was burnt to a cinder. I struggled with this culinary disaster, urged on by the thought that the beans would give me added momentum during the epic struggle up Grindsbrook Clough. It was one way of making flatulence work for you!

Fortified with this explosive mixture I hoisted my rucksack onto my back, shook hands with Ben and we were on our way. Kinder Plateau was reached without undue difficulty. We were not rushing things bearing in mind the weight on our backs. I had the advantage over Ben in that I was considerably taller and my longer legs meant that I would take several thousand steps fewer than him over the journey but he kept pace very well.

I performed the now familiar ritual of taking a compass bearing for the River Kinder and we squelched off into the quagmire of peat. The cloud level was low which meant that once again visibility was poor. I introduced Ben to the joy of bog-hopping between clumps of peat. With his slightly shorter legs, he had to make more of an effort each time. On several occasions I jumped onto a heap of peat only to find that there was no way forward, and when I swivelled back to return to the previous peat hag I realised that, because of the murk, I wasn't sure from which direction I had come. It was like puzzling out a maze, with endless back-tracking. The fellow walkers that we had met climbing Grindsbrook Clough, or standing apprehensively looking at the peat hags from the edge of the plateau, had disappeared. They had probably taken one look at the terrain and gone home!

At this point I nearly came to grief. AW's advice that at any time the Kinder Plateau is not really an undertaking for a solitary walker came true with a vengeance. But for Ben I may not have been here to write this tale. Whether it was due to the weight of my rucksack or the atrocious conditions I do not know, but I seemed to sink further into the peat than on my previous crossings. I jumped, realising too late that the selected peat hag looked extremely suspect. As I landed, my boots disappeared into the

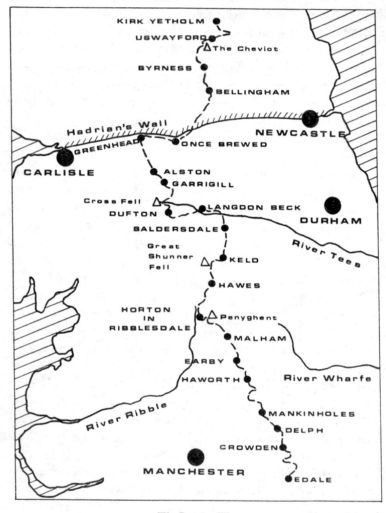

The Pennine Way

morass and in an instant I was up to my thighs and still sinking. Ben, to his eternal credit, saw my predicament quickly and, since he was on a firmer footing, he quickly grabbed my hand. Tugging with all his strength he managed to extricate me from the bog's grip. I dare not stop to think what might have happened if I had been on my own. Perhaps I would have been found centuries later, preserved in a grave of peat like a prehistoric man. I did hear later of a young Pennine Way walker who suffered a similar fate to mine on the plateau. Apparently she had the sense to throw herself forward and spreadeagle herself across the bog to prevent herself from submerging. The filthy state of her clothes would have been a small price to pay for her safety. I was merely covered in mud up to above my knees.

The River Kinder was reached safely and soon we were feeling the spray from Kinder Downfall. Visibility below us was better than I had had previously and we could see the grey waters of Kinder reservoir to the west. There were groups of walkers sitting around, chatting, eating or simply looking at the view. Most of these we surmised would have wisely taken the route around the plateau's edge or walked to this spot from the Snake Road. Our journey to that road was made easier by avoiding Featherbed Moss. Thanks to my previous experience we were able to follow the relatively firm route taken by the runner. We could see in the distance other walkers manfully squelching through the peat on the main path. There were many more people around than during my training walk when the weather had been much worse.

Crossing the road we headed for Bleaklow which is as notorious as Kinder Scout (2088 feet), if not worse. The section of path leaving the road had undergone repair with fencing stakes laid across it. I would have preferred peat as, in my view, those stakes when wet are far more lethal. More than once I did the splits as my boots slid along them. We shortly crossed the line of a Roman road known as Doctor's Gate. This formerly linked the forts near Castleton in Derbyshire and Glossop; it would have been a wild journey across the Pennines in those times.

AW's wicked sense of humour comes into its own as this stage of the walk is tackled. He gleefully informs us that it is commonly considered the toughest part of the Pennine Way. Mud, rain and wind will be experienced, true nature in the raw. Never fear, he tells us, worse is to follow. And if that isn't enough, he reports that lives have been lost on Bleaklow. Was it time to go home?

As we approached the Devil's Dike, I recalled AW's comments about this section: 'Roll your pants up above your knees.' And no wonder because the Devil's Dike is a gruesome, waterlogged channel running between mounds of peat for about three-quarters of a mile. Wooden steps make the descent into the dike's deep channel less arduous, but you then have to negotiate its muddy bed until Alport Low is reached. The only landmarks are two posts protruding from a hill of peat at the end of the Dike. There are no helpful steps here to assist the clamber from the depths. We struggled upwards over the clinging peat, our boots often slipping on the soggy slope. We stood clinging to the posts, thankful that we were able to look around us once more. The view of peat hags as far as the eye could see did not offer any comfort. Low cloud and mist were obscuring the higher reaches of Bleaklow. A line of posts on top of the hags flatter only to deceive as they do not mark the route. They merely signify the parish boundaries. (Those of you who are now thinking that this is a good place to avoid will be pleased to know that the surface of the bed of the dike is now much improved and stone markers lead you to Bleaklow Head.)

Having been up Bleaklow on my training sessions I had worked out a reasonable way to tackle the climb. This was not via the peat hags, which would soon sap vital strength, but by following the beds of the streams that run between them. Although it increased the distance by weaving in and out of the hags, the ground was reasonably solid and walking was much easier.

After a period of steady climbing through these meandering channels a group of stones could be seen through the gloom. These weirdly shaped boulders were the Wain Stones and although not signifying the summit, gave reassurance that we were near to it. A humorous sketch by AW in his guide depicts two of the boulders apparently in the act of kissing each other. 'This is the only bit of sex in the book,' he says wryly: (what a spoilsport!). In a way, it was lucky that the mist was down because the view from these stones to the barely discernible Bleaklow Head is not one to be enjoyed. It is akin to being in mid-ocean, with the waves substituted by mounds of peat. Like AW, I needed no reminder that this was not one of my favourite places. Chatting to a group of walkers resting on the stones we found that they were also filled with trepidation at this daunting sight.

We tentatively squelched our way across this sea of peat to attain the highest point of Bleaklow (2060 feet), our legs nicely soaked and stained by the morass. Once there we had to find the route down to the Longdendale Valley. If the weather had been kinder, we could have taken a bearing towards Holme Moss television mast which stands roughly five miles to the north. But of course . . .

We headed north and, much to our relief, eventually found the valley of Wildboar Grain. No wonder AW says that everyone who gets onto Bleaklow is glad to get off again. From AW's guide I knew that this valley ran into Torside Clough, which in turn would take us down to the reservoirs near Crowden Youth Hostel, our stopping place for the night.

Torside Castle stands about two hundred yards to the west of the path through Torside Clough. This is not actually a castle but a prehistoric mound which may have given the name to Bleaklow. It is derived from the Celtic 'hlaew' meaning a burial mound, or hill. Ben and I were relieved that, after that awful crossing of Bleaklow Head, it had not proved to be our burial place. As we descended Torside Clough we came out of the low cloud and got our first view of the valley and its reservoirs. The path became exceedingly steep and rocky as we dropped down towards Reaps Farm.

Unfortunately, this was the scene of Ben's demise. So intent was he on taking in the impressive view over Longdendale that he did not watch where he was putting his feet. What happened next taught me a lesson that I have never forgotten. Whilst extolling the virtues of the wonderful view Ben missed his footing and pitched forward to the ground, putting out his hand to lessen the impact. In so doing he dislocated his little finger. I was walking in front at the time so I did not see this happen. A surprised voice behind me said, 'Ouch, I've bent my finger!' Without more ado he grabbed the injured finger and, remarkably, pulled it back into position. This, I thought, was a minor miracle. I was totally unprepared for what came next. Not having learnt his lesson, he fell in exactly the same way a few moments later, this time letting out a loud yell. I turned to look at his now grotesquely shaped finger with a nasty gash at its base. He was obviously in considerable pain but I was no expert in replacing dislocated digits. Rooting inside my rucksack I found my first aid kit and bound the injured finger to the others. I had no idea if this was the accepted practice but it was all that I could think of at the time and hoped it would at least ease Ben's pain and prevent further damage. I have since read AW's strictures about this many times. He ends *Fellwanderer* with the words: 'Don't forget to watch where you are putting your feet, and you'll be all right.'

We made our way gingerly down to Reaps Farm, carefully watching where we placed our feet. Once on to solid ground we made better progress across the end of Torside Reservoir and along the far side of the valley to the Crowden Youth Hostel. After checking in, I explained Ben's predicament and asked if there was a hospital in the area. We were told that the nearest was at Ashton-under-Lyne on the outskirts of Manchester. I rang for a taxi to ferry Ben to the hospital and duly saw him off, with a promise to arrange that there would be some hot food available on his return. The evening meal was a rather subdued affair for me as I was concerned about Ben.

There was a bright spot, however, for whilst checking in we had overheard an elderly gentleman telling everyone within earshot that he was seventy-four years old and delighted to be walking the Pennine Way. He was accompanied by a mere strippling of sixty-six in his first attempt. Whilst I was silently eating my meal, I overheard the loquacious old fellow telling anyone who cared to listen how superbly fit he was and what had motivated him to walk the route at his age. It became obvious, however, that he was not too hot on route-finding as he and his companion had completely lost their way on Kinder Plateau and never made it to the Downfall. Instead, they had blundered from the plateau not knowing where they were and had to make an unscheduled overnight stop at a pub somewhere. They had managed to reach Crowden on their second day, already a day behind schedule. I wondered what problems might lie ahead for them, and I was eventually to find out as I encountered them in the most unexpected places. They were to prove a wily pair and I conferred on them the nickname of the 'Brothers in Law'.

Shortly after we had finished supper, Ben returned with his hand heavily bandaged and a splint on his injured finger. He had received a painful tetanus jab where it hurts most and been sent on his way with the sobering thought that they considered him mad to be attempting such a venture. The warden did Ben proud and provided a hot meal for him. Then later, suitably fed and watered, Ben telephoned his wife to give her the sorrowful news – and assured her that it would not distract him from his task. She probably tried to persuade him to go home, but you know how stubborn men are.

We then had a stroll around the hamlet, but the only photograph I got was of a bearded old goat chewing in the evening light. A little reconnaissance for the following morning was accomplished and we found the path that would take us on the next stage of our journey. This led up to Laddow Rocks and onwards to the dreaded Black Hill. Why 'dreaded'? Well, AW calls it in his *Companion* 'a desolate and hopeless quagmire', something I cheerfully reminded myself of before I went to bed. 'A frightening place in bad weather, a dangerous place after heavy rain.' And knowing our luck . . .

Day Two: Crowden–Delph

Next morning we were allocated some cleaning tasks, according to the YHA rules. Consequently we were amongst the last to leave and noted that the 'Brothers in Law' had got away much earlier. Ben's hand wasn't giving too much pain from its injury.

It is quite a stiff climb onto Laddow Rocks but the view from there down the valley and over Longdendale is very impressive. On a fine day the flat top of Kinder Scout can be seen on the southern horizon. On this occasion, yes, there was low cloud and rain was beginning to fall. We could see below us into the valley where Crowden Great Brook flows from the flanks of Black Hill. Lo and behold, the 'Brothers in Law' could be seen making uncertain progress along it – despite the fact that it was not the official route. They were going slowly and we saw no more of them that day.

We began the descent from the rocks on pretty rough going. I kept my eyes on the boulders underneath my feet and noticed that Ben was doing the same. Had he learned AW's important lesson? Some fellow walkers had commiserated with him at supper the previous evening after hearing of his accident, and one chap had mentioned AW's dictum which must have made Ben ruefully wish that he had been told it earlier. Now, however, he appeared to be heeding the dictum that: 'Fellwalking accidents happen only to those who walk clumsily. If you want to look at a view, *stop*, look and only then move on.' Ben carefully watched where his feet were landing and he made frequent stops to admire the view.

Once in the valley the ground softened and became quite boggy. We crossed the Crowden Great Brook high up and made our waterlogged way onto the lower slopes of Black Hill. It was impossible to see its flat top which was under cloud and the rain did not boost our spirits. The climb stiffened with detours neces-sary to either side of the wide, eroded path in order to find a firmer footing. This practice is frowned on by AW who did not approve of people making wider and wider paths round eroded sections. We were earning ourselves a black mark in his eyes, for our behaviour was exactly what turns paths into motorways.

I have already described the bleak conditions at the top of Black Hill in the opening chapter. May it suffice to say that once on the relatively flat summit (1908 feet), it took us a good twenty minutes of bog-hopping to reach the Ordnance column. You may have reached the conclusion that all the high ground on the Pennine Way consists only of oozing peat. Never fear, it does get better. Ben had not complained at all of his injury. He had covered the affected hand with a plastic bag whilst crossing the boggier sections which prevented his bandages from being dirtied by the ever-present peat.

As we sat at the base of the trig point on the only bit of solid ground available, the sun actually broke through the clouds. With our spirits lifted, we made short work of our lunchtime sandwiches provided by the Youth Hostel. We had met quite a few walkers during our climb but none of them apparently wanted to leave the path and fight their way to where we were sitting. It is surprising how quickly a shared challenge or adversity fosters companion-ship. Although barely halfway through our second day together, Ben and I knew a great deal about each other and were firm friends. As we sat chatting and enjoying the warmth of the sun, I felt glad once again that he was with me. We were actually perched on the county boundary which passes over the summit and were about to cross from Derbyshire into my adopted county of West Yorkshire. The clouds for once had moved away and the landmark of the television mast on Holme Moss was clearly visible about a mile away. Why had that mast been hiding in cloud when we needed it to guide us from the summit of Bleaklow? Now that we did not need it, there it was staring us in the face. Isn't life perverse, I thought.

I was jerked from my reverie by Ben gathering up his gear ready for departure. It was decision time once more. We had to choose between two alternative routes for the next few miles. The main route lies through a series of what can only be described as treacherous bogs. These bear the names of Featherbed Moss (equally as bad as its forerunner), White Moss and Black Moss. Having battled my way through them during my training walks, I suggested to Ben that the alternative route past the Wessenden Reservoirs would be preferable. Although I had no previous knowledge of that stretch, it certainly had to be better than the main route. If AW was right, the first part of the Wessenden route would be bad but once the A635 Holmfirth–Greenfield road was reached, conditions underfoot would be good.

We agreed to take the Wessenden alternative as AW is seldom wrong. The next challenge was to get off the summit of Black Hill in the right direction. Luckily, a pile of stones stood virtually on our compass bearing, so we struck out for this. After another period of squelching, weaving and hopping we got clear of the peat and were able to follow piles of stones marking a dry channel that took us down towards Dean Clough. We found the boundary ditch which runs to the road without difficulty and, before we knew it, we were clear of Black Hill and had the firmness of tarmacadam under our boots on the main road. According to AW a chap called Mario occupied an ice cream stand at the nearby junction with the Meltham road. Mario had probably retired to the Bahamas with his takings for he was nowhere to be seen when we arrived. We had to be content with chewing on the remainder of our packed lunches.

Once across the road we could see the broad, dry track running down to the distant reservoirs and made good progress down to them. The scenery was impressive around the reservoirs with several small waterfalls cascading from the surrounding moorland. We then passed the 'fleshpots of Wessenden', as they are described by AW, which consist of Wessenden Lodge, an imposing house.

I assume that any habitation would appear as a 'fleshpot' after the trials of Black Hill.

All good things must come to an end. A sign told us to leave the track and strike out across the moorland. With reluctance we dropped into the valley below the track, crossed a pleasant stream and made the steep climb onto the moor itself. As we passed Swellands Reservoir the conditions underfoot were reasonable, with young summer bracken and heather much in evidence.

Our destination was the Oldham to Huddersfield road, the A62. There are many reservoirs in this area which serve Huddersfield and Manchester's needs. As we reached the road, we passed the fifth of these, Redbrook Reservoir, which appeared to be very popular with yachting enthusiasts. We joined the main road at the head of Standedge Cutting where it runs between steep embankments up to the watershed between Yorkshire and Lancashire. Below the road run three tunnels. When these were constructed in the nineteenth century, they provided a vital link between the industrial areas of east Lancashire and West Yorkshire.

A detour of roughly two miles along the road to Delph brought us to our designated stopping place for the night, Globe Farm Bunkhouse. This is in a good position, sheltering beneath Standedge Edge and having extensive views over Greenfield and Oldham. We were made very welcome and the food was excellent. After supper Ben and I walked to a nearby pub with two chaps also staying in the bunkhouse. They too were walking the Pennine Way and we spent a pleasant couple of hours swapping stories. I was later to team up with one of them, John, for part of the walk.

Day Three: Delph–Mankinholes

The sleeping quarters at the bunkhouse were somewhat cramped. Ben spent an uncomfortable night tossing and turning with pain from his injured finger. By morning, it had swollen badly and turned rather an ugly colour. The weather, in contrast, was cool but clear to start with and got pleasantly warmer as the day progressed.

Our route up until lunchtime took us along the gritstone edge of Standedge, over the M62 roaring-way and across another gritstone bastion, Blackstone Edge. At this stage of the walk we were following the western fringe of the Pennines that forms a barrier between Lancashire, West Yorkshire and Calderdale. We were pleased that the weather had for once relented and we had at least some views over industrial Lancashire. Conditions underfoot varied from dry and grassy to boggy and we were able to maintain reasonable progress.

The M62 was crossed by means of a narrow footbridge strung across the gorge at Windy Hill on the crest of Saddleworth Moor. When the motorway was built in the late sixties, the constructors had to cut through rock to produce this steep-sided gorge. The motorway was designed in such a way that snow was not supposed to build up on the higher stretches; I don't know if this was successful, but the gorge at Windy Hill gave a good impression of a wind tunnel. The wind, which had been strong all morning, tore through the channel, buffeting the footbridge which swung quite appreciably from side to side. Crossing it was not for the faint hearted and my knuckles were white with gripping onto the hand rails. The sight of heavy traffic roaring beneath us did not provide any comfort.

Staggering from the bridge we began the long pull up to Blackstone Edge. As we did so, I recalled an incident that had happened during my earlier reconnaissance of this section. I had approached the motorway from the opposite direction in thick mist. Coming down from Blackstone Edge, a stretch of open, featureless moorland is crossed. Unable to see any land-marks, I was relying on my compass and, as often happens in such conditions, there was an accompanying eerie silence. All of a sudden I heard a swishing sound in front of me which was most disturbing. Wracking my brains as to what the noise might be I suddenly and miraculously stepped out of the mist to find the motorway directly below where I was standing. Thankfully there was a fence that stopped me from falling down the embankment and when I had recovered from the shock I realised that the sound I had heard was the traffic rushing through the gorge.

That particular sensation was similar to when one is on a mountain in thick mist and the clouds suddenly part to reveal a panoramic view for thousands of feet below: it happened to me as

I was descending Pillar which overlooks Ennerdale in the Lake District, of which more later.

To return to our passage up the Pennine Way, Ben and I reached the top of Blackstone Edge and, since the weather was still on our side, we stopped for a while to admire the view of Rochdale and Manchester below us. Leaving the Edge we crossed a Roman road which has one of the best preserved sections in the country. The stones have stayed in remarkably good condition for nearly two thousand years. The Aiggin Stone nearby marks the summit of the old road and AW shows a picture of it in his guide sadly toppled over. By saying in the guide that 'it seems odd that the local archaeologists have not thought to re-erect it', I suppose it was inevitable that someone would do just that. I hope he would be pleased.

The walking is easy from this point to the main A58 linking Halifax with Rochdale. Skirting round an old quarry, the road comes into full view, with the welcoming sight of the White House public house, a convenient watering-hole. Ben and I approached it at lunchtime and spent a pleasant half-hour outside with a well-earned pint to accompany our sandwiches. We struck up a conversation during our meal with a friendly couple who were walking a few miles of the Way before returning to their car. They said that they envied us attempting the whole distance, but when we jokingly offered to change places with them they hastily declined.

According to AW, the next three miles are the easiest part of the Pennine Way and so it proved. A good flat track passed three reservoirs before rejoining the rough moorland which was now becoming pretty familiar. Still traversing the western fringe of the Pennines, good views over Bacup and Todmorden opened up on our left as we approached the stone sentinel of Stoodley Pike. A short distance from the Pike we crossed a stone-flagged path that was an old trackway running from Crag Vale in the Calder Valley to Mankinholes which nestled below us. This path now forms part of the Calderdale Way, a fifty-mile circular walk around the Calder Valley.

Our route from here should have taken us down to the Youth Hostel in Mankinholes, but fate took a hand. To be precise, Ben's hand. The swelling around his affected finger was increasing by the hour and it was turning all colours of the rainbow. He obviously needed immediate treatment so, checking the map, we decided we had to head for either Todmorden or nearby Hebden Bridge to find a hospital or health centre. Although Ben must have been in considerable pain all day, he had not complained once and I felt the least I could do was to help him get some treatment. Despite his predicament, however, he insisted that we should first pay our respects to the monument of Stoodley Pike. In pitch darkness we climbed the steps inside to the viewing balcony, approximately one-third of the way up its 125 feet. This towering obelisk was built during the Napoleonic wars to commemorate the Peace of Ghent and it stands by the side of the Pennine Way footpath on a hill overlooking the Calder Valley. Many similar towers around Yorkshire's hills were built at that time. The view from the balcony was panoramic and, as conditions were clear, we could see for many miles in all directions and were loath to leave our lofty vantage point. The descent through the pitch black interior was hair-raising; I'm a bit surprised EC laws haven't put a halt to such an adventure. I earnestly hoped that Ben would not fall and damage his finger again or, worse still, break an arm or a leg. After what seemed an age, although it was only a few minutes, we reappeared into daylight at the foot of the tower, blinking at the brightness.

We made our way into the deep-sided Calder Valley where the lines of communication – namely canal, railway, river and road – squeeze their way through a narrow gap. The footpath intersected the A646 between Todmorden and Hebden Bridge. Not knowing the area, we asked about medical facilities at a nearby filling station. The owner couldn't have been more helpful: he rang the health centre in Hebden Bridge and booked an appointment for Ben. He also arranged for us to be taken there by car, thus saving us a walk of two miles, and told us the times of buses back and where to alight. I have never forgotten his generosity and whenever I drive along that road, which I have done many times since, I salute his thoughtfulness.

Ben and I were met in the health centre's reception by a smiling nurse who cheerily welcomed us. Apparently they were used to frequent visits from walkers whose feet had rebelled after three days' abuse and were considering changing the name of their centre to the 'Pennine Way Blister Unit'. Ben explained that blisters were not his problem and held out his injured hand. The nurse grimaced and whisked him away for examination.

A short time later he was back with a face as long as a fiddle. A quick look at his finger by the medics had been enough. He had been told to go straight home and report to his local hospital. This, of course, was the kiss of death to his Pennine Way aspirations and he was understandably very despondent; much preparation has to go into these long long-distance walks. My problem was that I would lose a companion and new-found friend.

Another out-patient recognised that we were walkers and re-marked on Ben's heavily bandaged hand. We started chatting and it appeared that he had been a walker in his younger days and was particularly fond of the Lake District. He recounted an experience of having to carry a particularly heavy young lady down from one of the fells. The unfortunate girl had broken her ankle and he had staggered a great distance with her on his back. I suppose I should have been grateful . . .

The next task was to get Ben home. We found a telephone and he gave his wife prior warning of his unscheduled return. Fortu-nately we were not too far from Harrogate and his journey would not be a long one. Ben and I took a disconsolate walk to the bus stop. I didn't feel that any comforting words would lift his spirits, so I had to be content with suggesting that we keep in touch and promised to inform him of my progress. We waved goodbye sadly as his bus pulled away.

After seeing Ben off, I had to get to the Mankinholes Youth Hostel in time for my evening meal. I caught a bus back along the main road towards Todmorden, from whence I had a brisk road walk to Mankinholes. I reached the hostel in time for supper and explained to the warden the reason for Ben's non-attendance. Unfortunately he would not let me eat Ben's share which was a shame since I was ravenously hungry.

Although I missed Ben's friendly chat during supper, I was otherwise entertained – by that canny pair, the 'Brothers in Law'. Once again, I was rather surprised that they had found their way here, as they were not doing very well when last seen approaching Black Hill. They had some hairy adventures to recount like being half submerged during their crossing of Black Moss which we had fortunately avoided. To illustrate their predicament, the older of the two brandished a broken walking stick that he had snapped whilst trying to heave himself out of the peat. Despite their misfortunes, they still seemed in high spirits and were determined to carry on.

I also met some young walkers who were doing the Way much more quickly than I could. One couple had walked the twenty-five miles from Crowden that day, thereby condensing two of my stages into one. Another pair, who were walking in the opposite direction, had come from Kirk Yetholm in just twelve days, including a rest day. One of them was paying a high price, for although he was wearing trainers, his feet were an ugly mess.

Day Four: Mankinholes–Haworth

My abiding memory of the hostel at Mankinholes is of the warden oversleeping the following morning. He was awakened by impatient walkers hammering on his bedroom door demanding breakfast.

As I set out on my first day alone, the rain, which had been falling since dawn, conveniently stopped. I found a path on the edge of the moor near the hostel that returned me to the main route at Stoodley Pike. Then I took the same journey into the Calder Valley that I had taken the previous afternoon. Wishing to thank the kind proprietor at the filling station I made a short detour along the A646 to tell him how Ben had fared, but unfortunately I had to leave a message as he was not there. I returned to the Pennine Way path disappointed that I had not been able to thank him for his kindness.

According to AW, the Calder Valley marks a change in conditions on the Pennine Way. The lonely peat moors are left behind to be replaced by a much easier terrain, which I was led to expect until Malham where the limestone country would be reached. I did find the going much easier, but there were one or two sticky sections whilst crossing Haworth and Ickornshaw Moors.

I tackled the steep climb out of the valley with the comforting feeling that things were about to improve. Much of the route was along paved paths that ran between stone walls, something unique to the area. My lack of a companion to talk to did not last long. Before I reached the top of the valley, I came across John, a young walker from Sheffield whom Ben and I had met at Globe Farm a couple of days previously. I explained how I had lost my earlier companion and when we discovered we were staying at the same locations until Malham we joined forces.

The next section of the route was quite complicated and we had to follow AW's instructions closely to avoid straying from the path. I could still see Stoodley Pike standing proudly above the Calder Valley whenever I turned round for a backward view. On its higher reaches the valley levels out slightly and we made good progress through meadows until we reached the crest of Pry Hill. This signifies the top of the valley and to our right appeared the towers of the two churches in the village of Heptonstall lying about one and a half miles away. The squat tower of the old church (circa 1260) stands side by side with its taller Victorian counterpart. This pair kept making an appearance, as if keeping a watchful eye on our progress, until Heptonstall Moor was reached. Another deep valley lies beyond Pry Hill and as we descended into it we could see rich woodland carpeting much of its floor. Through this attractive setting flows the lively Colden Water which we crossed by a fine old stone footbridge.

It is here that the Calderdale Way is crossed again. Another climb followed towards the hamlet of Colden which is flanked by the now familiar paths passing between stone walls – in fact, dry stone walls. AW has an interesting paragraph about these paths in his guide. Dry stone walls abound in the area and are a tribute to the craftsmanship and skill of their builders.

In a short time Long High Top was reached and we were on open moorland once more, but the going was reasonable. We followed one of the many paths that cross Heptonstall Moor; these were used as packhorse routes and salt ways. Ancient crosses also mark routes used by the monks of Whalley Abbey. As it leaves the moor, the Way passes the Pack Horse Inn that still stands on the Hebden Bridge to Colne road. Nearby is the head of Hebden Water which flows south-eastwards through a wooded valley past the local beauty spot known as Hardcastle Crags, a valley that has been popular since Victorian times. Time would not permit a detour to sample these delights as we had the challenging climb onto Haworth Moor to contend with; another day perhaps.

Many of the watercourses that flow from the surrounding moorland are dammed to form numerous reservoirs, some of which we had already seen. We were about to pass three of these that are interlinked and controlled by Halifax Corporation. The Walshaw Dean Reservoirs, as they are known, are quite picturesque and provide a reasonable distraction during the long pull out of the valley. The reservoir lodge was undergoing renovation, a fine stone building being fitted with a new stone-slabbed roof. Although it is a long way from the road, it occupies a fine position overlooking the lower reservoir and Alcomden Water. We called out a greeting to a chap lying precariously on the roof up a ladder. He paused in his work to respond that he thought we were right barmy to be trogging about the countryside with huge packs on our back. We told him that we stood less chance of breaking our backs than he did if he happened to fall from his ladder. With a broad grin and a rude gesture he sent us on our way.

As we left the reservoirs behind, however, the familiar battle with boggy peat was resumed during our steady climb to the watershed that overlooks Stanbury and Haworth Moors. John was making good progress in the conditions with his long legs that were a good deal younger than mine. I was struggling to keep pace with him and was glad of the occasional respite when we stopped to take in the view over the wide expanse of moorland behind us. The reservoirs looked quite small in the distance, but we could still make out the profusion of rhododendrons on their flanks. They provided a welcome oasis of colour amidst austere surroundings. We passed several walkers during our ascent, including a couple walking the Pennine Way in the opposite direction. They were adopting a more leisurely pace than those would-be record breakers that we had met at Mankinholes. They had the good sense to allow time for exploring surrounding areas of particular interest to them.

The weather was quite humid that afternoon and John and I were sweating unprettily as we reached Withins Height. Unfortunately the now overcast conditions hid the fine views we should have had down to Haworth and over Stanbury Moor. What we could see was the nearby ruin of Top Withens. Deciding that this would make a good spot for a late lunch stop, we hurried down to it. A persistent wind, one that reeked of consumption, whistled around the moor and we were glad to get some shelter from it. As we took our well-earned break, molested by those ravenous, sandwich-partial sheep mentioned earlier, I tried to picture Emily Brontë struggling up here from Haworth in her long skirts and high-laced boots. I could imagine her sitting in solitary silence, a thick shawl clasped around her shoulders and her teeth chattering. She would probably be doodling with her quill pen as she dreamed of some hunky male taking her in his arms in a passionate embrace. Longing for her hero to ride past on his white horse, she may have gazed at the farmhouse where we now sat, and imagined herself and the object of her desires living in it. Thus was sown the seed of Heathcliffe and *Wuthering Heights*. In case any Brontë lovers take umbrage, this is purely my personal version of the creation of her most famous novel!

As we sat munching, I mentioned that the mileage indicators in AW's *Companion* showed that we had recently passed the fifty-mile point. Although there were still many miles to cover, a celebration was called for. John and I toasted each other with strong, and by now, foul-tasting coffee from my flask. So elated were we that extra-large pieces of sandwich were thrown to the ever-watchful sheep, who were pleased to join in our celebrations. It would not have surprised me to learn that those far from dumb animals had already worked out that this was the magical fifty-mile point.

When John and I and the sheep were replete, it was time to leave the Way and make what turned out to be a four-mile detour to the Youth Hostel situated between Haworth and Oakworth. This was undertaken with the knowledge that we would have to retrace our steps the following morning. Some walkers choose to follow the Way to Rush Isles Farm near to the Haworth to Colne road, from where it is roughly a mile to Stanbury which has a bus service to Haworth and Oakworth. They are also able to return by bus the following morning and rejoin the Way at the same point. Having walked a distance of thirteen miles from Mankinholes to Top Withens, I appreciate that this could be a wise choice if you are feeling the strain.

We took the path that dropped steeply to the Brontë Falls, another tourist attraction. Unfortunately this turned out to be little more than a trickle, but perhaps we caught it on a bad day – although I would have thought there'd been quite enough rain for it to put on a better show. A broad, level track took us to the outskirts of Haworth and within easy reach of its main tourist attraction, Brontë Parsonage. This is well worth a visit as it is now a museum with many of the rooms laid out exactly as they were when the Brontës lived there, depicting life in those austere times. Across the churchyard, bulging with gravestones, stands the Parish Church where the Rev Brontë was the rector for many years. The cobbled main street of the village is flanked by shops and cafés and is thronged with tourists throughout the year. Haworth certainly is indebted to the Brontës as the shops are packed with souvenirs of the family and almost all the articles seem to have acquired a Brontë connection. There was even a bakery at the bottom of the main street that used to make Brontë biscuits.

John was fascinated by the village and its literary connections, but as I lived only a few miles away I knew it quite well already. When planning the walk, the thought had crossed my mind that I might go home for that night. However, honour prevailed and I had decided not to cheat by sneaking off. I now firmly banished any thoughts of a first-class supper with my family, a luxurious night in my own bed and, in the morning, a pile of clean clothes to pack.

Leaving the village, we made our way along the road from Haworth to Oakworth, and after about a mile we reached the hostel which stands well back from the road. It is a very handsome former mill-owner's house, with an imposing stone exterior. Inside is a beautiful oak-panelled staircase and hallway, overlooked by some fine stained glass windows.

As there were not many staying that evening we had a free choice of meal, as opposed to the normal set menu, which was very enjoyable. After supper, John and I struck up a conversation with three Australians who were walking in the area. We discovered that the Brontës' fame had reached the other side of the world.

Day Five: Haworth – Earby

The following day the sky was overcast at breakfast but cleared later and we enjoyed sunshine, blue skies and a temperature in the seventies. No, it was not too hot. No, I promise I didn't long for overcast skies and a cooling mist . . .

We did not wish to join those walkers who caught a bus to rejoin the Way a little further on. We decided to bag additional miles, and walked back to the point where we had left the path at Top Withens the evening before. The bus fare that we saved would, we decided, be spent on some extra liquid refreshment at a convenient watering-hole later on. Once we had regained the path at Top Withens, it was easy walking down to Ponden Reservoir that lies beside the Haworth to Colne Road. The last section of the descent is very steep with good views of the reservoir and valley below. Recalling Ben's accident, I remembered to watch where I was treading and stop for the views. Nearby was Ponden Hall, which is another reminder of the Brontës as this was supposedly the Thrushcross Grange of *Wuthering Heights*. It looked well preserved with an interesting stone frontage but we were anxious to get going so did not stop to look around. This is one of the few places on the route itself that provides refreshment and accommodation.

We knew from the *Pennine Way Companion* that the next obstacle was Ickornshaw Moor which stood between us and the village of Cowling. For some reason, no reference is made by AW to Cowling, apart from suggesting that walkers use the tower of its church as a guide off the moor in good visibility. Perhaps he got fed up with the signs as you cross the moor and approach the village; these implore you to sample the delights of its accommodation and tea shops.

Wainwright's description of Ickornshaw Moor is apt for it is just as he depicts it: an arduous stretch with paths that are conspicuous by their absence. He is quite right in commenting that, despite its drawbacks, it is a doddle compared to Kinder and Bleaklow. We made reasonable progress across the peat which was fairly dry for a change. The sunshine encouraged John to don his shorts and wide-brimmed sun hat. He was unfortunately brought down to earth when he got a bootful of water by not watching where he was treading. At least he didn't pay the same price as Ben for his carelessness.

There is not much of interest on the moor itself but as it stands high up, there are decent views from its flat top. On a good day you can make out Pinhaw Beacon to the north and behind it in the far distance some peaks of the Yorkshire Dales. It was comforting to know that we would soon be amongst them, out of this peaty terrain and into the lovely limestone country around Malham.

As we dropped down to Cowling, the broad outline of Earl Crag dominated the skyline to the east. Superimposed on this gritstone edge were the twin monuments of Wainman's Pinnacle and Lund's Tower. At the point where the Way joins the A 6068, the Keighley to Colne road, Cowling bombards the walker with arrows painted on everything in sight including a fence, the pavement and kerbstones. Perhaps they are put there to ensure that Pennine Way walkers take the correct route. On the other hand they may have had the devious intention of luring them away from the centre of Cowling. Whichever purpose they serve, they lead to a series of field paths that skirt the village, ending at the road to Lothersdale.

By a remarkable coincidence, the direction signs disappeared abruptly and we were left to use the OS map and *Companion* to follow the route to Lothersdale across farmland and along lanes. The signs had obviously served their purpose of relieving the walker of his cash or ushering him away from the village. Cowling obviously had no further use for us, or was glad to be rid of us. To be fair, I must point out that this situation is much improved, as a good system of direction signs now leads the way to Lothersdale.

It was pleasant, firm walking over the fields and meadows decked with buttercups. Lothersdale is a lovely village and, tucked away between attractive hills, does not reveal itself until the unsuspecting walker is almost upon it. As we approached, the first intimation of the village was the appearance of a tall, well-preserved mill chimney rising from the valley like a solitary finger. As we descended steeply down the hillside, the mill came into view in its most attractive setting. Unfortunately the mill wheel no longer works, but the mill building is still used and the adjacent cottages are well kept, with pretty gardens and window boxes sporting a fine array of blooms.

As we had already travelled a fair distance that day and had worked up a thirst, we tried to get a drink in the village, but annoyingly the Post Office-cum-village shop was closed. To add insult to injury the friendly looking public house was also shut. So much for AW's comment that an inn and a shop add to the joys of Lothersdale. John was so thirsty he asked at one of the houses for a drink of water, but was told it was unfit to drink. We were not acting very sensibly as we had broken one of the golden rules that tells us to always remember to fill up our water bottle, or carry supplies of liquid in the form of cans, cartons of juice, or energy-giving drinks.

It was with reluctance that we dragged ourselves away from Lothersdale, still perspiring and gasping for a drink, the saved bus fare still clinking invitingly in our pockets. We were to sweat even more as there followed a long pull up to Pinhaw Beacon. The going was good as we climbed from the valley across meadowland dotted with attractive copses and gurgling streams. After a while we reached the higher moorland approach to the Beacon. We crossed this on a wide track that kept us away from the worst of the peat.

As we stood on Pinhaw Beacon (1273 feet) we were rewarded with superb views in every direction. The beloved Yorkshire Dales were coming ever closer although a slight haze prevented us from seeing much further than Penyghent to the north. We were able to see views ranging from Pendle Hill in Lancashire, the Bowland Fells to the west and the fells around Wharfedale and Ribblesdale. The limestone hills above Malham could also be seen dominated by Fountains Fell. Pinhaw was a place to rest, take stock and drink in the wide-ranging countryside that Yorkshire and Lancashire have to offer. And talking of drink, we were both gasping by now.

Having toiled our way up there, it was a wrench to leave that fine viewpoint but we were only a few miles from journey's end for that day. This was at Earby, hidden in the valley that runs from Skipton to Colne. So we came down from Pinhaw and skirted Elsack Moor, the last stretch of moorland before joining the pastureland that heralds the start of limestone country. We, unfortunately, had to make a detour here which proved to be decidedly muddy, from the main path down to the industrialisation of Earby.

Our stay that night was at a Youth Hostel which comprises two converted terraced cottages. It turned out that John had arranged for his wife Anne to join him for the evening, to relieve the daily monotony of foot-slogging. She was there to greet us on our arrival, and after we had showered and changed we all went out for a meal, I having accepted their kind invitation with alacrity. No criticism of hostel food intended, but the thought of a change to more sumptuous fare was irresistible. Anne drove us to a nearby pub with a good restaurant and we enjoyed a first-class dinner, which was most welcome after the privation of the last five days. I fear that we must have bored Anne rigid with tales of our journey but she had the good grace to appear interested.

Thanks to the relaxing interlude – and the fact that we had spent the saved bus fare many times over on glasses of this and that – we returned to the hostel for a good night's sleep.

Day Six: Earby – Malham

The weather, which had been indifferent at the start of the walk, appeared to be improving. In fact the conditions on the following morning were ideal. The sky was blue, the sun shone and we were cooled by a light breeze. How long would this continue, I wondered?

Having forsaken a healthy diet, I normally eat a full, cooked breakfast each morning during long-distance walks. It sets me up for the day and only necessitates a light lunch. At Earby hostel I tucked into a large plateful of bacon, egg, sausages and fried bread. Then, during our climb back to the Pennine Way path, I suffered pains in my chest which I put down to indigestion, heartburn or an impending heart attack. I agree with Mike Harding's comments in his *Walking the Dales* that if you are going to expire, it might as well be in style, whilst walking the hills, rather than growing old and infirm and having to be looked after like a baby. Thinking what will be, will be, I pressed on. If I was stricken, at least it would be whilst doing what I enjoyed. You will have gathered by now that it was merely indigestion, otherwise I would not be writing this story. Also, you will have deduced that I am a confirmed hypochondriac.

Regain the path I did and headed with John towards Thornton in Craven which lay one and a half miles away in the valley ahead. We were onto grass now and were descending a fairly steep slope when I nearly came to grief. My feet slid on the rather slippery grass and my rucksack took me off balance, depositing me flat on my back in the middle of the field. A flock of sheep grazing nearby had been watching our progress idly, apparently unconcerned but as I lay spreadeagled on the ground, they suddenly broke into lusty bleating, which could only be interpreted as laughter. It prompts me to say that sheep are not as dumb as they are made out to be.

John, laughing too, pulled me to my feet and checked that I was sound in wind and limb. Only my pride was dented.

As we approached Thornton, the path crossed the line of a Roman road that is now merely a grassy path that leads to nearby Elslack. Thornton is a pleasant village but unfortunately spoiled by traffic that thunders through it on the main A56. We didn't linger, therefore, but found the path out of the village for the Leeds and Liverpool Canal, which it then follows for a mile or so. There were many boats moored on the canal, people sunbathing and contented families of ducks. This stretch of canal is also popular with anglers, that is if they can find a space to fish.

We left the busy stretch of canal for more field paths that took us to Gargrave that stands on the A65 running from Skipton to Settle. In the summer, Gargrave is often busy with traffic rushing to and from the Lake District.

According to AW, we now had to lick our wounds, rest and refuel. John and I did the latter, luckily having no blisters to lick. We ate our sandwiches by the attractive stone bridge over the River Aire. In springtime there is a profusion of daffodils and blossoms of every hue here. Gargrave, as AW hints, is a place to savour, for all too often one rushes through it on the drive to the more spectacular Lake District. The Dalesman Café stands on the main road where the Way crosses it and is a well-loved haunt of cyclists and walkers.

In front of us we had the prospect of a lovely seven-mile walk to Malham, and this began at the foot of Eshton Moor. Once over the crest of the moor we enjoyed a splendid view along the valley of the infant River Aire. Walking carefully to ensure no slip-ups on my part as we descended the grassy slopes of Eel Ark Hill, the river was soon reached. John and I then enjoyed a delightful riverside walk that took us past the hamlet of Airton with its attractive stone bridge and onwards to Hanlith. Here we passed the impressive Hanlith Hall which displays some intriguing stone carvings on its frontage. We were not far from our objective of Malham at this point and John's anticipation was increasing. He was rewarded during the final section of the day's walk with the dramatic view of Malham Cove, its sheer limestone face dominating the skyline beyond the village of Malham. About half a mile from the village, we passed near to Aire Head Springs where the River Aire emerges from an underground water course that runs from the Water Sinks situated two miles away near Malham Tarn.

Malham is one of the most visited villages in Britain. If you venture there on a Sunday or a Bank Holiday, make sure that you arrive before ten o'clock in the morning or you won't get into its only car park. Malham stands in a beautiful limestone setting, but suffers the ravages of tourism in the shape of its souvenir shops and roads clogged with cars.

However, none of this was in our minds as we entered the village along the lovely Malham Beck. We were spurred on by the realisation that we were at the critical point of the walk. Was it not common knowledge amongst the aficionados that if you reach Malham the odds that you will complete the whole walk will have swung in your favour? So here we were, one-third of the distance completed, standing a good chance of reaching Kirk Yetholm. To celebrate our achievement, we spent the latter part of the evening in the Buck Inn. Unfortunately, however, there was another reason for our visit to this popular Pennine Way watering hole. John and I were to part company as he was staying for two nights in Malham. Looking forward to his first visit to the area, he had planned to explore the surrounding countryside on the following day.

As we sat down at the table for our evening meal at the Malham Youth Hostel, suitably scrubbed, we found that there were only two other walkers for company. These turned out to be a married couple, Ian and Sheila, who were walking part of the Way. By coincidence they lived alongside the RAF camp at Duxford near Cambridge where I was stationed during my National Service; needless to say, we had a lot to talk about.

John and I were soon to discover that Ian, although of slim build, could eat like a horse. The first course of our meal that evening was soup which was in plentiful supply. When we had all consumed at least four helpings each, the warden deposited a large pan on the table telling us to eat up or it would go to waste. It was still half full of soup and everyone laughingly agreed that this was too much of a good thing. Everyone except Ian that is, who said he would happily finish the remaining contents. To our amazement, not only did he polish off every last drop, but he even scraped out the pan and the dregs from the ladle! He appeared to have no problem eating the rest of the meal.

After supper, Ian produced his party piece, in the form of a tea bag. He claimed to hold the world record for the number of cups of tea obtainable from one bag – sixteen! As I kept company with Ian and Sheila for much of the remainder of the walk, I was able to witness his remarkable prowess. However, I am glad that I never had to sample the tea that he produced after the third cup.

That evening I rang Ben to see how his injury was progressing. His arm was in a sling, he told me, but the swelling in his hand was going down. Apparently, the helpful Edgar Peel of the Pennine Way Package, was trying to claim on insurance and get a refund of the balance of Ben's fee. When I told Ben how much I was enjoying the walk, especially now I was in limestone country and the weather was good, he said that he was longing to join me. Unfortunately his wish was never fulfilled.

I felt sad that, having lost Ben as my walking companion through bad luck, I was now going to lose my second comrade in arms through his taking a rest day on the following day. We expressed the hope of meeting up once more but this looked unlikely according to our respective itineraries. My rest days were to come much later, but they were more accurately short days, as I was to walk a few miles on each of them. So, it was with some sadness that we drank to each other's success at the end of our last evening together.

Day Seven: Malham – Horton in Ribblesdale

I left Malham, after saying goodbye to John, as I had entered it, along the Malham Beck for a short distance. This was because I wanted to see a lovely stone clapper bridge that spans it. It is known as Prior Moon's bridge and has associations with one of Yorkshire's best-known landmarks, Bolton Priory, that stands on the beautiful River Wharfe. Prior Moon was in charge of the priory at the time of its dissolution in 1539. During its active life of nearly four hundred years, extensive areas of land and considerable property had been acquired. The great sheep ranges around Malham were among its acquisitions and the priory's retainers would have made frequent visits to the area to keep an eye on their investments.

After a short road walk, I joined the well-trodden field path leading to Malham Cove. Thousands of visitors to Malham each year walk this route to gaze at the great limestone buttress and the nearby strip 'lynchets', or mediaeval cultivation terraces, on the surrounding slopes. The cove needs little introduction as it is one of the most photographed sights in Yorkshire. Not so well known is the fact that it lies on the Mid-Craven Fault, a great fracture of the earth's crust. In simple terms, the limestone has been pushed upwards causing a displacement of several thousand feet. This has resulted in the limestone of the cove being higher than the rocks that it should be beneath. If you stand on top of the cove and look towards Malham you will see below the characteristic landscape of Yoredale Shales and Millstone grit. On top of the cove is a fine limestone pavement, one of five such preserved formations in Yorkshire. This is a mecca for geologists and students who come from far afield to study the features and development of the landscape. A series of stone steps leads up the side of the cove – quite a test of endurance for the unfit walker. The effort is well rewarded with the view that opens up to the south. On the rugged, sheer face, climbers of varying skills cling like limpets. There is a common misconception that the stream which runs from Malham Tarn and disappears below ground at the Water Sinks re-appears from under the cove. People are hoodwinked by Malham Beck which actually passes out from under the Cove, and flows southwards to Malham. The stream from Malham Tarn that flows underground at the Water Sinks forms the watercourse mentioned earlier that emerges at Aire Head Springs.

The traverse of the limestone pavement on top of the Cove should be made with care as the uneven rocks – which are known as 'clints' and are divided by deep channels or 'grykes' – can be treacherous, particularly when wet. It would be such a pity, I thought, to end my walk at this stage by breaking a leg. Once across the pavement I made a slight detour into the Dry Valley which squeezes between the weathered limestone formations that overshadow it. This valley is a dramatic representation of sculptured limestone and formerly had a stream running through it which plunged over the Cove. To leave the valley, I had to clamber up a steep rock-strewn barrier to reach the grassy moorland beyond. The morning was again warm and sunny and there was a slight breeze. As I walked along the springy turf passing Water Sinks and onwards to Malham Tarn I decided I could not wish for more pleasant walking conditions. There was a slight haze hanging over the tarn, but this added to the atmosphere. The Pennine Way is certainly not all about slogging through peat.

Malham Tarn is set in superb surroundings, but shouldn't really be there: after all, how can you have a lake in the midst of limestone? The answer lies in the remarkable geological structure of the area which straddles the North Craven Fault. A bed of Silurian slate has been pushed up by the fault and it is on this impervious rock that the tarn sits.

On its northern bank stands a grand house that formerly belonged to the Victorian industrialist Walter Morrison. He was fond of entertaining and amongst his guests were Charles Darwin, John Ruskin and Charles Kingsley. Tarn House is now owned by the National Trust and is used by the Field Studies Council as a training centre. As I passed, an outdoor class was in progress with the teacher explaining the wonders of nature to a group of children. I would have liked to have listened to the talk, but I had a fair way to go and two stiff climbs ahead.

My contented mood was punctured by the climb past Tennant Gill Farm onto the slopes of Fountains Fell. To be accurate, the ascent of the fell is a long drag, with the peat re-appearing as an added obstacle. As I neared the top, who should I come upon but my new-found friends, Ian and Sheila. We made our way together to the flattish summit and investigated a hole which was poorly fenced. I dropped a stone down it to test the depth and estimated it to be around fifty feet. Coal mining was prevalent here centuries ago and the hole may have been one of the numerous shafts that were sunk. The fell is named after Yorkshire's largest and grandest monastery, Fountains Abbey near Ripon, on whose land it lay during the monastic period. It would have been a testing journey for the monks sent to inspect their property. Whilst crossing the top of Fountains Fell, you should keep a sharp look out, because this is the place where AW lost his pipe in 1966. If you feel like mounting a thorough search you could be rewarded with a fine keepsake.

The view from the summit (2191 feet) is well worth a mention. This was superb in the fine weather that I was enjoying. Across Silverdale could be seen the extensive hump of Penyghent, its outline resembling the 'Sleeping Lion', as it is nicknamed. This was to be my next port of call and a reunion with the Three Peaks Walk. Ian and Sheila were having an extended stay for some refreshment, so I left them to relax and take in their beautiful surroundings. As I descended the rough, stony path into the sheltered valley, I came across two fellow walkers also enjoying their lunch. They were walking the Pennine Way as far as Hawes and were doing it in easy stages. It had taken them a fortnight since leaving Edale, but they were savouring the experience. I was introduced to the jungle telegraph that operates along the Way, walkers swapping items of interest as they pass. These fellows had heard about Ben and his accident and they asked if I had news of him. I also discovered that they had spent one night at Ponden Hall near Haworth and found it to be a good stopping place.

The road that cuts through Silverdale links Stainforth, a village near Settle, with Halton Gill that stands at the head of one of Yorkshire's lesser known dales. This is lovely Littondale, named after the village of Litton that lies a little farther down the valley. It is overshadowed by the better-known Wharfedale which it joins near the outstanding limestone feature of Kilnsey Crag. In my view, Littondale is a very striking dale that deserves greater recognition. One of the attractions is its abrupt ending below Horsehead Moor where you have to proceed on foot to traverse this barrier into picturesque Langstrothdale. Consequently, there is no flood of traffic clogging this quiet dale.

There is rather a boggy descent across fields at the base of Fountains Fell before the road is reached. A spell of firm roadside walking along grass verges took me to the track to Dale Head farm past some limestone outcrops that appeared to be popular with picnickers. A sign indicated that I must leave the road and join the well-trodden path up to Penyghent. The ascent from the road is steady at first, and the shape of the fell changes rapidly from this angle as you make a curved approach to it. The gritstone cliff that forms the southern edge of the summit reveals its variety of buttresses and crevices. Climbing becomes stiffer as you approach the junction with the Three Peaks path. I worked up quite a sweat before I reached the twin stiles spanning the wall to my left that marked the junction. As I paused getting my breath back, I was able to savour an already commanding view of Fountains Fell back across the valley. I recalled my earlier struggle in thick mist up the steep slope that loomed above me, unable to see more than a few yards. Today would redress the balance and I anticipated fine views from the top. Although the going was hard, I paced myself and climbed steadily to allow for the weight I was carrying. It was pleasing to discover that I was able to negotiate the steep clamber up the rocky gritstone section without too much difficulty. Perhaps it was the fine weather that kept my spirits up, or the realisation that an extended period of walking with a rucksack does make you fitter as the walk progresses. Was I smug? Well, slightly.

As the slope to the summit was reached, I was pleased to note that the bogs were drying nicely in the sunshine. At the trig point (2273 feet) I was not disappointed. The view was awesome. Through a slightly shimmering heat haze I was able to make out a number of landmarks ranging from Pendle Hill in the south, to Great Shunner Fell, my next objective to the north. The Howgill

Fells, Whernside, Ingleborough and Baugh Fell had come out of hiding to show themselves in all their glory. As I stood drinking in the surrounding landscape, I was brought down to earth by two young ladies who asked if I would take their photograph. They were camping in Horton in Ribblesdale for a few days and wanted to prove to their friends that they had climbed Penyghent.

Progress down the western flank was relatively smooth, although I watched the rocky ground carefully at the start of the descent. I did not wish to get down to Horton in record time by missing my footing. As the ground levels out the Way follows one of the numerous green lanes in the area, Horton Scar Lane, as it makes for Horton. This is the start of a loop in the route designed to lead weary Pennine Way walkers to havens of rest in Horton. A couple of miles extra distance must therefore be endured in order to enjoy a comfortable night's stay in the heart of Three Peaks' country.

That was just what I experienced at Hoyle Cottage, a lovely bed and breakfast establishment right on the Way itself. The nearest Youth Hostel was four miles away and Edgar Peel had done me proud on this occasion. I was made very welcome at this attractive white-walled cottage opposite the Crown Hotel, Horton's popular pub. After a glorious soak in a steaming hot bath, I had a big supper which brought on a satisfying feeling of contentment, but also extreme tiredness. I retired early, therefore, and was luxuriating in the enveloping softness of a comfortable bed when I was jerked from semi-consciousness by the sound of voices in the corridor. It sounded like late arrivals being shown to their room, but I was too tired to take much notice of their conversation and fell sound asleep.

Day Eight: Horton–Hawes

After a night spent sleeping like a log, I dressed and went down to breakfast the following morning to be met with two familiar faces. Who should be sat at the table but the 'Brothers in Law'. They had been the late arrivals the previous evening. I was intrigued to hear how they had managed to get this far, after their earlier disasters: apparently, they had stayed for the previous two nights at Lothersdale and Gargrave respectively. This explained their lateness in getting to Horton for they would have walked twenty-two miles from Gargrave. This seemed a pretty tall order, considering their navigational skills.

They appeared none the worse for their ordeal thus far and were going to make an early start for Hawes that morning. After chatting for a bit about the day's walk, they left me finishing a leisurely breakfast. Starting off a little later than usual, the first part of my journey was along another green lane, this one called Harber Scar Lane, one of a network of tracks used centuries ago by the monks of Jervaulx Abbey who bred horses in Horton. It was fine and sunny once more, making me appreciate my good fortune. Unfortunately, this was not to last all day.

I found it difficult to get into my stride; it had been easier when I had had a companion. I was now walking through an area containing numerous potholes, with several situated near the path. I paused to gaze down Sell Gill Hole, but even looking down one gives me a feeling of unease, and actually descending into one is unthinkable as far as I'm concerned. For people who like potholes there are plenty to choose from hereabouts; the largest and most distinctive being Hull Pot. This particular hole can be more conveniently examined following the descent from Penyghent on the previous day's walk, as it lies a short distance from the point where the Way joins Horton Scar Lane.

After an hour's walking, I came upon the 'Brothers in Law' sitting at the side of the track at its junction with the Three Peaks path which, after descending the slopes of Penyghent, was now heading for the road leading to Ribblehead. They were pondering over their map, obviously uncertain where to go next. One of them pointed along the Three Peaks path in the direction of the road and suggested that they should follow that route. Knowing the area fairly well, I pointed them in the right direction and on the map finger-traced the route to their destination at Hawes. I offered to walk with them, but they declined, saying that they would take their time and should have no further problems.

Satisfied that they could not go wrong on the straightforward route, I carried on and was soon climbing the winding path up to Cam End where the Roman road from Ingleton to Bainbridge is joined. At the approach to the climb, in Ling Gill, a fine packhorse bridge is crossed, recalling the times when this was a well-trodden route. The Roman road, or Cam High Road as it was known, is now a muddy, deeply rutted track. When trade was carried by packhorse, it formed part of the Lancaster to Richmond route, then it was replaced by the turnpike road that runs along the valley through Ribblehead. Its extensive erosion is a sorry sight, aided and abetted by the presence of motor cycles which have gouged the deep ruts which make walking almost impossible. I had ventured along it the previous winter on a raw, wet February day and had been passed by five motor cyclists who were merrily churning up vast amounts of mud and hurling it in all directions. I had to walk well away from the path to avoid a mud bath, and I then had to endure the whole thing again when the bikers returned fifteen minutes later, their raucous laughter and jeers almost drowning the sounds of their smoking machines.

The state of the path is obviously not helped by the pounding of thousands of pairs of boots each year – this section also forms part of the Dales Way. The two paths join forces for a couple of miles at Cam End and the Dales Way then drops down into the head of Langstrothdale past the remote farm at Cam Houses. It starts its journey at Ilkley and covers eighty-four miles before terminating at Bowness on Windemere.

On this stretch of the Pennine Way the 100-mile point is passed but unfortunately as I was now walking on my own there was no one to make a song and dance with. If I had tried such celebrations on my own, any passing walkers would have been inclined to rush to the nearest telephone (although there weren't, in fact, any for miles) and send for the men in white coats.

Putting aside my anger at the loutish treatment of the ground underfoot I was looking forward to another reunion with Dodd Fell. Memories flooded back of that hapless hour spent running around like a headless chicken searching for the checkpoint tent. The Pennine Way skirts the western flank of the fell, but I was able to see the fateful spot where we took a compass bearing for the summit. Here the Pennine Way runs in a channel between the lower slopes of Dodd Fell and the Snaizholme Valley and I met a walker who told me of the time he had found three feet of snow blocking the channel in early April. He was forced to walk along the higher slopes of the fell to avoid the snow and had noticed several dead sheep embedded in it. That was a sobering reminder of the harsh conditions that can affect a hill farmer in the Yorkshire Dales.

My progress, since leaving Ian and Sheila on the summit of Fountains Fell, had been good, and as I only had the descent into Hawes remaining, I stopped for a late lunchtime snack. The sunshine that had accompanied me for so long now deserted me. Menacing black clouds loomed overhead and a chill wind was blowing. This was not the time to stop and admire the view, I decided as the cloud began to envelop me. My stay was brief, therefore, and I was soon on my way down to Hawes to escape the worst of the elements.

As I entered the pleasant market town at the head of Wensley-dale which I had become familiar with through my walks around the Yorkshire Dales, I was in for a surprise. No sooner had I reached the market place than who should I see a short distance away? You have surely guessed right – there as large as life were the 'Brothers in Law' walking along the road. I was puzzled as to how they could have overtaken me. First, they were not fast walkers, taking into account their age and lack of map reading ability; second, I had made good time and was sure that they had not passed me. There was only one possible explanation. They must have taken the Three Peaks path to the road and got a lift into Hawes. It now became clear how they had managed to keep up with me so far. They were obviously not above a little bending of the rules. I did not attract their attention to the fact that they had been rumbled, deciding instead to keep my peace. I also did not wish to embarrass them into explanations for their remarkable progress since I felt that their secret would be exposed sooner or later. AW would certainly have taken a dim view of their actions.

I strolled around Hawes market and shops which are a magnet for visitors. It was mid-afternoon and the local Youth Hostel did not open until five o'clock. I never tire of browsing in those shops which cater for a variety of tastes, ranging from walking, reading and souvenir hunting to rope making. This ancient craft is still carried on here, as is cheese making for this is the home of Wensleydale cheese. Unfortunately the Hawes Creamery where the cheese is made had been taken over by a large dairy company and plans were in hand to close it and move production elsewhere. This caused a public outcry but spurred people into action and fortunately local business people purchased it and retained this proud heritage, re-naming it the Wenslydale Creamery. Traditional methods are now being used and customers are not only enjoying an improvement in quality, but also an opportunity to see cheese making in action, as it now boasts a visitor centre.

Hawes was the home of Kit Calvert, a famous Yorkshire character who died a few years ago. He ran the Hawes Creamery for a time, but in his youth he worked in a local stone quarry. Life was hard and pay was low, but Kit, being an enterprising lad, bettered himself by means of his skill and wits. The stone that was hewn with sweat and toil from the surrounding quarries was used to build many fine Yorkshire houses.

The town stands amongst some of the finest Dales scenery, not least being the limestone features of Abbotside Common which was formerly owned by Jervaulx Abbey. Many of the surrounding fields are traversed by stone-flagged paths that were laid to provide a walkway for quarrymen. Not for their convenience, but to prevent their boots from wearing away the grass.

At the appropriate time I made my way to the hostel which had only recently been built. When AW wrote his *Companion*, there was no hostel and he recommended a nine-mile trip down the dale to the nearest one at Aysgarth Falls. He did add that there was a bus service and it was not obligatory to walk there and back. I was not the first to arrive at the hostel. There were two ladies waiting outside who were walking the Pennine Way and our paths continued to cross until we reached Bellingham. As it was a modern hostel facilities were good, including television. So much for the rigours of walking the Pennine Way!

Day Nine: Hawes – Keld

The following morning I headed for the bridge that spans the River Ure. Wensleydale is the only main Yorkshire dale that is not named after the river which flows through it. Its present name is taken from the village of Wensley that was sadly decimated by the Plague and subsequently lost its importance. The river's name is derived from the word 'Yore' and the dale was formerly known as 'Yoredale'. This name still survives since the building converted from the former mill which stands by the Aysgarth Falls further down the dale is known as Yoredale Mill. As I stood on Haylands Bridge, the river looked resplendent as it rushed beneath me, hurrying on its journey to Bainbridge, Leyburn and beyond.

It was now my turn to take one of those stone-flagged paths across the fields to Hardraw whose claim to fame is the highest waterfall above ground in England. It is just under one hundred feet high now, but in former times may have been slightly higher. The tale goes that the limestone rim of Hardraw Force was washed away during a flood and although the owner had it re-built, there still remains quite a deep channel in the rock at its top. This is of no great significance except to say that a fall of *over* one hundred feet sounds much more impressive. A more interest-ing fact is that the only access to the waterfall is through the Green Dragon Inn. There cannot be many pubs with such an impressive waterfall in their back garden, but it certainly provides a splendid attraction for its customers. For a small fee (60p at the time of publication), you can enter the grounds at the back of the pub and gaze upon the cascade in wonderment before retiring inside for a taste of the local brew. Access to the Force can be obtained between 9am and dusk. I did not pause for a visit as I had the ascent of Great Shunner Fell on my mind.

As you leave the hamlet of Hardraw, the gradient increases where the lower slopes of Great Shunner Fell are encountered. Although it is a long drag to the top of this barrier that divides the head of Wensleydale from that of Swaledale, the climb is not too onerous. AW says that, favoured with fine weather and singing larks, the ascent can be quite delectable. Unfortunately, I have never done it in good weather so I must take his word that there are good views from the summit to the Lake District mountains to the west and the rest of the Yorkshire Dales to the east. I'm afraid that the only things I saw on this occasion were fellow walkers appearing out of the low cloud.

During my steady progress to the summit I met a young walker who had spent the previous night in the porch of a church. When the vicar arrived to open the church that morning, he almost fell over the sleeping walker. When they had both recovered from their surprise, the vicar told the man he would have been more than happy to have put him up at the vicarage. A very kind thought – but somewhat too late. The young man told me that he was wandering around the Yorkshire Dales for a short holiday with no pre-planned route. He was travelling wherever his fancy took him.

Other walkers that I met included a man and two women who were walking together from Kirk Yetholm south to Gargrave. I learned that one of the fairer sex was seventy-two years old but she appeared fit and sprightly. No sooner had I said farewell to them than I came across three Dutchmen who had also walked from Kirk Yetholm. As they had approached me at a good pace, I christened them the 'Flying Dutchmen'. This seemed a good day for walkers doing the Pennine Way in the reverse direction.

I left the boggy summit which, at 2340 feet, was the highest point so far, hoping to get below the cloud and enjoy some views of the upper reaches of my favourite dale. The view down Swaledale at this point is, I think, one of the finest in the Dales. The stone-built villages of Thwaite and Muker nestle in the narrow valley, flanked by meadows filled with wild flowers and the green fellside rising above, criss-crossed by the stone walls and spattered with the characteristic stone barns.

On entering Thwaite, walkers are met by numerous signs including terse instructions which seem intent on shepherding them in single file through the adjacent fields. You will have noticed signs as you enter towns stating that they welcome careful drivers: there should be a sign erected outside this village saying that Thwaite hates visitors. You are made to feel distinctly unwelcome amidst an abundance of 'No parking' and 'No cycling' signs and in one meadow I was forced to walk between two lengths of twine which defined the footpath. Before any landowner charges out in attack, I do appreciate that these conditions may have been brought about by damage to property and crops. It is probably a familiar case of a few irresponsible walkers spoiling things for the majority. AW sums up the situation in his book, *Ex-Fellwanderer*: 'Erosion of footpaths is a problem . . . erosion is not caused by too many walkers as is often assumed, but by clumsy walkers ... damage is caused by parties of three or four trying to walk abreast and maintain conversation.'

Despite this, I did have a look around this tiny village that was named by the Vikings who settled in the area, its name being the Norse word for a clearing. This hardy race inhabited the upper reaches of the valleys and the higher ground, as they were basically hill farmers. The Danes and Anglo-Saxons preferred the valleys and gave names to settlements which ended in 'ton'. There are several such names along Swaledale such as Fremington and Grinton. The main church of upper Swaledale is in Grinton and stands at the end of the corpse road which descends from Tan Hill, and forms a section of the Pennine Way. The simple coffins were carried along this ancient track for burial in Grinton churchyard.

Just as Haworth owes much to the Brontës, Thwaite is indebted to the Kearton brothers who were two of its favourite sons. Richard and Cherry Kearton became famous naturalists and their achievement is marked in various ways in the village including the Kearton Guest House which implores you to sample its delights.

I noted that AW had similar feelings towards Swaledale as I do, for at this point in his *Companion* he introduces a little question and answer session. First, he asks: which is the most beautiful of the Yorkshire Dales? His answer is Swaledale. Second: which is the next most beautiful? The answer, Wharfedale. I agree with him on both counts.

As I was not pressed for time that afternoon I made a short detour to Muker, an attractive village lying at the foot of Kisdon Hill. The tea shop, village store and Literary Institute give it a pleasant air. It is very popular with visitors and is jammed with cars during the summer months. Who did I see emerging from the pub but the 'Brothers in Law' who were still making remarkable progress. I did not wish to approach them as their secret would be revealed, but I did enjoy a good chuckle to myself.

I made my way from Muker back onto the Pennine Way and started up the steep climb to Kisdon Farm that stands high up on the impressive hill of the same name. In my opinion, this is the beginning of the first of the two most enjoyable sections of the Pennine Way – the walk along the Swale Gorge to Keld. Words cannot adequately convey the beauty of the area, but suffice to say that the views from this high-level path are magnificent. The infant River Swale cuts its way between surrounding hills that, in autumn, offer a blaze of colour, before making an almost right-angled turn into the main body of the dale at Muker. Walking was rough along the flank of Kisdon Hill, but I was rewarded with views of Swinner Gill, Rogan's Seat and AW's Coast to Coast path which hugs the opposite bank of the river. The rocky track forms part of the corpse road mentioned earlier and I did not envy the bearers carrying the wicker coffins in years gone by. I found it hard going with only my rucksack to carry, so I imagined that the poor bearers would have required frequent rests on their journey. Large 'coffin stones' were provided at intervals so that the loads could be set down whilst aching limbs were recuperating. As the approach to Keld is made, the ruins of Crackpot Hall come into view in the valley and the path forming the high-level Coast to Coast route can be seen snaking up Swinner Gill onto the high moorland beyond. This path traverses the higher reaches of the former lead-mining area, crossing the desolate mine spoilage areas of Merry Field and Old Gang, before re-joining the river route at Reeth.

The Swale Gorge is evidently a popular walking area, borne out by the numerous people that I met during my traverse of it. Several family groups and other walkers were enjoying a six-mile circular walk which can be commenced at Muker or Keld. This popular circuit of the gorge encompasses the low-level riverside path which follows AW's Coast to Coast route and the higher-level path along North Gang Scar that I was walking. I did meet one most determined walker who was extending his distance considerably by a detour through Swinner Gill to view the desolation left by the ravages of lead mining. I noticed that some of the walkers in the family groups were not wearing stout shoes or boots, which was unwise because the path that I was on was often rough and stony.

Near the village of Keld the Pennine Way and Coast to Coast path merge for a mere hundred yards. This is the only part of both walks where they march together – a true crossroads. AW makes no comment in the *Companion* about the Coast to Coast Walk because, of course, he had not yet devised the walk or written his guide book. That book does comment on the Pennine Way but I won't say what he said about it since I'll leave that until later. Inevitably, this tiny stretch of path is always crowded with walkers, many of them standing around in groups and swapping stories.

The surrounding area has a large number of waterfalls created over layers of rock which have varying degrees of hardness. Keld is an especially good place for waterfalls, and four of them have the word 'Force' after their name, bearing out the Norse influence again. Near the approach to the village is Kisdon Force to which a signed path briefly diverts off the main route. When the bridge over the Swale is reached a superb view of East Gill Force is obtained, where the peaty-brown water surges alongside the Way to plunge into the main body of the river.

Keld itself is a throwback to earlier times. It has the appearance of being untouched by the passing years, its scattered stone buildings recalling a peaceful, bygone age. Some religious persuasions are catered for by its distinctive United Reformed and Methodist chapels, and Satan is kept at bay by the closure of its only public house around forty years ago. This was formerly the Cat Hole Inn, which was purchased by a local farmer, Jim Alderson, and converted to a house. There is still no pub in Keld and anyone requiring a drink will have to stay at East Stonesdale farm which has a residential licence and is a popular stopping place on the Pennine Way and Coast to Coast routes.

My destination was the Youth Hostel which was formerly a shooting lodge. I found it to be a comfortable, well-run hostel, with good food. I was delighted at the re-appearance of Ian and Sheila, who I had not seen since I left them enjoying a rest on top of Fountains Fell. It was remarkable that I had not met up with them in the intervening two days, but they assured me that they weren't trying to avoid me, and confirmed this by sharing my table at supper. They had stayed in Horton and Hawes as I had done but at different lodgings and had wandered around indulging in a little sightseeing.

Ian scraped the soup pan once more and produced innumerable cups of tea from his single tea bag. He promised that he did not carry the same tea bag from hostel to hostel.

After supper we walked along the river, which looked resplendent in the evening sunshine. It was a pleasant feeling to be surrounded by areas of such beauty on the Pennine Way.

Day Ten: Keld–Baldersdale

The following morning it was time to say farewell to Swaledale and head for the highest public house in England at Tan Hill. Sunshine and a slight breeze accompanied me across rough moorland pasture and AW's description of the 'juicy' ground underfoot was very apt. One benefit of the uphill test was the retrospective view of Swaledale which expanded with every step that I took. AW informs us that nothing as pleasing as this view will be seen for many a mile. This made me wonder what lay ahead. After crossing Lad Gill, ravaged moorland engulfed me. I passed an old quarry where the earth had been gouged out of the landscape; it is advisable to keep well clear of the mineshafts situated near the path. Like Fountains Fell, cheap coal was mined here by workmen who, struggling for survival, didn't apparently have the time or inclination to fill in the redundant shafts. They are unsafely fenced and AW wisely advises against passing this way in the dark.

A little further on an old mine track is joined which, according to AW, heads straight for the bar of Tan Hill Inn, but before entering I crossed from the familiar county of Yorkshire into the unknown reaches of Co. Durham. It was at moments like this that it came home to me how far I had walked – and how far I still had to go. The Tan Hill Inn formerly quenched the parched throats of coalminers, pedlars and merchantmen with their pack-horses, and sheep drovers – and now Pennine Way walkers. The inn had the appearance of recently undergoing an external facelift but its interior seemed unchanged by the passage of time, the olde worlde atmosphere could be cut with a knife. It is a friendly place where travellers have met for centuries and nowadays is just the spot to enjoy a relaxing drink with fellow walkers whilst girding your loins for the forthcoming dubious privilege of squelching your way across Sleightholme Moor.

All good things must come to an end and it was soon time to wrench myself from the lovely old stone fireplace, blackened by smoke from countless welcoming fires. There is no clean air legislation in force at this lonely spot. Once outside, the fresh air invaded my nostrils and I blinked in the bright sunlight. I gazed over the foreboding stretch of bleak, dull-looking moorland that stood between me and the A66 that cuts through the Stainmore Gap.

Fortunately, the spell of good weather that I had recently enjoyed had started to dry out some of the more treacherous bogs and my passage was therefore made easier. I crossed the moor with a feeling of relief for myself and pity for those less fortunate souls destined to make the crossing in foul weather. Even so, I was accompanied for part of this stretch by a group of walkers who continually complained about the hard going.

At Trough Heads Farm, another of those tantalising route decisions must be made. The main path heads for God's Bridge, which is a natural limestone rock bridge over the River Greta, before crossing the A66 at Pasture End. If, however, you fancy the delights of Bowes, you take the alternative path or the 'Bowes Loop' as it is known. This makes a wide detour to the east but it is well worth the effort if time permits. AW seems to have had a yen for Bowes and who was I to argue. Prepared to cover extra distance to sample its delights, I set off for East Mellwaters, forsaking God's Bridge which a walker in the Tan Hill Inn had told me was a beautiful spot.

I was not disappointed by Bowes' historic remains, but found the place itself fairly insignificant. The castle, or more accurately the remains of its Norman keep, stands proudly in isolation amongst fields that were formerly the site of a Roman fort. All but a few ramparts of the fort are long gone but the strategic importance of Bowes did not diminish when the Romans left. As I stood on that historic site and thought about the Roman legions marching through Stainmore Gap, so must have done the Normans who, realising how important it was to guard this important route through the northern Pennines, built their castle or watchtower here.

When I had had my fill of Bowes' history, I walked along the road which slices through the centre of the village – and bumped slap into the 'Brothers in Law' who seemed to be dogging my footsteps. They were conveniently staying here whereas I had several miles of open country to negotiate before my overnight stay at Baldersdale Youth Hostel. I struggled to keep a straight face whilst listening to the account of the hardships of their journey to date.

I bade my two friends farewell as time was pressing and set off on what turned out to be a difficult section of the walk. On the outskirts of the village I passed a building which is now a café but was, supposedly, the 'Dotheboys Hall' depicted in *Nicholas Nickleby*. The hardest task was negotiating the route for the path was indistinct in places and I was overcome with a nagging feeling that I would not find the hostel before dark. Much of this section is over rough terrain which makes the going tough, but luckily I was not hampered by boggy conditions.

Apparently AW had not been thrilled by the area to the north of the Deepdale Beck across which I was now struggling. He describes it as 'unattractive and featureless territory', but he is more enthusiastic about Goldsborough (1274 feet) which I reached after a further mile of toil. This distinctive hill thrusts itself above the undulating countryside and stands sentinel over Blackton Reservoir that nestles in the valley beyond. With a sigh of relief, I eventually succeeded in reaching the narrow road running into Baldersdale. A thankfully short journey then brought me within sight of the hostel, a converted farmhouse which stands at the head of Blackton Reservoir.

I was overjoyed to read a caption in AW's guide stating that Baldersdale is the half-way point of the Pennine Way. I now had cause for a double celebration, for I had found the hostel before nightfall and had also covered half of my journey. My mood was one of great elation as I virtually skipped along the road to my destination.

The hostel turned out to be well run by a capable young warden, but who should I see as I hurried to check in but Ian and Sheila. They wanted to know why I was looking so remarkably cheerful at the end of a long day's walk, so I jokingly told them that the first half of my challenge was completed and it would be downhill from now on to Kirk Yetholm. Unfortunately they were not walking the whole distance themselves due to time restrictions, but that did not diminish their pleasure at my achievement.

As the hostel was self catering only, my culinary prowess was put to the test. Purchasing some provisions from the hostel shop, my celebratory menu for supper consisted of soup, meat pie and beans, rounded off by two Eccles cakes. This was hardly sparkling fare, but I did have great entertainment watching Ian and Sheila struggling to create a mouth-watering meal from the most basic ingredients. Although Ian didn't mention it, I could see that he was suffering withdrawal symptoms since there was no large soup pan to scrape out. He made up after supper by seemingly drinking gallons of tea from the now obligatory single tea bag. The two of them toasted me with this innocuous-looking brew and wished me luck for the remaining half of my journey. As we relaxed after our meal they described their day's journey from Keld, having chosen the main route from Sleightholme over God's Bridge. They were full of praise for the bridge and waxed lyrical about the numerous wild flowers in that area.

The washing of clothes is obviously a regular necessity during a long walk if you wish to retain friends. Unfortunately, facilities vary at hostels. Some well-equipped ones have superb washing and drying rooms, complete with automatic washing machines and spin dryers. Baldersdale, being a small, relatively remote hostel, had limited facilities which meant washing the necessaries outside in cold water. The only luxury was a hand-operated mangle. There were adequate drying provisions, however, an absolute necessity for drenched walkers. Since my walk there has been considerable reorganisation and improvement within the Association. In fact, it was whilst chatting to the warden at Baldersdale that I first learned of the survey that was currently underway around the hostels. A new management team had been recently formed, which comprised the first professional managers employed by the Association. I believe that an investigator and an Area Manager were sent to each hostel to report on its current situation and then recommend improvements. The aim was an overall increase in annual revenue of fifty per cent to make all the hostels financially viable. I do know that considerable modernisation has taken place and the facilities at many hostels have been upgraded. Unfortunately, as happens in most businesses, non-viable hostels have been closed and an emphasis placed on improving others. As an impartial observer, I do feel that to some extent the original concept of hostelling has become rather blurred and some of the more remote hostels that came under the axe provided a spirit of friendliness and companionship that the larger ones sometimes lack.

Day Eleven: Baldersdale – Langdon Beck

When I set out from Baldersdale the next morning, to make my way to Middleton in Teesdale and my destination at Langdon Beck, I was looking forward to visiting the farm at Low Birk Hat. Talking to the warden the previous evening, I learned that Hannah Hauxwell had lived at the farm and that the warden had often been able to help her during the hard winter months. Television viewers will be familiar with the programme entitled 'Too Long a Winter' in which she was immortalised by Barry Cockroft. Now a national celebrity, Hannah has since moved six miles down the valley to enjoy village life in an attractive cottage.

Her farm of Low Birk Hat lies right on the route of the Pennine Way and apparently she loved to chat with walkers as they tramped past. Unfortunately, she was not around when I went through but lingering awhile in the farmyard I tried to picture it in the depths of winter, with the wind howling over Cotherstone Moor. Tearing myself from the scene, I turned my sights northwards and passed through a field that is now known as 'Hannah's Meadow'. Not far from the Balder Head–Romaldkirk road stands a small stone pillar bearing a plaque proclaiming this.

My journey to Middleton was one of anticipation for I was looking forward to my first view of the River Tees which several friends had told me was such a lively and attractive river. The going at the outset was not hard and I was able to enjoy a fairly relaxed pace, unlike the previous evening. There were several interesting features as I progressed through the Lune valley and onwards across Crossthwaite Common. The view from Grassholme Bridge across the rippling waters of Grassholme Reservoir is one to be savoured as the Lune valley at this point is in its most attractive mode. The rolling green carpet of the reservoir's grassy banks and surrounding fields is scattered with the darker hues of copses and a lattice-work of steel-grey stone walls. In the far distance, beyond Middleton, the high, austere moorland provides a subtle contrast to the lushness of the valley. In a nearby stone wall a wooden gate hung lazily from its broken rusty hinges, a victim of years of exposure to the insidious elements. All too often, these details are missed by a walker yomping along with head down.

Shortly after leaving the bridge I crossed the Middleton to Brough road. Here I met two fellow Pennine Way walkers who strode up behind me in determined fashion. They were considerably weighted down with their expansive rucksacks, but this had not prevented them from making very good time from Bowes from where they had made an early start that morning. Now well into their day's walk they could afford to relax and take a well-earned rest, for their destination was Newbiggin which was only about three miles past Middleton. I discovered that they liked to get away early in the morning and accomplish most of their day's journey by lunchtime. On this particular day they were planning to take a leisurely look around Middleton before strolling along the banks of the River Tees in the afternoon. Their approach differed significantly from mine as I prefer to keep up a fairly even pace and when I intimated this they laughingly said that it would not do for all walkers to be the same.

Wishing them luck as I left them I climbed through the pastures flanking Crossthwaite Common, following AW's guide closely, as they are bounded by an intricate pattern of stone walls. Eventually the route became clearer and the landmark of Kirkcarrion stood sentinel over my progress.

This is a distinctive tree plantation that stands proudly on top of a hill which was the site of a large tumulus, or burial ground. It was instantly recognisable for I had seen a photograph of it in the large-format illustrated version of AW's *Companion, Wainwright on the Pennine Way* illustrated by Derry Brabbs. In fact, I was often to find myself walking into a familiar scene - not the least of which was the green lane leading to Horton in Ribblesdale which is on the cover of that book, and it had been etched in my memory ever since.

I was now entering Teesdale which I found was a delightful area. Middleton came into sight, spread before me in its panoramic setting.

The forthcoming seven-mile walk along the River Tees to Langdon Beck ranks with the Swale Gorge as the most outstanding sections of my walk. That was a treat to be savoured since I stopped for a while in Middleton to explore its attractive streets. The weather, which had been dull with a light drizzle up to then, suddenly cleared and the sun came out. It was as though the little town was determined to be seen at its best. Glinting in the sunshine was the unusually monumental fountain which trumpets Middleton's history as a lead mining centre; in fact, the place owes much of its growth and present appearance to the London Lead Company which was very active in the area.

Looking forward to an enjoyable afternoon's walk, I ate my packed lunch perched on the steps of the ornate fountain which stands beside the enticing tree-lined main street. I played a game of sorting out the local people bustling about on their business from the visitors who perambulated at a much gentler speed. Although Middleton is a very pleasant place, it was no hardship to be on the move once more as I headed out of town in search of the delights of the teeming River Tees. I crossed the sturdy stone bridge over the river as I retraced my steps to the Pennine Way path that would take me upstream. The rushing waters beneath my feet were already hurrying towards Barnard Castle, paying no heed to Middleton, as they passed by the town. Their vibrancy eventually decreases as the river matures and threads its path through the sprawling industrialisation of Stockton on Tees and Middlesbrough.

The path that hugs the southern bank of the river proved a fine vantage point from which to see its magnificence. I was not disappointed. An exciting river here, the Tees surges over and through some impressive rock formations. Millions of years ago a sheet of dolerite intruded into the strata over a wide area of Upper Teesdale and formed what is known as the Whin Sill; this is responsible for the three dramatic waterfalls of Low Force, High Force and Cauldron Snout. All three are passed by the path and the cascades provide splendid spectacles, and an additional bonus are the intricate limestone formations on the river bed. The path also skirts lush meadows which were bedecked with wild flowers. I am no connoisseur but there must have been at least thirty species of blooms on view. You can tell AW was happy when writing about this stretch of the route because there are little humorous asides tucked away on each page. He warns against the hazard of falling over crawling botanists – intent, no doubt, on examining the flowers mentioned above; he says that they recoil and act unpleasantly if trodden upon. I kept my eyes skinned. However, a page further on, he warns courting couples and others likely to sink to the ground – including, I presume, crawling botanists – to beware of adders. In between these two pages of the *Companion* is an illustration of a young woman, back to the pen, looking at Low Force. I wondered, as I walked, if there was any connection.

As I reached High Force, there was a superb view overlooking the falls. The prospect from this bank is free; to view them from the opposite bank currently costs around one pound, which pays for the privilege of using the path that runs down from the High Force Hotel.

A foaming torrent of water, seventy feet high, crashes over the crest with a roar that invades the ear drums. AW thought that this is the river's finest moment. Personally, I consider Cauldron Snout the most impressive. Having said that, it was still a wrench to pull myself away and walk on up the river for about one and a half miles. At this point I bade a temporary goodbye to the Tees as I headed for my night's rest at Langdon Beck Youth Hostel. The beck from which the hostel takes its name is followed for a further half-mile until the Alston road is reached. Standing impressively some distance away was the modern stone-built hostel, the only other buildings to be seen were the hotel and the white-walled farms, typical of the area.

The hostel was run by a formidable lady warden, assisted by her quiet and retiring husband. As I was checking in, I mentioned that I had booked my accommodation through the Pennine Way Package. It was then that I was given some startling news. The warden told me that Edgar Peel had died suddenly that very day. This made me extremely sad as I had planned to go and see that kind man on my return and thank him for his help. Only the previous day I had sent him a postcard with news of my walk. I had been looking forward to going to visit him as he had clearly shown a genuine interest in everyone who had booked through him.

The evening meal, however, was a rather amusing affair. We did not queue to be served nor have our food brought to the table. We were served through a hatch in the kitchen wall and the husband, whom we never saw apart from fleeting glimpses, would open the hatch prior to each course, place the food on the shelf and then slam down the hatch behind it. This act became part of folklore amongst Pennine Way walkers and was referred to in several visitors' books at succeeding hostels. There were references to 'the Dragon of the Langdon Beck Hostel' and 'Mr Invisible', her better half; I wondered how many hatches he got through in a season. I personally found no fault with the way that the hostel was run and I had a good laugh at the slamming hatch which threatened to chop off the fingers of anyone who was over anxious to snatch their food.

After supper that evening I enjoyed swapping tales with fellow hostelers who included a variety of walkers and cyclists. I was particularly intrigued to meet a nun whose interest was acid peat bogs, rather an unusual hobby for one of that calling. She was spending her holiday studying the geology of Upper Teesdale. Despite my earlier comments, it seemed a popular hostel. Walkers doing the Pennine Way in the opposite direction told me that they had not enjoyed the Cheviot section but things had improved since then. They were very impressed with Upper Teesdale, particularly Cauldron Snout which I would see the following morning.

Day Twelve: Langdon Beck – Dufton

The following morning dawned sunny and warm, with a cooling breeze to keep perspiration down to a reasonable level. Walking on such a bright morning made one revel in such beautiful surroundings. Although not as dramatic as the section from Middleton to Langdon Beck, Cauldron Snout excepted, the upper reaches of the Tees were still a sight to behold. The river rippled between ever-narrowing rocky clefts, its waters a deep, shiny blue under the sun's rays. How different from the bog-hopping of Kinder and Bleaklow which now seemed a world away. It is funny how the mind soon blots out uncomfortable experiences. What a shame Ben wasn't with me to experience all this. He had certainly drawn the short straw.

The lone building passed that morning was Widdybank Farm

which offers refreshment and camping facilities for weary walkers. Its unusual name is derived from a 'widdy', or slate pencil, for a small layer of Skiddaw slates had been mined in the area; there is also a ruined pencil mill nearby.

At this point I was overtaken by five young Pennine Way walkers dwarfed by their heavy packs and striding purposefully with heads lowered. A brief conversation revealed that they were aiming to complete the walk in fourteen days and that up to then things were going according to plan. I kept my thoughts to myself and wished them well as they hurriedly strode ahead. Having a goal is a good thing in my view, but when it entails a forced march with no time to look around, as it appeared in their case, a lot of satisfaction is sacrificed although perhaps achieving their targeted completion time would have been reward enough for them. It also brought home to me how many walkers I was meeting who appeared to carry everything but the kitchen sink. To be fair, those young people could have been back-packing, but they were in too much of a hurry for me to find that out, or to congratulate them on passing the 150-mile point.

Accommodation is virtually non-existent between this farm and Dufton, twelve miles away across wild country. Many walkers hole up here in bad weather before the long trek to High Cup overlooking Dufton. On this part of the route, walkers actually head in a westerly direction which is not desirable for laggards like myself who want to progress northwards and get to journey's end as soon as possible.

After leaving Widdybank Farm, the river twists and turns and walking becomes difficult on its rocky bank. Negotiating the wide loop under Falcon Clints is helped in parts by the presence of duck-boards which relieved the strain on my ankles. Beyond the loop a roaring sound could be heard, shattering the peaceful-ness of the surroundings. As I turned the corner, 150 feet of foaming water confronted me. I had reached the impressive Cauldron Snout that cascades from Cow Green Reservoir. Negoti-ating the steep scramble up the side of the torrent, I dared not dwell on the possibility of slipping on the wet rocks and falling into the foaming mass.

From the top of the climb it is only a short walk to the reservoir that caused a storm of protests from naturalists prior to the commencement of its construction in the late 1960s. Amongst its opponents was AW who was disturbed by the prospect of submerging many acres of attractive countryside. Probably the worst effect of this ravage of nature by man was the destruction of countless rare Alpine plants, for which the area was noted. Procrastination by civil servants, who could possibly have averted the onslaught, incensed many of the protesters. So vociferous was the opposition to its construction that it required a parliamentary Bill to decide the issue. The government of the time had to weigh the demand for preserving the natural beauty of the designated area against the need for controlling the flow of water down the River Tees, thereby providing a constant water supply to the extensive chemical and steel industrial sites in Teeside. They decided, in my opinion, to opt for maintaining the industrial prosperity of the region by providing a controlled and constant water supply to its heartland. To keep faith with naturalists some of the rare plants were moved to higher ground to escape the flooding.

In lighter vein, I did notice from my OS map that the county boundary dividing Durham and Cumbria, created in 1974, runs through the centre of the reservoir. I wondered if the residents of each county could only have water from their half!

The view over the reservoir stretched for many miles and on the skyline could be seen the adjacent humps of Great Dun Fell, Little Dun Fell and Cross Fell. The latter at nearly 3000 feet is the highest point on the Pennine Way. I gazed at those ramparts dominating the horizon with expectancy, tinged with apprehension.

At this point, I caught up with a group of walkers travelling part of the Pennine Way. I discovered that they lived under the shadow of Kinder Scout at Hayfield; at least they didn't have far to travel to the start of this 270-mile challenge. We joined forces for the walk to Dufton, which I was grateful for. I had heard it was a lonely moorland stretch to High Cup and companions were just what I needed. As we made our way towards the two farms of Birkdale, we met a local man walking his dog. He proved to be very knowledgeable about the area and, like so many dog-owners, knew all the best walks for miles around. He accompanied us for a few miles and, if truth be told, I think he relished coming across

Pennine Way walkers so he could impart his local knowledge, pointing out everything and anything of note. As we passed some mining spoil, he told us of the lead miners who formerly worked the area. They would apparently stay on the moor, in even the harshest of conditions, from Monday to Friday, only returning to their families for the weekends. Their home during the week was a crude hut, with up to fifty men sharing a room. Privation and disease were rife, with life expectancy a mere thirty-two years.

As we parted company with him, the prospect of a desolate moorland trek loomed before us. In a short time we found the Maize Beck which would be our guide for part of the journey. After following its course for a mile, we had a decision to make. We could attempt to cross at the appointed spot on the map, or detour north-westwards to a footbridge which would add extra distance but keep our feet dry. Fortunately the waters of the beck were not too hostile and we were able to cross without mishap.

From that point the path began to improve and there were beautiful wild flowers in abundance. Our progress quickened but it was not long before we were smartly halted in our tracks. A mile or so past the bridge, the ground suddenly dropped away beneath our feet without warning. We had arrived at the geological phenomenon of High Cup. A vast basin lay before us through which we could look down upon the lovely Eden valley, with the Lake District hills forming a fine backdrop in the far distance. The horseshoe-shaped cleft is lined with vertical columns of the now familiar Whin Sill which has resisted the ravages of erosion.

This was an ideal spot to eat our lunchtime sandwiches, so we picked a comfortable vantage point on our lofty perch. Having time to study the rugged outlines of the great basin, the myriad fantastic rock formations were a source of wonderment. My eyes were drawn to a stone wall which soared up the opposite face of High Cup, its highest section appearing almost vertical. I felt great admiration for the builders of that drystone wall because it must have been a feat of endurance to get the stone to its higher reaches and then construct a wall that had obviously stood the test of time.

After skirting the northern edge of the escarpment, we began the three-mile descent to the village of Dufton. On the way we came across Ian and Sheila who had been ahead of us but were now just getting ready to start again after a rest stop. Catching up on our respective happenings since leaving Baldersdale, we jauntily descended into the village. The welcoming sight of Dufton's village green was soon upon us. A fine array of cottages surrounds the green and the pleasant hostel is sandwiched amongst them. At the time of AW's walk there was no such accommodation, and hostellers had to walk a further three miles to find a hostel at nearby Knock. The new hostel has made a typically dry Wainwright remark sadly redundant.

Another sobering observation by AW, however, is still very much the truth – that Kirk Yetholm was now further away than at the start of the day's walk. The day's route from Langdon Beck, as the ubiquitous crow flies, had been very slightly south of west.

As we were too early for the opening of the Youth Hostel, we lay on the grass basking in the pleasant sunshine. Someone mentioned that the next day's section, from Dufton to Garrigill, could be the most difficult of the whole walk if the weather were poor. I stopped chewing the long piece of grass that I had inelegantly sticking out of my mouth when that was said: surely not worse than Kinder Scout, or Bleaklow? But when I looked up into the soft summer sky, I was able to relax and continue to chew my grass ruminatively: the weather would continue to be fine for a few days yet. If I prayed hard enough, perhaps even to Kirk Yetholm.

But less than an hour later, as the group of us strolled out of Dufton to check the beginning of the route to Great Dun Fell for the next morning, the clouds began to swirl over the fells. That, I was informed, signified the famous 'Helm Wind' that blows down from Cross Fell. It was this wind, my informant nastily rubbed in, that may have given Cross Fell its original name of Fiends' Fell.

I have stayed in many hostels, but Dufton wins the prize for supplying the most resplendent meals. I found it difficult to get up from the table after supper; the food was first rate and very plentiful.

Among the hostellers staying was a group of schoolchildren in the charge of two teachers who kept them under strict control, and ensured they were kept busy with many jobs around the hostel. The children were walking to Garrigill the following day like myself. One of the teachers, a really outgoing type, talked non-stop throughout supper. We were treated to his virtual life story from his days in the Navy up to and including his recent walking exploits, which featured losing the sole from one of his walking boots. When he paused at last to draw breath, I took my opportunity to talk to the other teacher who I came to know as Mac McGregor. He was an experienced walker and told me about some of the forthcoming sections of the Pennine Way, particularly the last stretch over the Cheviots. I told him that according to the Pennine Way Package, I was due to complete that part of the journey in two bits and stay at an isolated farm known as Uswayford. Mac kindly gave me directions to it, such as needing to turn right at the fourth cairn past Windy Gyle before a trek through a forest. I asked him about the Cheviot itself but he did not advise a detour from the path to climb it – 'dull, uninteresting and very boggy'.

I overheard Mac telling his charges that one of the lessons walking teaches you is patience. I have never forgotten that piece of astute advice and agree wholeheartedly that impatience should be avoided, particularly when faced with a challenging climb. It is rare to be able to see the summit of a fell throughout a climb up to it. Most summits are deceptively hard to reach. I cannot remember the number of times that I have thought I am just below the summit when another slope looms up in front – and then another, and quite possibly another. The never-to-be-reached summit is particularly evident in bad weather. When this happens, you just have to grit your teeth and press on stoically until you achieve your goal. A good tutor of children was Mac McGregor.

Day Thirteen: Dufton–Garrigill

Although the following day dawned bright and sunny, these conditions unfortunately were not to last for long. Leaving the hostel in the lovely, clear morning air I was reluctant to say goodbye to the village green where I had reclined the previous sunny afternoon with my companions. The scene was just as idyllic that morning as I walked along the road that separates the two parts of the green, flanked by trees on either side, their resplendent foliage virtually forming a triumphal archway. Why was I delaying my departure with a final farewell when toughness and resolve were required? I stopped at the impressive village pump, the focal point of the green. I took a lingering look at the red sandstone structure impressively topped with a white sphere, eventually raising my eyes above the backdrop of white-walled cottages to the beckoning distant fells. How tempting it was to delay my plans and remain in these enticing surroundings for a further day. Were all Pennine Way walkers as easily diverted from their task? Could it be that my enthusiasm for the village was a ploy to avoid tackling one of the most testing sections of the walk? The mere thought of ruining poor Edgar Peel's hard work on my behalf goaded me into action. I could see other walkers heading towards the lane leading out of the village and forced myself to follow them. My procrastination meant that I was probably the last to leave, despite a hard seventeen-mile journey ahead of me. The realisation of this caused me to step out at a good pace. AW informs us in his guide that there is no accommodation until Garrigill, my destination that day, and I didn't wish to become stranded.

As I struck out along the lane that would take me past Coatsike Farm and Cosca Hill, Dufton Pike basked in the sunshine to my right and kept watch over me as I began to skirt its broad base. According to AW my initial surroundings would be quiet and peaceful and so it proved on that pleasant morning. Other Pennine Way walkers must have felt as invigorated as I did, for I had not caught up with any of them despite my fast pace.

Crossing the Great Rundale Beck that threads its way down the valley between Dufton Pike and Brownber Hill the ground began to rise, heralding the start of the ascent to Knock Fell. My feeling of contentment was quickly evaporating with the effort of climbing, but even more disturbing was the sight of thick mist beginning to roll down from the heights. It was not long before I was completely enveloped and had to resort to taking a compass bearing for Knock Old Man, a cairn not far from the summit.

Curiously there was not a soul around. I was now paying for my dilatory start by being behind all the other walkers. An eerie silence had descended and there was nothing for it but to press on alone hoping that my bearing was accurate. Longing for some company I stuck to my task up the rapidly increasing gradient. My breathing became laboured as I forged ever upwards thinking that the wanted cairn would never show itself. After what seemed an eternity, one loomed out of the mist, but a quick look at AW's guide indicated a line of cairns on the approach to Knock Old Man. Reckoning that this was a false alarm I carried on past more cairns until I reached a grander one which proved to be my destination, – and who should be sheltering beside it but my old friends Ian and Sheila. We had left Dufton separately since they were not staying at the hostel and apparently had not dawdled at the start as some people had done. I was both relieved and elated as I joined them for a cup of tea and a discussion on the prospects of finding the summit of Cross Fell. The interlude proved to be all too brief as Ian and Sheila suggested once again that I went on alone they were in no hurry and didn't want to hold me back. Too macho to admit that I could do with their company in the mist I smiled bravely and left them to their second cup of tea. Ian's tea bag was certainly going to get plenty of use that day.

Alone once more in the mist I tackled the steep, but thankfully short climb over the summit of Knock Fell (2604 feet) and eventually found the road leading to the radar station on Great Dunn Fell. This was originally a track to the surrounding mines which had been surfaced to provide access to the 'paraphernalia' as AW calls it, on top of the fell. The summit of Great Dunn Fell (2780 feet) is not in AW's top ten list of favourite places; in fact, he had no time for it at all. He felt that it was defaced and debased by the tall masts and attendant equipment. He would prefer to see a few sheep and a cairn on a mountain top.

As I approached the station, I was surprised to find a new encircling boundary fence under construction. It was eight feet high and was obviously there to keep walkers like myself from passing through. My map showed the path leading through the various buildings, but it was evident that a detour round the fence was necessary. This does not appear too onerous on paper, but unfortunately I became disorientated in the thick fog and found myself plodding round the large circular fence at least twice. I couldn't find the path leading from it and twice ended up at the spot where I had joined it. The first time made me cross, the second time even crosser, but also more than a little concerned.

Fearful that I could carry on circling the fence all day, I stopped to rack my brains as to how I could pick up the path again. I tried walking round the fence once more. Having taken a hopeful compass bearing, I left the fence and in the swirling mist blundered out over the fellside – and bumped straight into Ian and Sheila. They too had lost the path and had also taken a bearing towards Little Dun Fell. Could it be, I thought, that there was a multitude of hapless walkers circling the radar station in a state of bewilderment? Relief permeated through me as we teamed up and after about twenty minutes of struggling over featureless fellside we met up with the elusive path.

Determined not to lose it again, we stuck to the path like limpets, careful not to be diverted onto any wrong path. Progress onto Cross Fell was steady and we were soon straining our eyes for the numerous summit cairns we knew surrounded the trig point. AW this time describing them as 'furniture'. As the ground levelled out a minor miracle occurred. We walked out of the mist into bright sunshine. The features of the summit plateau stood out clearly before us and, hardly able to believe our luck, we made our way easily to the trig point which, at 2930 feet, is the highest point on the Pennine Way. We enjoyed a celebratory lunch in the large stone structure that acted as a convenient windbreak. Out came Ian's tea bag for the now familiar toast to our achievement. Unfortunately the mist was still below us, blotting out any surrounding views. Although this was a disappointment, we did not let it upset us unduly as we were grateful to find the summit clear.

I was pleased to discover that Ian and Sheila were staying at the same place in Garrigill that evening. We decided to complete the day's journey together. This also provided an opportunity to see how his tea bag would stand up to the strain of a hard day's use.

Before starting our descent, we met up with the school party from the Dufton hostel once more. They all made it safely to the top although one or two were limping slightly. We let them go first and followed their route past a row of cairns. They looked to be going in the wrong direction, but the masters were good guides and we soon joined the track that took us down to the cairned path that was formerly the old corpse road from Kirkland to Garrigill. The most demanding part of our day's walk was over and we were able to relax with the prospect of only an easy, though seven miles long, walk to come. Staying a few hundred yards behind the school party we were able to take in our surroundings and savour the thought of a good meal and pleasant evening at our destination.

There were signs everywhere that lead had obviously been mined extensively in the surrounding area. Spoil heaps, mine shafts, tunnels and ruined buildings were commonplace. One of the buildings was in a reasonable condition and contained fire-places. This I recognised as Greg's Hut which is used as an emergency shelter by anyone caught in bad weather, or behind schedule. I should have remembered this facility before rushing out of Dufton thinking that I had to reach Garrigill by nightfall at all costs. A few months previously I had seen a television series featuring four young people tackling the Pennine Way. They had run out of daylight on reaching the top of Cross Fell and had spent an unplanned night's stop in this hut.

The mist had now gone completely and the journey down to Garrigill along a good track was completed without difficulty. In the improved weather conditions, it was possible to see down to the valley of the River South Tyne, our next destination.

During our descent we caught right up with the now-struggling back-markers of the school party and I walked with Mac for the last couple of miles to where their minibus was waiting. Being the kind man that he obviously was, he had dropped behind their main group to accompany a girl who was hobbling painfully. She would never have made it without his continual encouragement over the last few miles. It reminded me of the scenes one sees on the telly of the closing stages of the London Marathon.

I bade those nice people goodbye and turned my attention to Garrigill, a village which straddles the River South Tyne. It lies off the beaten track, but is none the worse for that. Like Dufton it has a pleasant village green and I was looking forward to my night's stay at the local Post Office. Lying as it does at the foot of Cross Fell, Garrigill probably started life as a lead-mining settle-ment. Alston, my next port of call, also shares the same origins.

We were made very welcome that evening, the meal lived up to expectations and pleasant company was enjoyed, Ian keeping us well entertained with a string of humorous stories. Everyone staying at the Post Office that night was either doing stretches of the Pennine Way or the whole thing so we had much in common. As if we had not walked enough that day, we went for a stroll round the village after supper.

Day Fourteen: Garrigill—Alston

The following morning I did not hurry my breakfast which was worth savouring. Gone was the apprehension of the previous morning when I had had Cross Fell in front of me; I only had a short walk to Alston that day. Navigation would be simple as the four-mile journey basically follows the river. The Pennine Way Package had offered the alternative to an extremely arduous day's walk from Dufton to Alston, of staying at Garrigill, as I had done, and treating the short journey to Alston as a rest day. As mentioned earlier, two rest days are suggested to ensure a good chance of completing the walk and this was my first. Unfortunately it came a long way into the walk, but I had decided that the best approach was to press on through the earlier sections and cover a good deal of the distance before relaxing with a couple of easy days. Pennine Way walkers' choices vary in this respect; John, you will remember, took a much earlier rest day because he wished to acquaint himself with the limestone country around Malham.

I made a leisurely start at around ten o'clock, wondering how I was going to make a journey of four miles last all day. Just outside the village I joined a riverside path for an amble alongside the River South Tyne. What the day's walking lacked in quantity, it made up for in quality; it proved to be a charmingly attractive area. The young river's source at Tyne Head lay only a few miles away on the flanks of Tynehead Fell. I had unknowingly passed within two miles of that point the previous day whilst descending from Cross Fell. Looking at the river in its natural and unfettered state made me conscious of the dramatic change that would eventually befall it. Following its meeting with the River North Tyne near Hexham it would form the majestic River Tyne that had so long been the life's blood of the North-East, serving now defunct shipyards at Jarrow and Wallsend. For the time being the infant river was content to ripple towards Alston, its bed and banks strewn with boulders and overlooked by trees of differing hues. The surrounding meadows were speckled with wild flowers and I took the opportunity to stop and study some of them; so often one takes them for granted as one marches past. Here they added another dimension to an already attractive walk.

A couple of miles along the path I came upon a series of stone walls within a short distance of one another and my tranquil mood was soon to be shattered. As I neared one of the gateways in the walls a farmer on his tractor was pulling out of the field and bounding alongside the tractor was a large Alsatian which was barking menacingly. I gave the farmer a cheery 'good morning' whilst keeping a wary eye on his fierce-looking dog. He shouted a terse command at which the animal stopped barking, but approached me with a low growl. Stopping his machine the farmer demanded to know if I was one of the Pennine Way crowd. When I confirmed that I was he replied, 'I thought so. We get a lot of your sort through here.' Assuming that by 'your sort' he meant walkers carrying an assortment of rucksacks, I nodded. His dog, which I sincerely hoped was not as angry as its owner, was now circling round my legs, growling as it did so. 'Most of you shouldn't be let loose,' was his next retort. 'Staggering along with damn great packs on your backs looking absolutely knackered. Some of you couldn't find your way out of a paper bag, God knows how you expect to walk that Pennine Way.' I could appreciate that walkers passing straight through Garrigill heading for Alston after having tackled Cross Fell would not be looking too sprightly, but before I could reply to this insult the redoubtable farmer, now in full flow, continued: 'Walkers come knocking on my door at all hours asking to camp in my field. I can't understand why they can't make proper arrangements instead of wanderin' around like nomads.' When I tried to explain, whilst struggling to remain calm as the animal snarled and nudged at my ankles, that some walkers prefer the flexibility of staying wherever it is convenient, I was met with a snort. 'Can't they do a bit of proper plannin'; where would I be if I didn't plan my work? You should hear some of the horrific tales they tell me about wanderin' around like lost sheep.'

I reckoned he was about to expound my theory that sheep have more intelligence than some humans when he stopped to shout at the dog. Seizing my opportunity to escape I made a speedy withdrawal with a quick wave of farewell. Thankfully his dog did not chase me as his owner sat nonplussed on his tractor. Scurrying away, I breathed a sigh of relief at escaping with my ears and legs intact.

My leisurely stroll to Alston that had been so rudely interrupted seemed to be over all too quickly and I was soon at the Youth Hostel. It was now only lunchtime and the hostel itself would not open until five o'clock but the washing and drying room was open – so sensible. I took the chance to do some necessary laundry, and then ate my packed lunch. Trusting that my drying clothes would still be there when I returned, I went for a walk around the little town. I have always found hostellers honest people, except for an isolated experience at Bellingham, which I will come to later, and my clothes were untouched upon my return.

There was plenty of time available for a leisurely stroll around Alston's cobbled streets and for gazing in its shop windows. The place has a pleasant, unspoiled appearance and the shops are a boon for self-catering walkers, enabling them to replenish shrinking stocks of food. It claims to be the highest market town in England, but unfortunately there was no market that day, the lovely stone market cross standing in splendid isolation in the market square. In front of this eye-catching structure stands a neat line of round, squat stone pillars whose origin intrigued me. A row of tall stone buildings, some with white-painted walls faced me across the square. They are four storeys high and two of them house the shops of H. Kearton and Son. At the sight of these my mind immediately returned to Thwaite and their famous Kearton brothers. Determined not to be overlooked, the church spire thrusts itself above one of the more conventional three-storey buildings farther down the square.

As I surveyed the pleasant scene, I was joined by an elderly man who sat down beside me to pass the time of day. He turned out to be a local inhabitant who had lived in the town all his life and proved to be most friendly and informative. Having noticed me studying the market cross he enquired if I would like to know more about it. The original was erected in 1746 he explained, and the present structure was a grade two listed building. Unfortunately, due to wear and tear, and more recently to battering from passing lorries far too big to be sensibly allowed through the town's streets, it had required re-building three times. He went on to solve the mystery of the line of stone pillars. I laughed as he told me that they were of no historic significance, but merely protecting the building from the ravages of passing traffic. My earlier frustration at not being able to cover any more miles that day was now tempered by learning more about the little town from my companion; in fact, I was given its complete history since becoming a parish with its own church in the twelfth century. The town's growth was due to the silver and lead mined in the area, which also provided the incentive for building the railway line to Haltwhistle in 1852. That construction was completed a mere twenty-six years after the local population had cheered the arrival of its first stagecoach. He suggested that I visited their railway station, for although the line was closed in 1976 a short section of narrow gauge track is still in use as a tourist attraction. Although of modest length it is the highest railway of its type in England, at nearly 900 feet.

I was completely engrossed in his enlightening account and was quite sorry when it came to an end. However, his following remark brought a huge smile to my face. Apparently he had met a pair of elderly walkers in the square the previous day, who had proudly told him that they were walking the Pennine Way. When I asked if one of them had happened to mention that he was seventy-four years old he nodded, confirming my suspicion that he was referring to the one and only 'Brothers in Law'. I explained about their adventures and the remarkable progress they had made to forge one day ahead of me.

Bidding him goodbye with grateful thanks, I recommenced my tour which included a visit to the railway station but there was unfortunately no sign of a train. I finally headed for Alston bridge, which stands near to the Youth Hostel. This would be the starting point of my next day's journey. Enjoying the riverside setting, I looked over the stone parapet at the River South Tyne which would soon be swelled by the River Nent when they joined forces at the northern end of the town.

The afternoon eventually turned to evening and I was eager for the morrow and to be on my way again. After supper in the hostel, I overheard voices with a familiar accent coming from the self-catering kitchen. I went to investigate and found three ladies from Mansfield, the town of my birth, preparing a meal. More accurately, two were cooking and the third, who was suffering terribly from blisters, sat watching her companions. It transpired that they were walking the Pennine Way to raise money for their local hospice. They had never walked any great distance before and as far as I could make out had not done any preparatory training. Consequently they were plagued by sore feet. Things had got so bad that they had come by taxi from Dufton as the worst sufferer was unable to walk; they hoped that a day's rest would enable them to carry on and finish the walk. They must have achieved their aim, for on my next trip to Mansfield I was delighted to see them featured in a lengthy article in the local paper. It put great emphasis on their achievement as their feat had raised a good sum for charity. I felt pleased for them because they were very keen not to let down their sponsors by allowing the blisters to get the better of them.

It was these ladies who first told me about a fellow walker nicknamed 'Road-Runner'. Before my walk was finished his name was on many Pennine Way walkers' lips relaying stories of his great speed and stamina. Apparently this young man had been a great help to these ladies during their trip from Langdon Beck to Dufton. They happened to mention to the 'Road-Runner' at Langdon Beck Youth Hostel that they were apprehensive about finding their way across the moorland. Although he was due a rest day, he offered to accompany them for part of the way. In the event, he guided them the whole distance to High Cup and then returned to the hostel to make the official journey to Dufton the following day. Anyone that helpful was in my view worth meeting. I was to make his acquaintance later, but not for some time.

Day Fifteen: Alston–Greenhead

The first part of the following day's route hugged the picturesque valley of the River South Tyne, which had now become a welcome companion. Fortuitously I met Ian and Sheila, who had enjoyed the luxury of bed and breakfast accommodation the previous evening. I had only just set out across Alston bridge and we stayed together for the journey to Greenhead where they were also staying at the Youth Hostel. Discussion centred around our fitness and unimpeded progress. We agreed that we were lucky to have no serious problems with fatigue or blisters. After early rain the skies cleared and we optimistically decided that the weather would be kind to us for the rest of the day.

I had read in AW's *Companion* the previous evening that we were to spend several miles 'in the footsteps of the Romans', and this information was imparted to my companions who were suitably impressed. AW is referring to the Maiden Way, a Roman road which we were to meet about two miles farther on. This ancient marching road skirts Gilderdale Forest to the west of Alston en route for the fort at Carvoran that stands alongside Hadrian's Wall.

Maintaining a lively pace we were soon crossing the A689 Alston to Brampton road that threads along the valley, keeping close company with the disused railway that formerly linked Alston to Haltwhistle. We were to re-cross the road several more times that day. A study of my OS map revealed that Alston stands at an important route junction; no fewer than five roads emanate from it, hence its use as a staging post in former times. The railway was still in use when AW produced his *Companion* and utilised small unstaffed stations along the valley; these he says, combined with the bus service along the road offered a 'temptation to walkers to save their time and their feet'. Although there was now no railway I was confident that my two friends and I would not harbour such a notion. As they hurried on their way ahead of me, the 'Brothers in Law' would surely have thought otherwise, looking upon such an opportunity as manna from heaven.

It was hard to find our meeting point with the Maiden Way as its line was indistinct. According to the map we were to cross and recross it several times during our approach to the site of Whitley Castle, a Roman fort, where the soldiers would have rested their tired limbs before their final push to Hadrian's Wall.

Ian and Sheila were singing the praises of the river scenery, particularly when we made our way through the attractive meadows beyond the tiny hamlet of Kirkhaugh. They were bemoaning the fact that Bellingham, their finishing point, was looming ever closer but were determined to enjoy the remainder of their journey. This they felt would not be difficult if the forthcoming countryside measured up to the current setting. Unfortunately their expectations were somewhat deflated a few miles further on.

The easy walking brought us rapidly towards Slaggyford which nestles by the river. This we decided would be a good place to eat our sandwiches and admire the meandering, yet still lively river. Upon reaching the hamlet we relaxed on the riverbank, but I was rather put out by the discovery that my packed lunch was extremely meagre (for which I mentally docked the warden at the Alston hostel a few bonus points) and I wolfed it in record time. While I waited for Ian and Sheila to finish off their much more substantial tucker, I had time to sit and wonder who Slaggy was, and when he had forded the river, presumably in pursuit of some lovely prize on the other side. I have since been corrected in this assumption, for the name is derived from the river clattering over its stony bed.

The afternoon section of the walk began well enough as we veered away from the river and onto the rounded contours of Glendue Fell and Hartleyburn Common. It was here that we rejoined the Maiden Way, now more clearly discernible as it cut straight through the heathland, and we followed it for two and a half miles to our farewell intersection with the A689.

From this point onwards our surroundings deteriorated until the approach to Greenhead. AW's comment at the foot of the appropriate page in his guide of 'Uninteresting' warned of what was to come. In fact, AW exudes an air of despondency by proclaiming: 'If the remainder of the Pennine Way was like this (happily it isn't) here would be the place to pack it in and go back home.' What was this talk of giving up? Hadn't AW been my trusty guide and mentor over many arduous miles; encouraging, sometimes warning, but above all making me stick at my task? Such talk with a mere quarter of the distance remaining could be misconstrued by the faint-hearted as a call to rebel against daily rigours by ripping off their boots, crying, 'You can keep the Pennine Way' and catching the next bus home. Thankfully, my companions and I were above such actions and had the sense to realise that this was only AW's quirky humour at work.

We gritted our teeth, therefore, for AW is invariably right in his predictions and struck out across the 'tedious' stretch as he calls it that would take us to the A69 Brampton to Greenhead road. The path, indistinct and difficult to follow, initially led us through fields before depositing us on trackless moorland. Only the landmark of the trig point on top of Wain Rigg, at a modest height of 900 feet, served to relieve the monotony. However, we received a little light relief by chatting to a group of Pennine Way walkers that we came upon as they rested. They were still hoping to accomplish the whole distance despite two of their party dropping out at an early stage. Overcome with the pain of ripe blisters on the third day, one of the girls in the group had decided that she could go no farther. Her boyfriend, not wishing to leave her, had also dropped out. Their depleted party had remained intact thus far, but its members expressed varying reactions to the demands of walking every day for nearly three weeks. The more experienced walkers amongst them were quite enjoying themselves but some of the others, who had come along for company, were not as impressed. We were treated to the full spectrum of their feelings concerning the various sections of the walk. Wanting to press on we wished them well. I wonder if they ever made it to Kirk Yetholm.

The three of us had by now grown tired of the hummocky grass that had dogged our footsteps for so many miles during our crossing of the foothills at the northern end of the Pennines. In AW's opinion, the Pennine Way should end here, rather than progressing for a further sixty-five miles, and the final section should instead be called the Cheviot Way. However, he tells us not to argue the point as we are enjoying our walk so much. (Aren't we?)

During our approach to the A69 my eagerness to reach Greenhead was mounting with every step. I was greatly anticipating my first view of Hadrian's Wall, about which I had heard so much, but had never seen.

We were striding out as we crossed the road heading for the Roman road known as Stanegate, which signifies the beginning of 'Wall Country'. So intent were we in reaching our objective that I nearly missed AW's indication that the 200-mile point was rapidly approaching. Hurrying through the hollow depression that forms part of Stanegate we fairly leapt over the stile at the end of it to be confronted by the Vallum, a large ditch which formerly defended the south side of the Roman Wall. The beckoning 200-mile landmark lay a little way along the path running parallel with the Vallum near its intersection with the B6318. We hurried to the spot and stopped to recover our breath. Suitably refreshed Ian, Sheila and I performed our own version of a three-way Highland fling – quite an operation with our big packs jiggling around on our backs. Luckily there were no onlookers to observe our antics. We rapidly ran out of steam and sank to the ground, taking the opportunity to survey our surroundings. Annoyingly there were no remaining traces of the Roman Wall at this point and we had to wait until the following day for our first glimpse of it. A consolation was the sight of Thirlwall Castle, now sadly a ruin, standing above the path. This fourteenth-century pele tower stands on a green hill overlooking the footbridge spanning a burn heading for Walltown Quarry.

A detour was now necessary to the Greenhead hostel – a converted church – which lies a quarter of a mile off the path. It was a long quarter-mile for tired legs: perhaps that Highland fling hadn't been such a good idea after all. Unfortunately, I was feeling somewhat below par by the time we reached the hostel. This was due to a head cold which had very suddenly developed. I had no idea how I managed to acquire it. I had suffered no early warning signs; it had just sneaked up on me. Not being able to concentrate very well on the good chat which always seemed to follow the supper, I went to bed early.

Day Sixteen: Greenhead–Once Brewed

I awoke the next morning feeling much better for the good night's rest, and raring to get going. This I attributed to the tablets that Ian had given me the night before. He was a man prepared for any eventuality.

At breakfast I met a young man who was walking the entire length of Hadrian's Wall, seventy-three miles from Bowness-on-

Solway to Wallsend-on-Tyne. He was being sponsored, the money raised going to Cancer Research. Waving his toast and marmalade around in the air, he explained the construction of the Wall which is approximately fifteen feet high and eight feet thick, with a six-foot parapet. Seventeen forts are spaced evenly along its length and at every Roman mile is a small fortification known as a milecastle.

Ian and Sheila were to accompany me once more as they were also having a leisurely day's walk in order to explore the Wall. Our common destination was the hostel at Once Brewed. We were licking our lips in anticipation of a journey through history along the boundary of the great Roman Empire. Our day was to be extremely gratifying, but also surprising, because the actual appearance of the Wall was very different from what I had imagined.

We were to find it in various states of disrepair along the seven-mile stretch that we covered. Its line follows an escarpment that appears man-made, but is actually a series of crags that necessitate alternate climbing and descent. They are very similar to the escarpment at the northern edge of the Cleveland Hills, which I was to meet later on in AW's 'Coast to Coast' route. On that walk the path undulates like some giant roller-coaster as it overlooks the flat plain of Teeside that sprawls away to the north.

The day started bright and sunny; perfect for views along the Wall and of the striking Northumberland scenery. AW puts the previous uninteresting afternoon behind him and he becomes quite excited as he tells of the joys to come. We were to walk for one and a half miles before our expectations were fulfilled by having our first sight of the Roman Wall. Eagerly we marched alongside the Roman Ditch that marks the original line of the Wall, quickly skirted Walltown Quarry where the Wall has unfortunately been destroyed by quarrying, to finally feast our eyes on the first section of the impressive stone rampart. Although sadly a shadow of its former majestic self at this point, its massive bulk undulates over the escarpment, reaching around half of its original height (fifteen feet) in places. AW calls this 'a great moment', and he was obviously thrilled by this impressive view.

As the Wall climbs from its starting point it skirts a disused quarry which is being landscaped with a view to creating a recreation and amenity area for visitors. Currently, the scheme is still being developed and is due to open in mid-1995. The reasons for the long development period are that the infill used in the levelling of the area required several years to settle and the young trees subsequently planted needed time to mature. When completed, the site will include a picnic and recreational area and an unmanned Northumberland National Park information point, as well as car parking and toilet facilities. Although the development has taken a long time to come to fruition, the long-term aim of providing a tidy facility for visitors will have been achieved.

Whether AW would have approved of the scheme is debatable as he would not have enjoyed the sight of people swarming around the Wall en masse, undoubtedly leaving their all too familiar legacy of litter and exhaust fumes. He would, however, have relished the sight that confronted us a little farther on. Part of the Wall was being renovated by a group of enthusiasts. The work was being done painstakingly and progress appeared to be very slow; there was miles to be done stretching in front of them – a daunting task. During the intervening years they will have made significant advances; they certainly earned my admiration for their tireless efforts.

Alongside the Wall a military road ran, replacing the Stanegate and acting as an artery for supplies to the fortifications. I didn't envy the Romans their task of manning the Wall or transporting provisions in the depths of winter. The weather we were enjoying was pleasantly warm and dry.

The sixteenth day was the second of my official rest days and I was torn between two courses of action during my eight-mile journey to the Once Brewed Youth Hostel. The first, and by far the easiest, was to head straight for the hostel and spend a relaxing afternoon waiting for it to open. This would be restful, but rather dull. The second involved joining Ian and Sheila on a trip to the Roman Fort at Housesteads; this required a two-and-a-half-mile detour along part of the following day's route, which would then need to be retraced. I plumped for the latter, even though my day's mileage would come close to that of a normal one. A rest day was not really required, and the fort seemed too close to miss. It also meant that I could remain with Ian and Sheila who had only one more day left.

We carried on our intriguing journey in the footsteps of the Romans, even walking on top of the Wall where its dimensions and solidity allowed. AW helpfully indicates such sections with arrows in his sketches, but we were keeping a wary eye open for arrows of a different kind; those that could be fired from the bows of warlike Celts. It was exciting to walk along this Roman monument and marvel at its skilful construction in a pre-mechanisation age.

Our undulating and physically demanding progress was accompanied by remarkable views from crags that tower above the surrounding countryside. Some have intriguing names such as Windshields, Peel and Hotbank and all carry their burden of the man-made stone rampart. The highlight was a view over the shimmering blue waters of Crag Lough from Highshield Crag. Ringed with trees and a backdrop of rolling Northumberland hills it forms a memorable setting.

Our visit to Housesteads proved very worthwhile. The ancient five-acre site, shaped like a playing card, formerly included streets, barracks for the legionnaires, granaries and a commandant's house. It now displays, in addition to its ruins, more modern attractions such as a visitor centre, museum, picnic site, shop and refreshment kiosk. The museum houses an original plan of the fort and many artifacts portraying the military and civilian roles that it played in those times. We were also interested to learn that the nearby milecastle at Sewing Shields was undergoing painstaking excavation and would soon become an additional attraction. Ian, Sheila and I agreed that the visit had crowned one of the best days of our walk.

Retracing our steps along the Wall to Once Brewed we surveyed the extensive Wark Forest in the distance, which we would encounter the next day. Before checking in at the hostel we visited the adjacent Tourist Information Centre, from where I got some excellent literature about the Wall and its other attendant forts, and later spent a happy couple of hours reading it. At the Centre, I asked about the unusual names of Once Brewed and its chum down the road, Twice Brewed, and was told that originally there had been an inn and a bothy in the surrounding hamlet. The inn stood in West Twice Brewed and the bothy a quarter of a mile away in East Twice Brewed. Ale supplied by the inn was fermented twice to give added strength, hence the name; the bothy was provided for walkers, who could obtain refreshment there. This bothy was replaced by the Youth Hostel which was opened by a lady from a local Methodist family. At the opening ceremony she expressed a wish that nothing stronger than tea would be consumed in the hostel and that it would be brewed only once, thus giving rise to the name of 'Once Brewed'. I was confident that Ian would ensure the brewing of large amounts of tea during our stay, but was less convinced that it would qualify as a single brew.

Although the hostel is a new and impressive purpose-built building it unfortunately lacked a corresponding atmosphere. This I attributed to the way that it was run – on a seemingly tight budget. Food was in short supply; portions were measured and small and did nothing to satisfy Ian's rapacious appetite. When he had the temerity to ask for more bread with his soup, he was tersely told that there was none available. Amazingly, we were restricted to one cup of tea with our supper, but Ian came to the rescue, as I knew he would. We were later able to supplement our liquid intake by a visit to the inn at Twice Brewed to sample the strong ale.

Day Seventeen: Once Brewed–Bellingham

Next morning I managed to get another half-slice of toast at breakfast to supplement the one I had been rationed to. (A note to all wardens who might read this: one slice of toast is not enough for a grown man who has many miles in front of him.) A group of friends whom I had met along the Way, including Ian and Sheila, assembled for a photo-call after breakfast. We were now entering the last stages of our walk and wished to have some record of our respective companions; something to bore our relatives and friends back home.

The day's walk was to the little Northumberland market town of Bellingham (pronounced Bellinjam) and it would be my last opportunity to accompany Ian and Sheila as their journey ended there. Apparently the hostel in which we were to stay that evening was, according to Ian, rather cramped. He had been telling me frequently that on his previous stay there he had slept in a broom cupboard as space was so limited. Never being absolutely sure whether his stories were true, I wondered what I was letting myself in for. I would leave Ian and Sheila with some regret as they were a great couple and good company. Ian had kept my spirits up with his mealtime antics and his humorous tales. I will always remember their companionship, which was particularly welcome during our foggy climb to Cross Fell, together with the sobering thought that I could still be blundering round that fence on Great Dunn Fell to this day.

With this in my mind I set off with them to join Hadrian's Wall for the last time before leaving it a few miles farther on to head northwards. Once again we were treated to sunshine and a slight breeze, perfect walking weather. The familiar pattern of alternating climb and descent was recommenced as we passed Crag Lough and Hotbank Crags once more. The appeal of those superb views had not diminished. At Rapishaw Gap, within sight of the picturesque Cuddys Crags, we said a reluctant goodbye to the Wall and obeyed AW's instructions to drag ourselves from it and cry; 'On to Bellingham!'

The walk then became less interesting as undistinguished moorland stretched before us. Views of Broomlee and Greenlee Loughs added some variety before we found ourselves enveloped by the brooding pine trees of the Wark Forest. As Northumberland has many such forests, I was to spend a great deal of time walking through them during the next couple of days. The first experience of walking along forest tracks in warm sunshine was a pleasant one, but, after the 'nth' mile of this, I did long for the fells and open spaces. I was even prepared to settle for a return to the peat and a little bog hopping. This I was to have in plentiful supply when I reached that final barrier, the Cheviot Hills.

In his *Companion* AW explains at length the background to the Border Forests, which I was now in. Apparently it was the largest of Britain's forest plantations at that time, yet the least known. The main problem associated with the forest industry, if one can so call it, is that after planting there is a wait of at least forty years before you can reap what has been sown. Although there is an undoubted benefit in creating these forests from what was previously a wasteland, by the employment and prosperity it has brought to the area, AW echoes my sentiments of forest walking, when he describes a forest as a prison and the fell as liberty.

Normally there is little difficulty in following the route along forest tracks and if you are in a hurry time can be made up. However, problems do arise when one's track comes into one of those wide clearings – where the great logging lorries turn – and one finds three paths leading out the other side. Which to choose? I did manage to get lost during a later stage when trying to pick my way through the forest above Byrness, as the track indicated on the map turned out to be a narrow offshoot path that headed into a dark cluster of spruce trees.

The relief of emerging from the Wark Forest was tempered by the lack of a distinct path through the open countryside. But things soon improved, and we came upon the delight of Warks Burn, a pleasant stream which is a tributary of the North Tyne. It lies in an attractive, wooded glade which made a wonderful change from staring at Sitka spruce for hour after hour.

The following section proved a complicated one until a road was reached. Concentration was required to follow an indistinct route through pastureland and AW calls this task 'cross country rambling'. After a spell of road walking we headed over more fields until the landmark of the unfortunately named Shitlington Crags came into view. We stopped at a nearby farm which displayed a sign with a welcoming message that tea and refreshments were available. The lady appeared glad of some company and we enjoyed a leisurely half hour chatting on the lawn of the farmhouse and admiring her garden furniture which consisted of a commode and a curious assortment of old tables and chairs. The tea was very satisfying and it was hard to terminate this pleasant interlude in the sunshine.

The remaining distance to Bellingham was covered quickly. It stands in pleasant countryside and the approach is particularly impressive as one drops down to the River North Tyne which flows just outside the middle of the little town. A sturdy stone bridge over the river was undergoing reconstruction, but there was room to pass over it and make our way into the village. I was eager to see the hostel that Ian had told me so much about, but as it lay on the opposite side of the village, that pleasure was to come later.

An important feature of Bellingham is that it is the last major place on the Pennine Way where supplies can be replenished. My first job, therefore, was to do the victualling in the welcoming shops, the hostel being self-catering. While I was thus engaged, Ian and Sheila wandered round to assess the merits of the four public houses, in one of which we planned to have our farewell drink later that evening. Before making our way to the hostel, there was a little time to inspect the Early Norman church. This was sturdily built to repel attacks, and has narrow windows in its thick walls. Bellingham's history is interlinked with the border disputes and Scottish raids that were prevalent centuries ago. The church was seriously damaged by fire during two particularly punitive raids by marauding Scots.

The hostel, when I finally saw it, was a revelation. It had the appearance of a simple wooden hut that had been banished to the outskirts of the village. A YTS party was staying, as were some fellow walkers from abroad. These included an American who was hoping to complete the Pennine Way in fourteen days. Then he planned to attempt it again and halve that time. Rather him than me, I thought, but he had the advantage of Marine training. AW certainly would not have approved; he would have sent the chap off to the local running track to complete his time trials.

Space was at a premium in the communal area that also served as a dining room but we just managed to squeeze in. The adjacent dormitories were thankfully larger than the broom cupboard that Ian swore he had slept in on his previous visit, but the proverbial cat could not be swung around in the cramped kitchen where we grappled with pots and pans, struggling to prepare a decent meal. My greatest fear was of other hostellers squeezing past me in the confined space and propelling my prospective grub over the floor. At supper Ian had a captive audience for what was his farewell performance with the single tea bag. They could hardly escape his swansong as there was nowhere else to retire to, except to bed. Ian's humour was infectious and everyone enjoyed the cosy and pleasant atmosphere, and many tales of walking exploits were exchanged.

As I mentioned earlier, this hostel was the only one where any of my belongings went missing. We noticed that items such as soft drinks, tea bags and small personal articles had a habit of disappearing, but I was cross about my map and its case which I was unable to find when we returned from our celebration at the pub later that evening. Ian kindly gave me his map case and the missing OS map of the Cheviots, insisting that he had no further use for them.

Day Eighteen: Bellingham – Byrness

At breakfast the next morning I made some porridge for Ian as a parting gesture. He said that it was the best he had eaten on the Pennine Way – a fine compliment for he took his porridge very seriously. The warden had been conspicuous by her absence for most of the time. She did not live at the hostel, for reasons of space, and her house was quite a distance away. We had to suffer the indignity of walking there to reclaim our membership cards before we could start our day's walk. I was, however, still full of optimism, reckoning that if I could reach this far I must surely finish. Only the thought of crossing the exposed and demanding Cheviots seemed daunting, but I thrust that to the back of my mind as the day's task of reaching Byrness came first. Instead, I started a countdown: only forty-five miles left.

I bade a very sad farewell to Ian and Sheila, for they had been ideal companions. We had liked to walk at much the same pace, and had enjoyed talking when we felt like it, but were also content to swing along in silence at other times. As usually happens on these occasions, we made promises to keep in touch which, apart from one short correspondence, sadly did not materialise. I often think of them because they feature prominently in my slide lecture about the Pennine Way. I am indebted to Ian for his popularity amongst my listeners as I recall our introductory meal at Malham Hostel and subsequent adventures. I wonder if they will read this book.

As they disappeared from sight, my attention reverted to the job in hand and I made my way to Hareshaw Linn along the attractive Hareshaw Burn, a detour recommended by AW. I was not disappointed, for following a pleasant walk up the wooded valley, a waterfall came in view to greet me. The sun was shining and a slight accompanying breeze kept my spirits high although these were somewhat dampened by then having to backtrack a considerable distance to regain the main route.

I took my time over the four miles of pleasant countryside walking to reach the Bellingham to Otterburn road that takes a different route out of the village. Disused quarries and shooting butts were much in evidence. Part of the track follows an old wagon-way that served the quarry and colliery situated near to the road. The colliery had been in use for over two hundred years until its demise around forty years ago. Many raw materials had been hewn from this area including ironstone, limestone and coal. One of the quarries still has traces of an accompanying lime kiln.

The journey between this road and the next one linking Byrness to Troughend was awkward to negotiate as no clear path was visible. I found the countryside to be a pleasant mixture of forest and hill. I crossed three summits, namely those of Lough Shaw, Deer Play and Lord's Shaw, all of which are of moderate height but they do have the advantage of affording the first views of the Cheviot Hills, that final barrier of the walk. AW advises caution at this point, claiming that it is too early to start getting excited by the prospect of journey's end. He reckons that the Cheviots are the toughest test of all. Personally I would rank them alongside Kinder and Bleaklow, although I do appreciate that they cover a much greater distance. However, as I descended to the Troughend road I obeyed AW's instructions and tried to contain the excitement that I could feel welling up inside.

The next landmark, approximately a mile past the road, was the monument on Padon Hill. Although not directly on the route, I had only to make a short detour to the summit, and though the hill was of no great height, around 1250 feet, I was perspiring freely in the heat of a warm, early summer afternoon. The stone monument appeared to be a solid construction, roughly the shape of a salt or pepper pot. It was erected in memory of the Scottish Covenantor Alexander Padon who held religious gatherings at this remote spot in order to escape persecution.

A convenient fence runs alongside this section of the path which must be a great help in bad weather. I had no real need of it as visibility was good and I was continuing to enjoy the remarkably fine weather that had accompanied me for most of my walk – what a pity I had had to struggle over those early stages in such appalling weather. I realised that my mind was being inextricably drawn to the Cheviots still in front of me. Perhaps their notorious bogs would have dried out a bit after the extensive spell of good weather. Following a period of respite during the descent of Padon Hill, I then worked up a fine lather whilst climbing the final hill before Byrness, Brownrigg Head. AW makes the rather unkind remark that this is a place to vacate quickly. I found it no worse than many other hills and at least the surrounding boggy landscape was definitely drying out under the hot sun.

Following a mile of descent from Brownrigg Head it was time once again for some more forest walking. The next three miles were through Redesdale Forest which encloses the hamlet of Blakehopesburnhaugh and the village of Byrness. The former has the longest name of any settlement on the Pennine Way and is a test of pronunciation. I am glad that I was not born there, or lived there: what a mouthful every time one had to give one's address. And could one get it all out smoothly if stopped by a police patrol car on the way home in the evening?

It was cooler in the forest, but I found the endless rows of pines intensely boring. In fact, AW's comment that you can't see the forest for the trees is very apt. I was thankful to emerge from the claustrophobic place and follow the River Rede for a couple of miles to reach Byrness, which is little more than a collection of forestry cottages arranged in neat rows. Two of the cottages are converted into the Youth Hostel.

The roadside café and store was the first place I headed for at the end of the hot, tiring day's walk rather than the hostel. Sweat was pouring from me and I had a raging thirst, the drinks that I had carried with me having been consumed due to the heat. It was too early for the hostel to open so I made for this convenient watering hole. When I tell you that I drank a litre bottle of mineral water virtually straight down, you will know how thirsty I was. A few minutes later I paid the ultimate penalty for bolting that large amount of fizzy liquid: eruptions began to tune up in my stomach and took a long time to abate.

As I checked in to the hostel I recalled the cryptic entry in the Pennine Way Package which referred to the fact that baths could be taken by prior appointment with the lady warden. I felt tempted to ask her if I could take advantage of the offer, but restrained myself. The lady was much more helpful than the warden at Bellingham hostel.

At supper I met another two fellow Pennine Way travellers. One had damaged a leg muscle which had delayed his progress by four days. He planned to catch a bus to the finish at Kirk Yetholm to make a pre-arranged rendezvous with a friend. His companion was planning to complete the walk on foot in the correct way. They had heard about Ben and his finger (what an age ago that seemed); one had met the 'Road-Runner' and knew of his assistance to the three ladies from Mansfield. The Pennine Way grapevine is truly remarkable.

Amongst further acquaintances made at the hostel was a Scotsman who was walking the Way from north to south. Apparently he had covered the twenty-nine miles over the Cheviots in nine hours, which seemed a remarkably good time to me. He confirmed my hope that the conditions underfoot were as good as could be expected, reporting that the peat had dried out considerably. The character who topped them all was Canadian and something of a masochist, for in his rucksack he carried a fifteen-pound rock in addition to all the normal gear. Obviously he wanted to do the Pennine Way the hard way. When I asked him what on earth possessed him to carry a darned great rock, he replied, 'Well, it's something to do.' If the Cheviots had not been drying out so rapidly I could have visualised him sinking into a peat grough up to his neck with all that weight.

Later that evening I accompanied my new-found friends to the local hotel for a couple of hours' relaxation and to forget about the formidable task awaiting me the next day.

Day Nineteen: Byrness–Uswayford

The following morning I awoke early to find another hot, sunny day in prospect. On the one hand this was a welcome sight, as the drying of the bogs would continue and visibility would be good. The downside would be losing another few gallons of sweat.

As I set out, my thoughts were mixed. Here I was on the last lap of my journey with high hopes of finishing in style. However, the thought of twenty-nine miles of tough country with virtually no habitation was a sobering one. I trusted that my route finding would not be found wanting, but there was the comforting fact that I was to break the crossing at the remote farm of Uswayford, high among the Cheviot hills. That was assuming that I could find it and, as I set off, I tried to recall 'Mac' the schoolmaster's precise directions to it.

I am relieved that AW found the initial climb out of Byrness confusing, because I certainly did. I had done as he instructed and had girded up my loins as never before, but this did not prevent me from getting lost in the forest. I missed the official path that appeared to be nothing more than a narrow gap between pines that were shrouded in eerie darkness and extremely uninviting. Consequently I spent quite a time plodding along forest tracks, which I generally think look identical in these situations. Finally I got back onto the proper route, picking up the path as it emerged from the forest. This diversion did nothing to bolster by spirits for if I couldn't find my way at this early stage, what hope was there on the exposed hills?

Pulling myself together, I said goodbye to the forest at last, glad that those infernal trees were behind me. A short climb up the remainder of the steep path took me to the summit of Byrness Hill (1358 feet). Even without the hot sun doing its worst on my pale complexion, my face was very sore from the many nicks with a razor blade that I had inflicted that morning. My electric razor had decided that it had had enough of the Pennine Way and had stopped working. Consequently I had had to resort to a small disposable version which had proceeded to cut my face to ribbons.

Therefore, I stayed on the exposed summit only long enough to look back, with considerable satisfaction, over the last of the forest to the valley of the Rede spread out below.

As often happens, the anticipation of an event is more awesome than the event itself. So it proved with the Cheviots, although I must admit that I did have the benefit of good weather and reasonably dry conditions. I found it hard work but enjoyable, and the Border fence between England and Scotland provided a lifeline for much of the way. In misty conditions, I could imagine clinging to that fence like a limpet. The scenery was impressive with myriad rounded hills stretching in all directions. Peat groughs abounded and some were many feet deep. I thanked providence for the reasonable solidity of the ground. As I was emerging from a particularly deep chasm of peat I was staggered to see a chap hurtling towards me on a trike, or three-wheeled motor cycle. He paused just long enough for me to ask what on earth he was doing riding such a beast up there. He replied that he was a shepherd looking for his sheep. Apparently he had overslept that morning, jumped on his machine and was trying to make up lost time. Wishing him well in the search for his sheep I bade him goodbye and watched him ride his bucking bronco into the distance. The ATV (all-terrain vehicle) is now standard equipment for all hill shepherds, hence the tyre tracks all over the hills.

I now turned my nose towards the north and set off at a brisk pace to find the Border fence which was to be my companion, on and off, for the rest of the day. There was no one about apart from the ubiquitous sheep, and I amused myself with quirky thoughts about the oddly-named hills that I passed. Houx Hill – did it really exist or was it just a hoax? Ravens Knowe – what did the ravens know that I didn't? Ogre Hill – no giants in evidence, but its name rhymed with toga, which was appropriate as I was about to pass some ancient Roman camps not far beyond. Just before the Chew Green settlement, the path crossed the border into Scotland for the first time. This gave me a definite thrill, and I smiled to myself as I read AW's comment in the *Companion* that it is just as soggy as England!

At Chew Green, however I passed back into England and joined Dere Street, a high-level section of Roman road. I have recently walked through the Scottish Borders and met up with other sections of Dere Street. Some, I am sad to say, are no longer recognisable, even as footpaths. However, the day that I passed through Newton St Boswells a section was being officially re-opened by Magnus Magnusson only a few miles from the town. I should also explain that much remedial work has been carried out and more is planned, but like most things it takes considerable time to accomplish. It would be a great pity if this Roman arterial route from the great legionary fortress at York to the Firth of Forth were allowed to disappear. It was used to control the south of Scotland for more than a hundred years during the Roman occupation. Dere Street continued as a main route between England and Scotland until the Middle Ages, so the road built by Agricola remained vitally important to trade for many centuries after the departure of the Romans.

Brownhart Law and Black Halls were the next two hills to be passed and once again my sense of humour began to run amok: less said about my rhyme for the latter the better. Brownhart Law triggered thoughts of the 'Brothers in Law'. Where were they? Had they succumbed to the Cheviot peat or were they still maintaining their remarkable progress? Then came Lamb Hill – at over 1500 feet – an apt name considering the local sheep popula-tion. This was followed by the even higher Beefstand Hill and Mozie Law – reminiscent of the Wild West – 'mosey down to the old corral'. Plea Knowe and Foul Step came next (who dreamt up such names?) – a request that I watched where I was putting my feet? As I approached Windy Gyle, I met several walkers, some doing the Pennine Way and others out for a circular walk. I was glad of the company up there on the summit (2034 feet) which was reached after a stiff climb. In bad weather, I could imagine that AW's warning of the lack of shelter – 'nor are there any rocks to crawl under or holes to creep into' – must be extremely apt.

Taking a short break I noticed in AW's *Companion* that the 250-mile point had been passed prior to Lamb Hill and had gone completely unnoticed due to the ridiculous name game I had been playing – but it had certainly helped to pass the tedium of that stretch.

Leaving the top of Windy Gyle, I concentrated on Mac's instruc-tions for leaving the path in order to drop down to Uswayford. As one would have expected, they were very accurate and I found the farm without difficulty. It lies in a lovely spot surrounded by rolling hills and attractive pastureland.

Unfortunately the welcome on my arrival was not courteous and I was abruptly asked if I had booked accommodation. I told the lady that Edgar Peel, God rest his soul, had made a booking for me and she visibly softened. I gathered that her attitude was caused by inconsiderate walkers. Apparently some made a booking and never appeared; if the weather was fine they just carried straight on to Kirk Yetholm. The opposite often happened when walkers would just appear at her door without a prior booking and expect to be accommodated. It transpired that four other walkers were expected that evening and she was concerned that they would not turn up. This probably explained the fact that I was not offered a cup of tea after my hot, tiring day. She spent most of the next two hours looking out of the window through a pair of binoculars for a sight of my missing fellow guests. When I enquired about the possibility of a bath I was told that there was not enough hot water. The long-lost walkers finally made an appearance just before eight o'clock which eased the atmosphere a bit.

After supper, which was delayed due to the late arrivals, I found out quite a lot about Uswayford. The farmer told me that they were eighteen miles from the nearest shop and, worse still, twenty-two miles from the nearest pub. There was no power supply and they relied on their own electricity generator at the back of the farmhouse. We were warned not to turn on any lights in the middle of the night or the noisy generator would automatically start up and wake the household.

There were more than 1200 sheep and 150 cattle on the farm and a good class of sheepdog was essential. Consequently there were several border collies in evidence and the farmer was a keen breeder. I was leapt upon by numerous pups whenever I left the house. In fact, my stay was quite pleasant once the initial difficulties were overcome. The food was good and wholesome, as one would expect on a farm.

Day Twenty: Uswayford–Kirk Yetholm

As I awoke the following morning, the realisation quickly dawned on me that this was to be the last day of my walk. My feelings were mixed. I looked forward to achieving my goal of Kirk Yetholm, but I had become accustomed to my daily routine and the challenge that each day brought. Would I find it hard to readjust after nearly three weeks of walking and living out of a rucksack? That I would find out soon enough, but the immediate task was to find my way back to the path and cover the remaining sixteen miles to the journey's end.

The remarkable weather was true to form for the final test, the sun shining yet again. Was a fortnight of sunshine something of a record for the Pennine Way, I wondered? There was a spring in my step that morning and I was eager to put those remaining miles behind me. From AW's description, the final part of the route was not too arduous. Once Auchope Cairn was attained after about six miles' walking, it was downhill all the way to the end.

The testing peat groughs were soon in evidence once more, but AW said that there was no point in beating the breast or sitting down to cry. I was certainly in no mood for sitting down, and I fairly leapt up and down those formidable obstacles. It is strange how unknown reserves of energy can be summoned when the moment of triumph is there for the taking.

I was soon approaching Auchope Cairn and was so intent on reaching my destination that I decided to give the two-mile detour to The Cheviot a miss. It may have been the highest point of the Cheviot Hills – 2676 feet – but it didn't look very inspiring and I was in a hurry. My decision was also tempered by AW who advises that The Cheviot should only be included for the record, or to satisfy the conscience. If the weather was bad, he didn't think it should be attempted at all.

Feeling that I had all the advice I needed, I pressed on to the summit of Auchope Cairn (2382 feet). I was soon to receive a setback for the next hill, known as The Schil, although nearly 400 feet lower than the one I had just left, proved to be a stiff climb. Clearly there was hard work still to be done, although one was gradually reducing altitude. The steep slope down the far side of The Schil actually saw me breaking into a run. I could never have imagined doing this when I had ploughed my way across Kinder Plateau on that energy-sapping first day. As the ground levelled out I passed a survival hut, not as spacious as Greg's Hut on Cross Fell, but obviously very welcome in a storm. Some kind benefactor must have sited it there for Pennine Way walkers in a state of collapse with just a few miles left to go. Perhaps after a period of respite in there they could summon enough strength to stagger the last five miles.

At the bottom of the slope of The Schil, the path divided. The official way went down into the attractive Halterburn valley and, as I had been told by Mac, this was the best way if the weather was bad. But good fortune still smiled on me, so I took the right-hand path and strode along Steer Rigg. My momentum was temporarily slowed by the pull to the top of White Law, but from that hill's summit it really was downhill to the edge of the Cheviots, and I broke into a trot once more – that is until I suddenly thought how awful it would be to break an ankle so near to the end, and dropped back to a more sedate pace.

They say that the longest mile of any walk is the last one and so it is on the Pennine Way. As I dropped down the last hill on the Cheviots, I saw cars parked where the path ended in the valley below. I wrongly assumed that this was the finishing point of the Way. There was a sting in tail, for on consulting AW's *Companion* I discovered that I still had some road walking to do.

Feeling deflated, I was immediately faced with the prospect of another slope to climb, albeit on tarmac. My legs suddenly lost their spring and I found this last unexpected obstacle a real drag. After what seemed an age, the road descended into habitation. I paused a moment to enjoy the marvellous sight of the buildings of Kirk Yetholm. Again I smiled at the thought of AW's cryptic comment that any village would look wonderful to someone who had walked 270 miles to reach it. As I covered the last few hundred yards to the village green I half expected to see the ancient Kelso bus waiting for me, as shown in the final drawing of AW's splendid guide.

I was not ready to catch any bus yet as the official finishing point, the Border Hotel, beckoned and I had my final duty to perform.

Shedding my rucksack with great relief, I hurried into the bar to claim my free drink on AW as all Pennine Way walkers have the privilege of doing. The lady behind the bar eyed me suspiciously when I made my request. She asked for proof that I had walked the whole Pennine Way, although it was obvious from my weather-beaten appearance and my well-used walking gear, let alone the sweat on my brow, that I had not just driven there in my car. Proof was requested in the form of AW's *Pennine Way Companion*. I happily produced it, showed the completed log at the back – and was rewarded with my free half pint of bitter. A full complimentary pint was the original prize but the ravages of inflation have obviously eaten into AW's generous donation. Now convinced of my authenticity, the landlady signed my *Companion* to signify my receipt of a free drink and handed me a book containing the signatures and dates of the Pennine Way completions. I added my own details and casually studied the recent entries. Imagine my surprise when two signatures leapt from the page. They were those of the wily 'Brothers in Law' who had finished *two days ahead* of me! I should have guessed that those two were capable of anything.

Carrying my well-earned drink from the hotel into the glorious sunshine, I sat on the village green to savour my moment of achievement and to send Ben a postcard. Moments later a young walker came tearing down the hill into the village. I have never seen more sweat on a man and, judging by his rapid pace, I reckoned that he must be the 'Road-Runner'. He was obviously making a bee-line for the hotel and liquid refreshment. It was mid-afternoon, the official closing time for licensed premises in England prior to the relaxation of licensing laws. A local wag stopped the rushing walker in his tracks, explaining that if he was dashing for a pint, he was unlucky as they had just stopped serving. Panic stricken, our hero was about to throw himself at the hotel door when he realised that he had been conned. It dawned on him that he was, of course, in Scotland where bars stay open. Tearing off his rucksack he leapt into the bar to claim his reward from AW. He too must have been thwarted by the laconic landlady who had obviously asked for the same proof that he had completed the 270-mile walk. Within half a minute he hurriedly re-emerged, tore open a pocket flap of his rucksack and returned to the bar, brandishing AW's book.

A few moments later he came out with a drink in his hand and a grin on his face, and crossed over to where I was sitting. He was indeed the 'Road-Runner' and I was not surprised to learn that he had accomplished the complete twenty-nine mile journey from Byrness in less than eight hours. He smiled when I told him of his fame amongst fellow Pennine Way walkers, and that he had earned admiration from everyone who had come across him. He picked up his copy of AW's book, and turned to the Kirk Yetholm page, and read: 'The satisfaction you feel is intensely personal, and cannot be shared: the sense of achievement is yours alone simply because you have earned it alone.' We sat there companionably, drinking the last of our hard-earned beer and reflecting on our own achievement. One thing I know I had learned – as AW had told me I would – was not to give up.

As we relaxed there in the sunshine, I couldn't help thinking that we had both possessed an abiding companion throughout our triumphs and tribulations. AW had been ever-present through the medium of his book, continually encouraging, restraining, and sometimes even warning of impending doom. Most of all, our spirits had been lifted by his wry wit and humorous observations.

When I reflect on the Pennine Way, I realise that it was not just my own triumph, it was also AW's.

CHAPTER SIX

My Introduction to Lakeland

All good things come to an end, as the saying goes. Upon returning home the euphoria began to wane as I struggled to readjust to sleeping in the same bed each night. It seemed strange not to have to pack my rucksack each morning and be on the march once more. AW sums it up by saying that you will for a time feel lonelier than ever you did in the remoteness of mountain and moorland. Although it was great being back with the family again, my mind inevitably started working on the tantalising subject of where I would go from here. Having completed my first long-distance footpath, my appetite was whetted for more. But for obvious reasons – amongst them time and money – I had to bide my time.

In the meantime, there was the pleasant task of getting the photographs developed that I had taken on the Pennine Way. The camera I had taken was old and the results were pretty appalling, but beauty, as they say, is in the eye of the beholder. Just like holiday snaps, they were put into an album, labelled, and thrust in front of everyone who came within reach. Looking back I realise how poor they were and how most of the long-suffering friends who saw them probably could not have cared less. It is true that, as AW says, one's achievement is a personal thing and to the outside world it means virtually nothing.

It did not take many polite murmurings to make me realise that taking quality photographs required parting with some money. So I bought myself a better camera, which I still use, and switched to colour slides. Now eager to try out my new acquisition and capture anything on film, I decided to return to AW's *Walks in Limestone Country* and explore as much of Yorkshire as possible. At every opportunity, I would visit the Dales with my camera, and so began the compilation of my slide collection.

Although thoroughly enjoying my weekend walks I still had the nagging feeling, after a few months, that I must get down to planning another challenge. Many interesting alternatives seemed available, making it difficult to single out one in particular. Then the realisation dawned that I knew absolutely nothing about AW's home patch, his beloved Lakeland. It seemed logical to familiarise myself with this area next. The first thing I did was to buy AW's seven Pictorial Guides to the Lakeland Fells* which soon became my inseparable companions.

My first venture into that unknown territory, armed with the appropriate guides and OS maps was a three-day expedition which is imprinted on my memory as a complete washout.

It took place in February as the intention was to capture vistas of stunning, snow-capped mountains. The reality did not live up to my expectations as I suffered some of the wettest weather endured by man. This provided an introduction to Lake District rain which I soon discovered doesn't mess around. It relishes its task as it cascades vertically downwards, pounds itself into the ground and rebounds ferociously to a height of several feet. This is to ensure that if it doesn't drench you on the way down it will complete the job on the way up.

My choice of route on that ill-fated trip was influenced by a combination of some beautiful photographs that I had seen in a Lakeland calendar and by selecting from the Personal Notes in Conclusion at the end of AW's guides some of his favourite places. I planned to spend the morning of the first day travelling from home and locating my pre-arranged accommodation in Ambleside, which would allow only a short walk that afternoon. With this in mind I searched for an easily accessible, attractive location which would afford a simple circular walk. The ideal spot appeared to be Tarn Hows which nestles amongst the fells near Coniston and is circled by footpaths, with Black Fell rising behind. I had been attracted to it by one of the stunning photographs in the calendar, and also by an enticing sketch by AW in his guide to *The Southern Fells*. AW describes the view from the summit of Black

* *See* Appendix 4, page 240.

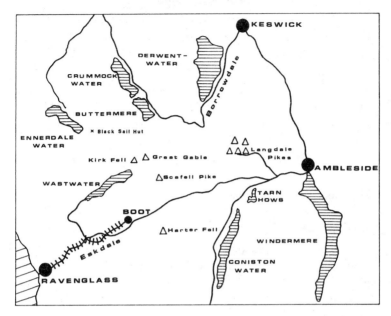

The Lake District

Fell thus: 'The lovely countryside around the head of Windermere is delightfully pictured, this being the best viewpoint for the sylvan charms of the area between Ambleside, Wray Castle and Hawkshead. Southwards, Coniston Water is seen above the indented and wooded shores of Tarn Hows, which appears as beautiful as ever but a trifle foreign to the district.' Not knowing the area I was intrigued by his remark concerning Tarn Hows and hoped that all would be revealed during my visit there.

It was with great excitement that I set off from Yorkshire on what I was convinced would be an unforgettable experience. This turned out to be true but for entirely the wrong reasons. My arrival on that first day was accompanied by rain battering the roof of my car. The Lake District didn't appear very pleased to see me.

Imagine my deflation, therefore, as I approached Tarn Hows a little later along a soggy footpath in torrential rain with the mist closing in. Things can only get better I optimistically reasoned, praying that the sun would eventually make an appearance. A murky stretch of water reluctantly appeared out of the mist, as the rain, which was obviously enjoying itself, increased its intensity. Water was insidiously creeping into the hood of my jacket and into my boots. As I squelched around the featureless expanse of water it appeared to be almost foaming. The battering by multitudes of watery cannon balls was causing its surface to erupt. AW's comment that one can find peace up here amongst the hills brought a wry smile to my lips. I fervently hoped that he had never been to Tarn Hows in such deplorable conditions.

Not surprisingly there was no sign of any fellow idiots. People obviously had more sense than to blunder around in a grey haze whilst becoming remorselessly saturated. The rain had by now achieved its objective of seeping into every nook and cranny about my person. It would have been as effective to dispense with my clothes and let nature take its course. At least that way I would enjoy an invigorating cold shower as I walked. What a sight for unsuspecting eyes it would make. I could imagine incredulous fellow walkers, crazy enough to venture out in these conditions, staring at my goose-pimpled form with soggy sandwiches poised before their gaping mouths.

The path, which in places was waterlogged, eventually left the waterside and I blundered into a wood whose foliage at least kept some of the rain at bay. I realised that the omens were definitely against me as my watch strap promptly snapped, and I then had to scrabble around the drenched undergrowth to retrieve the vital section.

On emerging from the wood I found that the rain had now eased to a steady downpour. Be thankful for small mercies, I thought. Shortly afterwards I was surprised to meet another walker lurching towards me, providing a good imitation of a drowned rat. We exchanged commiserations and questioned our sanity before disappearing into the mist once more.

A track, marginally less of a quagmire than the path I was following, came into view, and I hoped this would return me to my starting point. It would be an understatement to say that I couldn't wait to get into the dry. The nagging thought of what account I was to give my colleagues upon my return to work tugged at my nerve endings. Hadn't I been boring them to death with details of my anticipated trip to this watery jewel set amongst the Coniston fells? How demeaning it would be to admit that my visit had been a soggy failure.

Dismissing such negative thoughts I convinced myself that today had been an unfortunate exception. Tomorrow, the rain was bound to relent and the sun would wreak a remarkable transformation. I would then have plenty to tell my friends about. With renewed optimism I splashed through the remainder of my journey. I was even able to ignore the miserable clamminess of my sodden clothing: this will fade into insignificance, I told myself, visualising the delightful moment when I would luxuriate in the eagerly anticipated steaming hot bath.

The perplexing question returned as to why A W considered Tarn Hows foreign to the district. Could it be, I wondered, that when viewed from the top of Black Fell, it looked small and irregular in comparison to Coniston Water and Lake Windermere? I was unfortunately no wiser for I had seen very little of it that day. I had to leave the question unresolved as my mind was soon engaged on the immediate problem of shedding my sodden walking gear and getting it dried for the next day's foray, which would be an exploration of the Langdale Pikes.

I had read in A W's guide *The Central Fells* that 'No mountain profile in Lakeland arrests and excites the attention more than that of the Langdale Pikes.' With such a build up it had to be included in my itinerary. In support of A W's claim was the beautiful winter photograph of those mountains, which I had removed from the Lakeland calendar, framed, and hung in my office. In order to see them at their best I planned a route around them using A W's guide. Pavey Ark (2288 feet) was to be my first objective, and my choice of ascent was influenced by his enthusiastic text: 'The view of the Ark across the waters of Stickle Tarn, at its foot, is superior to all others of this type in Lakeland.' From Stickle Tarn I planned an ascent via North Rake which A W describes as 'a surprising and remarkable grassy breach in the crags, cleaving them from top to bottom on their north side, and affording a simple route of ascent'. It was the last phrase that particularly appealed to me as I had no desire to go rock-climbing.

As the following morning dawned, the enveloping grey blanket of cloud still hung overhead and the rain continued to beat down in its determined fashion. A crystal ball was not required to tell me that my anticipated views of those distinctive peaks thrusting into a clear blue sky were not going to materialise. I cursed those beautiful photographs. As I put on my reasonably dry clothes, I wondered how long they would remain in that condition.

I made my way into the Langdale Valley, my views severely restricted by an overhanging mist. On the roof of the car was the now familiar beat of the rain. Massive black humps eventually appeared out of the gloom behind the white-walled buildings of Millbeck, indicating that I had reached my destination. They presented a foreboding sight with their upper reaches shrouded in mist; where were my stunning snow-capped peaks?

In such weather conditions I was not relishing my task as I reluctantly pulled on my boots and prepared to leave the warmth and comfort of the car. From the Dungeon Ghyll New Hotel I set off on the steep climb up Stickle Ghyll, which is the Ordnance Survey's name for what AW calls Mill Gill, heading for Stickle Tarn. AW's comment that the Pikes appear pugnacious was very true. The sharpness of the gradient, even in the initial stages, was certainly giving me a fight. 'I must be mad,' I muttered as I slowly ascended into the enveloping gloom, the only sound being the rushing water of nearby waterfalls. After a while the slope relented and the ground levelled out to reveal an eerie amphitheatre that contained the inky-black waters of Stickle Tarn. This provided a respite from struggling past those swollen waterfalls below on a path cascading with surface water.

Two massive bulwarks loomed over the tarn, their shapes barely visible in the semi-darkness. This was my first introduction to Pavey Ark and Harrison Stickle whose steep rocky faces disappeared into those dark waters. Snow was just discernible many feet above me. At least I had been granted one wish, that of snow-covered peaks. This was, however, a mixed blessing. In good weather and small doses, snow is a boon to the photographer and walker. Large amounts in poor conditions accentuate its nasty habit of obliterating footpaths, making route finding a severe test of skill and temper.

The latter applied as I left the tarn and headed for the top of Pavey Ark. I was soon struggling through deep snow, trusting that I would find the summit in these conditions. After a period of stumbling over hidden obstacles and slipping on wet rock, I emerged on the top cursing lustily.

This was immediately curtailed as I came face to face with three elderly male walkers staring at me. Could this be retribution in the form of the 'Three Wise Men'? I was greeted with the following profound remarks. 'Why have you come up here on a Tuesday? It always rains on Tuesdays.' This rather unusual greeting came from three gentlemen who lived in Blackpool and, following early retirement the previous year, made regular trips to the area each Tuesday. I pointed out that we should have met down in the valley and then they could have saved me the trouble of struggling up there in pouring rain. They omitted to explain why they always came on Tuesdays and ignored their own advice!

I warmed to their friendliness and dry humour, accepting their kind invitation to lead me round the remainder of the Pikes. I told them that I had planned to visit Harrison Stickle (2403 feet) next, the highest of the Pikes, and then Pike o' Stickle (2323 feet), and they helpfully guided me along that route. Desperate for photographs of any kind, I foolishly took out my camera and recorded them staring out into the mist amidst the snow-covered surroundings. I took a few more shots of murky views as we made our tour of the tops and later paid the price of stupidity. Remarkably, the photographs came out all right, but the ever-persistent rain had found its way into my camera. When I attempted to use it the following day it was partially paralysed, refusing to wind on the film. Eventually I found that it would work if I gave it an encouraging slap.

My new-found friends knew the terrain very well and the conversation was a welcome antidote to the miserable feeling of being soaked to the skin once more. The views from the top of Harrison Stickle and Pike o' Stickle were still unfortunately non-existent. Taking into account the conditions, we decided to retreat and avoid further saturation. A steep uneven descent to the Dungeon Ghyll Hotel began and I was able to catch glimpses of the sodden Langdale Valley through the mist. Ever mindful of Ben's fate on the Pennine Way, I kept a close watch on where I was putting my feet. The rocky path was treacherously slippy and I had no wish to break the record for the quickest descent to the valley. Below us, what should have been a most inviting sight, according to AW, was reduced to a murky representation of one of the most visited valleys in Lakeland. A faint, grey expanse could just be discerned in the far distance – the northern end of Lake Windermere.

Returning to the valley we said our goodbyes and I was left with the empty feeling that there was just one more day left for the weather to redeem itself. Not even a full day's walking remained as I had to return home towards the end of the following afternoon. It was with a heavy heart that I headed for Eskdale and my final walk the next morning.

There was, however, an 'up' side to the day's events. I mentioned earlier that, against all odds, my camera shots later came out. They were subsequently included in my slide lectures on the Lake District, helping to depict the area in all its subtle moods. Introduced as my 'cupboard' slides, meaning those normally dispatched there never to see the light of day, they add an ethereal quality not normally seen.

My tribulations on the first two days also made me realise that walkers are optimists, believing that the sun will always beat down on them out of a clear blue sky. The realisation that life is not like that fostered the idea of a series of cartoon slides depicting the nasty things that can shatter this delusion. Some have already been mentioned such as rain and snow. That arch enemy of walkers, mist, which seemed to be ever-present during those fateful two days is amongst the nastiest. Not only can you not see things through it, as demonstrated by my struggle up Pavey Ark only to be rewarded with the non-view of a blank, grey wall, but other people can't see you. For the lone walker, this may produce a feeling of stark panic, which should be resisted at all costs.

There are, however, a few simple rules that can help you to avoid this. Don't run round in ever-decreasing circles or you will inevitably disappear! Shouting for your mum should be avoided as she won't hear you and it only serves to expend vital energy. Try to stay calm and look for a landmark, if you can find one. If you can't, just follow the simple rules of map and compass reading. These are easy for anyone with a PhD in geography because you must first tackle the thorny problem of three 'norths'. Always remember that these are true north, grid north and magnetic north. To help you to remember which is which, true north can't be altered, grid north follows the vertical lines on your map and magnetic north insists on moving around. If you successfully match up your 'norths' you will get home safe and sound, if you don't, a prayer to the almighty might help.

Imagine my chagrin on that third Lake District morning when I awoke at Eskdale Youth Hostel to find that it was 'more of the same' as far as the weather was concerned. I could not believe my bad luck, another drenching seemed inevitable. Fears of swamp fever and foot rot welled up inside me. A swift check of my toes thankfully confirmed that they were not joined together.

Listening to the weather forecast during breakfast I was aware of fate's subtle ironies. The rain was due to cease later in the day, possibly with the cloud cover breaking up. If this meant that the sun would actually put in an appearance; it was sure to arrive too late for me to enjoy. I realised that no purpose would be served by worrying about the weather and that I must press on with my day's plan.

I had been drawn to Eskdale by AW's vivid description of the valley in his guide to *The Southern Fells*: 'But precedence must be granted to Eskdale, the one valley that gives full allegiance to the Southern Fells and in some ways the most delectable of all. This is a valley where walkers really come into their own, a sanctuary of peace and solitude, a very special preserve for those who travel on foot.' Not only did I wish to see part of this highly recommended valley – unfortunately time did not permit a full exploration – but I had also discovered in *The Southern Fells* an ancient route out of it that would take me to another area that I was longing to see. This route follows the old corpse road from Boot, which stands one and a half miles down the valley from the hostel. It leads over Eskdale Moor, past the lonely Burnmoor Tarn and into Wasdale Head at the north eastern end of Wastwater. My objective was a view of the impressive fells that encircle Wasdale Head, all vividly described in *The Southern Fells* and *The Western Fells*. Their names captured my imagination; Great Gable, Kirk Fell, Lingmell, Yewbarrow, Scafell and Scafell Pike. I was determined to see them in spite of the wretched weather.

Despite Eskdale lying under cloud and suffering persistent rain, my walk from the hostel to Boot was enough to convince me of the latent charm of this valley, so loved by AW. I vowed to return and see it in better weather.

A little while later I set out from the attractive village of Boot still accompanied by the now obligatory rain and low cloud. I threaded my way along the narrow street flanked by the white-walled cottages which managed to be picturesque even in the gloom. At the end I was confronted with a steep, stony path down which water was flowing freely. I was definitely being accorded a typical welcome to the sodden Eskdale Moor. My prospective journey along the old corpse road seemed prophetic, the way my luck was running.

Once through the gate at the top of the steep slope the path headed determinedly for higher ground and open moorland. For the first mile it climbed gradually, following the valley of the Whillan Beck. From the amount of water flowing along the rough, stony path, one could be forgiven for thinking that the beck had changed its course. The views across Eskdale must have been impressive in decent weather; also the hills surrounding the Duddon Valley which were just discernable. Resisting the temptation to capture them with my ailing camera, I was convinced, in a rush of optimism, that the sun would shine upon my return.

As it climbed the desolate moorland, the water-logged track widened. This proved to be a mixed blessing as it became boggy in addition to its roughness. Undeterred, I continued my progress along the shoulder of the moor, frequently hopping from stone to stone over boggy channels. The dark waters of the diminutive Eel Tarn could just be seen as I battled with the inhospitable terrain. At this point I met a couple with two children who told me they were making for Illgill Head which overlooks the famous Wastwater Screes. I had seen many photographs of these dramatic slopes which plunge down to the shore of Wastwater and disappear into Lakeland's deepest and darkest lake. I would like to have taken a close look at them for myself but time did not permit.

Bidding goodbye to the family and wishing them luck, I covered the short distance to the fell's crest and stood gazing over the serene and lonely Burnmoor Tarn. Under grey skies it appeared sombre, its rain-spattered surface rippled by the wind. A feeling of peace and solitude prevailed as I descended into this natural basin, flanked on two sides by protective fells. This place was thankfully not on the tourist routes. Later that day, under the sun's rays, the tarn was to undergo a remarkable transformation when its waters turned a rich, deep blue. This unforgettable sight was complimented by the varying shades of fawn and brown provided by surrounding grasses and bracken. The reason for waxing lyrical over this inspiring scene is that it represented the only sunlit view of my three-day tour.

Anxious for my first view of Wasdale Head, I splashed my way around the head of the tarn, the swollen waters covering the way ahead. Thankfully the invisible path was marked with piles of stones and, with boots full of water, I reached Bullat Bridge which, according to my map, spanned the source of the Whillan Beck. Unfortunately the meagre wooden structure was totally inadequate for the present width of the beck, reaching no more than halfway across. All was not lost, however, as some resourceful person had provided stepping stones for the remainder of its width. Duly tip-toeing over the uneven stones, I didn't care much if I slipped into the water as I had already reached saturation point.

As I climbed the next rise, a backdrop of the fells surrounding Wasdale Head began to unfold. This was the sight that I had been eagerly anticipating. I longed for brighter conditions as the steel-grey shapes came closer, their tops enveloped by drifting clouds. Descending the steep path, I could see the imposing mountains circling the lush, green valley below like faithful sentinels. I studied each one in turn, but was unable to see Scafell or Scafell Pike which were hidden in cloud. That most inspiring of Lakeland's fells, Great Gable stood proudly between Kirk Fell and Lingmell, tempting me to its hidden summit, but today time and weather were against me. Gable would have to wait, which was a great pity as AW gives it a glowing testimony in *The Western Fells*. 'Great Gable is a favourite of all fellwalkers and firm favourite with many. It is a good name for a mountain, strong, challenging, compelling, starkly descriptive, suggesting the pyramid associated with the shape of mountains since early childhood. People are attracted to it because of the name.'

Progress became hazardous down the slippery path, and once in the valley bottom I followed the swollen waters of the Lingmell

Beck, looking for a convenient place to cross. It was with relief that I eventually found a footbridge and walked the last bit to the Wasdale Head Hotel. There was hardly a soul around as I passed the hotel, imagining the difference on a fine summer's day when the spot would be crammed with cars. I wondered how the local people fared at the surrounding farms during heavy snow in this idyllic, but isolated setting.

At this point I had to decide whether to have my lunch in the comfort of the valley or climb to a vantage point on one of the fells around me. A steep path rising up the front of Kirk Fell caught my eye. Time would not permit a climb to its summit, which seemed just as well judging by the angle of ascent. As it had finally stopped raining, I took out AW's *The Western Fells* once more, confident that it would not get a soaking whilst I read what he had to say about this climb. The sketch of a walker climbing a steep gradient on all fours and gazing backwards between his legs met my eye. This depicts AW's impression of the ascent from Wasdale Head, part of which I was about to attempt! The caption beneath the sketch of the struggling walker reads: 'Looking backwards (between one's legs) there is a superb upside-down view of Wasdale Head.' His description of the ascent is no more reassuring: 'a straight line is the shortest distance between two points. This route is the straightest and therefore the most direct ascent in Lakeland. It is also the steepest – a relentless and unremitting treadmill, a turf clutching crawl, not a walk.'

Always one for a challenge, I took a deep breath and struck out through the bracken at the foot of the fell. As the slope steepened gravity began to take its toll and I bent double and hauled myself upwards with the aid of tufts of grass. I had never experienced such an energy-sapping climb, even the ascent of the east face of Whernside paled into insignificance beside it. My tortured lungs demanded frequent respite as I clawed my way towards a suitable halting place for my lunch stop. During these rests I would turn round to take in the ever-expanding panoramic view below me; I didn't dare venture the 'upside down' approach of AW's walker because I feared I would get dizzy and end up sliding all the way down. With lungs bursting and my whole body protesting I reached Highnose Head, where, thankfully, the steep grass slope momentarily levelled out. I decided that 1500 feet of torture was sufficient and that this would be the perfect spot to eat my lunch.

The reward for my labour was the magnificent, albeit hazy, view of Wasdale Head, its patchwork quilt of verdant fields laid out beneath me. Cloud still drifted over both me and the nearby summit of Great Gable, its craggy top remaining obstinately out of sight. From my lofty perch I could see over Wastwater to the coastal plain, noticing that the sky was perversely clear over the sea. It was to remain so for a time, the clouds that hung over the summits refusing to make way for the sun. I formed the impression that those surrounding barriers of rock are highly productive cloud factories. The slightest breath of moisture-laden air from the Atlantic is enough to generate a moving shroud that clings to their upper reaches.

As I hungrily consumed my sandwiches I tried to make out what details I could of the views that would be magnificent in good weather. Paths wound up the valleys on either side. To my left the one to Sty Head Pass fought its way across the flank of Great Gable. It resembled a snaking ribbon on its strenuous ascent to Styhead Tarn, from whence it would descend into Borrowdale. The path on my other side squeezed its way up Mosedale, between Kirk Fell and Yewbarrow bound for the Black Sail Pass, that gateway to Ennerdale. Making a promise to return to this superb area of Lakeland to appreciate fully the delights expounded by AW, it was time to leave my high-level pulpit and return down to earth.

Back in the valley I detected a slight clearing of the sky above Wastwater. I chose the route on the opposite side of the Lingmell Beck to that which I had taken on my outward journey, foolishly ignoring a sign warning that the path was liable to flooding. This was to prove my undoing, as the path came to an abrupt end at the confluence of the beck and one of its now raging tributaries. The footbridge beckoned a tantalising hundred yards downstream. Rather than backtrack I once more filled my boots with water, which was now becoming a habit. I had paid the price for not taking the recommended route.

A short time later having completed the return climb to Burn-moor Tarn, the rain stopped, the clouds departed and I was bathed in unaccustomed sunshine. My camera then began working overtime as I captured anything within range. Eskdale Moor and the hills beyond took on a whole new aspect as I splashed back along the track, cursing my luck at not being able to photograph those memorable scenes around Wasdale Head.

My frustration did help me to forget about my third soaking of the three days and the sunshine had a pleasant, warming effect. As I drove home in the late afternoon with the setting sun shining through my windscreen, those three sodden days in Lakeland would, I realised, remain forever in my memory.

Lightning never strikes in the same place twice, according to the old adage. Optimistically hoping that the same was true about rain I returned the following May to the scene of that earlier débâcle at Wasdale Head. I planned to spend some more time sampling the so far elusive delights of Lakeland in better weather. My intention that day was to climb Great Gable and walk from its summit down into Borrowdale.

What did I find on my arrival? It will be no surprise to you that I had an immediate reintroduction to my old adversaries, rain and mist. Acutely annoyed that the weather forecaster had not warned about this, I felt that retribution was called for. Those incompetents at the Weather Centre should be forcibly dragged to the top of Great Gable and kept there until they could get their forecasts right. The cloud factory was working overtime and visibility was minimal. As usual, the rain was happily hurtling itself at the ground in its regular fashion. I was now convinced that I had in some way angered the rain god who was unleashing his personal revenge upon me. What could I do to demonstrate to the sun god that I urgently needed his help? I know that primitive tribes perform rain dances, but that was the last thing that I needed at that moment. The only reference to Sundance known to me was as the partner of Butch Cassidy.

Frustration welled inside me when I realised that AW's much loved ring of mountains was hidden from me yet again, necessitating a change of plan. Forced to make a move and go somewhere, I opted for a valley route as there was once more no point in climbing into the cloud which covered all the surrounding summits. The best plan appeared to be to take the path from Wasdale Head through Mosedale and head for Ennerdale by way of the

Black Sail Pass. I could then reach Borrowdale by going over Loft Beck.

Entering Mosedale, I was once again struck by the lush green appearance of the surrounding vegetation. This was hardly surprising due to the countless rivulets of water cascading from the hills on either side. With the obligatory mist encircling me, the landscape took on a translucent appearance, with the path disappearing into an ethereal, grey curtain. In that peculiar half-light, one often has the strange feeling that the sun is about to break through, despite common sense telling you that there isn't a hope.

Thankfully the path was some way from the Mosedale Beck which had been transformed into a rushing torrent. It foamed as it hurled itself over a series of waterfalls at the valley entrance. So much water was pouring through the normally peaceful valley that my imagination switched into overdrive. I was convinced that when combined with the accumulated contents of the streams pouring from other valleys it would flood Wasdale Head and eventually engulf the narrow road running along the shore of Wastwater. Thankfully, I was escaping by a higher route.

Gradually changing direction the path skirted the aptly named Gatherstone Head. At that particular time, I would have loved to gather together some stones and hurl them at something to vent my frustration.

As the gradient steepened a hazy, hunchbacked figure slowly became visible in the gloom. This ghostly apparition was stumbling and lurching ahead of me, giving a realistic impression of Quasimodo touring his beloved cathedral. Drawing nearer to this awesome sight, I was greatly relieved to find that the hunch on his back was actually a bicycle. It was not one of the modern lightweight mountain bikes that are so familiar nowadays, but an old, heavy version complete with drop handlebars and primitive three-speed gears. Gulping air and looking on the verge of collapse the bearer of this monster stopped as I drew level and released his unforgiving load with a clatter to the ground.

Some moments later, as his breathing began to return to normality, he had recovered sufficiently to tell me that his name was Harry and that he was on a cycling tour of Lakeland with two friends. I suppressed a smile, for I would hardly have described it as such, more a walking tour with a bike on his back.

This view was confirmed when I discovered that his friends who were somewhere in the mist ahead of us were also carrying similar steeds. Due to their age and fitness, much of their journey so far had involved dismounting and lugging these brutes over mountain passes. Their circuitous journey around Lakeland apparently consisted of cycling between mountain passes, and whenever the path through the pass became too steep or rugged to cycle they had to dismount and resort to their Herculean routine. Harry looked to be well into his sixties and unequipped for his present ordeal. He was nearly all in and, taking pity on him, I offered to help him carry his testing load. This gesture was gratefully accepted and with each taking hold of one end of the bicycle we made steady progress up what was by now a steep incline.

As I contemplated whether Harry would have made it alone up this demanding path his two companions appeared through the mist. They didn't seem too concerned about Harry's condition as they were evidently struggling themselves. It may have been kinder to suggest that they were doing themselves no good whatsoever, but I took the easy option and said nothing. I learned that they were several days into their tour and, despite the strain on their none too young bodies, seemed determined to complete it. In my opinion, Harry would be lucky to reach their destination at the Black Sail Youth Hostel.

The path became even steeper and their tortuous progress slowed to a crawl, with frequent stops. At last the gradient eased and the path brought us into the head of the pass. A well-earned rest was called for as we divested ourselves of our unwelcome burdens. I learned that the three companions made many such trips around the country, staying in Youth Hostels wherever possible. They appeared to be undaunted by their present predicament and, as their breathing returned to normal, became very talkative.

A cold, clammy feeling crept over me as I cooled down but this was pushed into the background by the strange sensation of *déjà vu*. Here I was once again, high up in Lakeland, talking to three fellow travellers whom I had just met whilst staring into thick mist. Could they be a re-incarnation of the 'Three Wise Men' of Pavey Ark? Surely not, I thought, as it wasn't a Tuesday.

According to AW we had just ascended the initial part of the commonest route from Wasdale to the top of Pillar. As a joke, I suggested that we should complete the climb now that we had come so far. This made their already ashen faces turn whiter than ever and they vehemently turned down my offer. If they had attempted such a foolhardy task they would probably have collapsed under the weight of their steeds. Either that or died of shock as I nearly did whilst descending Pillar by that particular route on a later visit to the area.

Straining to follow the indistinct path in thick cloud on that occasion I was continuously buffeted by a howling wind that threatened to bowl me over. Suddenly, without warning, the cloud momentarily parted, giving me a heart-stopping view of a thousand-foot drop a yard or so away from where I had halted. In a flash, the view was once more blotted out leaving me with an unreal and terrifying feeling. My imagination ran riot: what would have happened if the wind had been blowing in the opposite direction and I had staggered from the path to end up over that precipice? Despite the temperature and the altitude I broke out into a cold sweat. Trying to cheer my battered spirits I joked to myself that this wasn't one of the easy Lakeland routes which, according to AW, are used by an assortment of day trippers, courting couples, earnest boy scouts, babies and grand-mothers. If my three soulmates had attempted it, they stood a good chance of finding out the nasty things that gravity can do.

We rested at the head of the pass for quite a while, and discussed a wide range of topics including hostelling and society's ills. Despite the fact that we were well and truly sodden, we agreed that it was preferable to die from pneumonia up there than to stagnate at home. One of their pet hates, I discovered, was unruly dogs that chased alongside their bikes yapping and snap-ping at their legs. I also admitted to an aversion to unfriendly canines that sometimes get in the way of walkers. Working on the theory that if you turn your back on them they will go for your ankles, I always try to stare them out and prevent them from getting behind me.

Eventually they suggested that I should carry on without them as I still had a good distance to cover to my destination in Borrowdale. Concerned for their safety I offered to help them down to Ennerdale. They wouldn't hear of it but asked me to call in at the Black Sail Hostel and tell the warden to put on the kettle ready for their arrival.

Bidding them a reluctant farewell I began what turned out to be no easy passage down the rocky valley. I had difficulty keeping my balance on the slippery surfaces, fearing for my friends following behind with their troublesome burdens. Reaching the valley bottom I had my first view of the forests that cover much of Ennerdale, the mist having prevented any views from the pass. AW had been saddened by the transformation from open valley, home to singing birds and grazing Herdwick sheep, to an area deformed by a multitude of conifers crowded in battery formation. This, in his opinion, constituted cruelty to the poor trees which were denied light, air and natural growth. On a recent visit to the area I noticed that the Forestry Commission has felled and tidied much of Ennerdale Forest.

As I approached the Black Sail Hut I was conscious of the evocative feeling that this hostel arouses. AW considers it to be the loneliest and most romantic of them all. People who have stayed there consider it to have a special atmosphere and intimacy that the larger hostels lack. Space in this former shepherd's hut is severely restricted. This promotes friendliness and tolerance, two vital ingredients required when strangers are thrown together in a confined space.

My heart sank at the lack of any sign of life in the hut. I would have loved to escape briefly the incessant rain and enjoy a hot drink. Also I wanted to alert the warden to be on the lookout for the cyclists who would now be struggling down the rocky path. The door was locked and there was no reply to my repeated knocking. Peering through the window I could see the basic furnishing and the legendary clothes rack that could be hauled to the ceiling to conserve space. Stories abound of communal evenings spent around the large table whilst steaming clothes suspended above dripped water onto the inhabitants below.

Disappointed, I searched for some form of shelter where I could at least eat my sandwiches out of the rain. The only dry place available was an outside toilet which was fortunately unlocked. So I perched there, listening to the rain beating on the roof and hoping that no one would come knocking on the door. I suppose you could call it eating at my own convenience!

I emerged from my refuge not relishing the prospect of facing the elements once more and, yes, it was still raining just as hard. There was no sign of the three cyclists and I was very concerned for their limbs on that slippery descent from Black Sail Pass. The thought of going back to check their whereabouts crossed my mind, but I really needed to press on as I still had to cross into Borrowdale. A feeling of guilt and unease pervaded me as I contoured the valley side, heading for Loft Beck where the path would ascend steeply and lead me towards the Honister Pass. AW suggests a last lingering look back over Ennerdale at this point. Unfortunately my brief visit had not done it justice and the foul weather had restricted any views. I strained to catch a glimpse of the full length of the valley but could see no further than the nearest dark green all-enveloping blanket of conifers.

Leaving the head of the beck, the gradient flattened out and I crossed the Brandreth fence. This is the remains of a wire fence which crosses the nearby mountain of that name. A short distance away a merging track descends from Great Gable indicating that I had walked around most of the base of this so far unseen mountain. At that point, fine views of the Buttermere Valley would normally be on display according to AW, but I would not enjoy them until my next visit to the area.

A gradual descent brought me to the line of a disused quarry tramway. The tracks have long since been removed, but the bed leads steeply down to the road that links the valleys of Buttermere and Borrowdale. Once the road was reached I could follow it into what AW describes as the fairest of Lakeland's valleys with its clusters of white cottages set amongst emerald pastures. My immediate concern on reaching Borrowdale was to find a convenient place to dry out. Fortunately I found a welcoming café where I spent a soggy half-hour dripping water, with steam rising from my drying clothes.

I hesitate to mention the location of the Youth Hostel where I spent that night, as it was there that I was introduced to the never to be forgotten Borrowdale soup. Not wishing to be the perpetrator of a stampede by soup lovers into AW's coveted haven, its name will not be divulged. Far be it from me to encourage the destruction of centuries of quiet harmony in the valley by creating an overwhelming desire to sample this rare phenomenon.

It is common knowledge that hostel wardens can work wonders despite a tight catering budget. My first sight of that extremely appetising vegetable-laden soup appeared to confirm this remarkable aptitude. Imagine my consternation when, putting this superb looking concoction to my lips, it passed over my palate without raising the slightest reaction from my tastebuds. This effect could only have been achieved by boiling it for hours to rid it of the last vestige of flavour, or by surgically extracting the taste. Never had what promised so much been enjoyed by so few. A study of the expressions of my fellow diners confirmed their common disbelief, as their bowls were universally pushed away from them, or the salt and pepper pots emptied over them. Another cunning ploy involved using the left-over carrots and vegetables from the main course in the carrot cake that made its appearance shortly afterwards. This was recycling with a vengeance.

Talking about cycling of a different kind, I struck up a conversation during supper with a young man named Jim who was on a lone cycling tour of the district. He didn't care much for travelling alone in the atrocious weather and asked if he could join me on my next day's walk. I readily agreed, providing that he didn't take his bike as I had no wish to repeat the cycle-carrying episode. He arranged to leave it behind and walk back to collect it the following day.

Having read that nearby Esk Hause is the highest pass in Lakeland but, according to AW, is rarely used as a through journey to Eskdale, I planned to try that route as something a little out of the ordinary. Still suspicious of the weather I figured that it would be the next best thing to walking over the mountain tops. I rang Eskdale Youth Hostel to ensure that accommodation would also be available for Jim.

Miraculously, the following morning dawned bright and clear, which made a welcome change. Jim, who decided to stick to the plan to accompany me, and I set out after breakfast and followed the line of the narrow road to Seathwaite. Unable to believe the transformation in the weather, I was crossing my fingers in the hope of completing my first Lake District day without a drenching. Was it time to let those weather forecasters off the summit of Great Gable? No, it was not yet propitious: the whole day was ahead of us and they still had time to get it wrong.

Our route passed alongside the attractive River Derwent and we made good progress to the accompaniment of birdsong and unaccustomed clear views on either side of the valley. Passing Seathwaite Farm and the popular car park at the end of the Borrowdale valley road, we joined the wide track that would take us up to Stockley Bridge. It is surprising the effect a little decent weather has on the spirits. I was contentedly admiring the towering slopes of Glaramara and Seathwaite Fell that lay ahead of us. Jim also appeared to be relishing his unaccustomed journey on foot. He normally stuck to the roads and valleys unlike my three friends who seemed to carry their cycles everywhere. Out came my camera to record some sunny Lakeland scenes at last.

With jaunty steps we passed the bridge where the paths and the lively river divide and headed up Grains Gill, one of the Derwent's tributaries. The path climbed steadily with the accompanying stream dancing merrily in the opposite direction on its journey to the northern end of Borrowdale where it feeds Derwentwater and Bassenthwaite Lake. The colours of the surrounding landscape had shed that dullness which is commonplace when subjected to continuous watering. Crossing a footbridge at the head of Grains Gill, we were faced with the prospect of climbing Ruddy Gill, so named because the iron content in the subsoil which lines the gill does give it a definite red hue. By the time we had puffed our way up that testing climb, I reckoned Ruddy had quite different origins; however, we knew that at the top Esk Hause would be within easy reach.

Progress was slower now and, passing a series of fords, we eventually reached a junction of paths. The strenuous part was over and we saw from the map that the path crossing ours led to the right past nearby Sprinkling Tarn on its way to Sty Head and Wasdale. I had seen the lower end of this path on my first trip to Wasdale Head as it skirted the lower slopes of Great Gable on its misty journey to Sty Head. It was fun fitting newly-discovered sections into the whole Lakeland jigsaw.

The weather continued to behave itself, and as we were making good time, we decided to make a short detour to Sprinkling Tarn. AW enthuses about this delightful sheet of water, advising a long halt to savour its charms. Thoroughly enjoying our break by those waters shimmering in the sunshine, I began to regret not grasping the nettle and tackling Great Gable which beckoned from across the valley, but at least I could now gaze upon its distinctive summit which had so far eluded me.

With regret, we had to leave that peaceful and inviting spot and press on to Esk Hause. We retraced our steps along the path that now made for the Langdale Valley. How frustrating it was on that fine day not to be able to sample the numerous alternatives afforded by the network of paths encircling the central Lakeland Fells. In such lovely weather one wanted an unlimited amount of time to wander at will. We stuck to our plan, however, and shortly turned right back on to the path leading to Esk Hause.

A short time later, standing on the pass, we were treated to a landscape which formed a rich tapestry of varying shades of grey, green and blue – all beneath a benevolent, clear sky. This was my first real taste of Lakeland beauty from the high fells, and Jim and I gazed around for several minutes without speaking. Esk Pike towered above us, its lofty grey pinnacle pitted and scarred. Around its base lay loose stones and rocks which it had shed when attacked by fierce weather and unfriendly walking boots.

At the start of our descent we passed the oddly named Knotts of the Tongue, which form a rugged battlement guarding the approach to Tongue itself. We were now traversing the gathering grounds for the River Esk, many streams tumbling from the hills which were crowding in on either side. This is truly the head of Eskdale, but the infant river has a great distance to travel before attaining the broad, flat reaches of the lower dale.

The steep cleft of Little Narrowcove soared upwards to our right, leading to the ridge between Ill Crag and Scafell Pike. The stream roaring from it formed a lurching mass of white foam as it discharged itself into the River Esk, which we were following, and the valley floor was becoming marshy. As we skirted the fellside, the marshland below us increased and widened out into the spongy mass of Great Moss which looked very uninviting. A time-check indicated that we were still ahead of schedule, and as the weather appeared to be settled we decided to be adventurous and climb Scafell Pike which lay temptingly above us.

According to the map, a path would take us up the next gully, Cam Spout, onto Mickledore Ridge which lies between the summits of Scafell and Scafell Pike. This looked to be a straightforward route on paper, but it did not indicate the multitude of loose stones lying in the channel that make the ascent doubly hard. Our climb up to the ridge was one of the stiffest that I have ever experienced, commencing at a sharp angle and getting progressively steeper; it was nearly a match for Kirk Fell. With feet slipping on the bed of stones we made laborious progress up that testing wall, pausing frequently to recover our breath. There was the consolation of a magnificent view whenever we rested. An added comfort was the knowledge that AW considers Scafell Pike to be the toughest proposition in Lakeland. Hoping that time would not turn against us we continued climbing.

As we scrambled over the final approach to the ridge, an unusual and amusing sight met our eyes. Perched on the rocks was a rusting articulated trailer with a distinctive red cross painted on its side. We assumed that it had been brought there by helicopter in case of emergency as a first-aid post or stretcher store. As one end was completely open and it was absolutely empty, it looked less than inviting. Fervently hoping that we would not need to use it, we agreed that it would be preferable anyway to remain outside if badly injured. At least one could die in more dignity that way.

From Mickledore, a well-trodden track took us over and around boulders as it approached the summit of Scafell Pike. Excitement welled up inside me as the cairn on top of England's highest mountain – at 3210 feet – came into view. We could see many fellow walkers resting in the nearby stone shelter, huddling together to escape the stiff wind. AW bemoans the harsh treatment meted out to this stone edifice on the roof of England by people with no respect for the glories of Empire or its monuments. We were simply glad to climb inside it and relieve the strain of our scrambling ascent. Elated by our achievement we shook hands and peered over the walls of the shelter to take in the superb views – it was truly one of those crystal clear days when one could see for miles, as far as some of Lakeland's furthest fells. Below stood Great Gable, and its close companion Green Gable, smaller now but providing a focal point amongst a sea of surrounding mountains. This produced a feeling of superiority at being able to gaze on Great Gable's summit (2949 feet) from above, and made up for it refusing me access on previous occasions. AW, as he gazed out from this vantage point, could put a name to all of the heights. In *The Southern Fells* he identifies no fewer than seventy-four peaks.

I was pleased to get a glimpse of Wastwater which was just visible behind Lingmell. This reminded me of that soggy trip to Wasdale Head. All the frustrations with bad weather and lack of visibility on that day were receding now that the balance had been restored. The tribulations of those earlier Lakeland episodes could now be looked back on with humour – time is certainly a great healer.

Surrounded by other noisy visitors who shared a common feeling of well-being, I was reminded of AW's observation that this is not a place for quiet thought and privacy. He suggests that the south summit overlooking Eskdale is the ideal place for those who crave peace.

When time dictated that we must leave our lofty spot, we began our descent down the shifting boulders, but this time with gravity easing the strain. With great care and in some trepidation, we renegotiated the gully of Cam Spout, knowing that its myriad loose stones were waiting to punish any unwary movements. It was like tiptoeing across a steep slope on a moving bed of stones but we achieved it with only an occasional slide, and as we passed the waterfalls near the base of the Spout we knew that the worst was over.

Renewing our acquaintance with the River Esk once more we followed it down to Brotherilkeld that lay beneath Hardnott Pass. An added bonus during this descent was the sight of the river tumbling through an impressive gorge and forming the Esk Falls. These are a match for any that I have seen on my journeys, although they do not possess the grandeur of High Force.

Crossing Lingcove Bridge our pace quickened, despite our recent testing climb, as we were keen to reach Brotherilkeld and the main part of the dale. When we reached the road, our expectations were completely justified. The sun beamed down transforming Eskdale into a glorious bed of green, overlooked by shimmering fells and crags. Dotted around the valley bottom were pockets of lush woodland, adding variation to the pastoral landscape. Ultra-bright white cottage walls shimmered in the sunlight, surrounded by foliage of every hue. No wonder AW was so taken with the area, it was a delight.

Ignoring the time, so keen were we to take in as much of this splendid scene as possible, we took the path that runs towards the Duddon Valley. Climbing a little way up the fellside, we turned to admire a spectacular vista of mountains which dominate the head of the valley. This view instantly became one of my Lake District favourites. Behind the foothills which we had recently passed, a semicircle of distinctive and graceful mountain peaks carved their irregular shapes in the skyline. This was the kind of view that I had anticipated on that first fateful visit to Lakeland. The mountains had vindicated themselves at last.

Nearest to hand were the unmistakable indentations of Crinkle Crags with the spear-shaped top of Bowfell soaring upwards behind them. In *The Southern Fells* AW gives a rather nice description of this pyramid-shaped summit, likening it to the female form, adding that it shows the rare characteristic of a graceful outline and sturdy shapeliness on all sides. Completing this admirable mountain backdrop were the peaks of Esk Pike, Scafell and Scafell Pike. It was hard to imagine that a short time ago we were perched on the highest point of that glorious mountain range.

Jim was enthralled by the hitherto unexperienced Lakeland views that he had enjoyed that day. He was now a converted walker and couldn't wait to climb another mountain immediately. Tempering his enthusiasm I reminded him that unless he wished to go hungry we had an urgent appointment for a meal at the Eskdale Youth Hostel, a little way down the valley. In desperation he looked around him and then, in a burst of enthusiasm, suggested that, after our supper, we should climb Harter Fell which stood directly above us. As I was so captivated by the surroundings I foolishly agreed.

As there were not many hours of daylight remaining, we hurried through the meal and, immediately afterwards, set off back along the valley. The evening sun had already cast a rich glow over Eskdale, adding lustre to those sparkling colours that we had enjoyed earlier, but I hoped daylight would linger long enough for us. My camera, which had been working hard all day, recorded our perfect surroundings. If our luck held, I anticipated some fine shots of the gathering sunset. At the base of Harter Fell, the first hint of dusk was already noticeable. Realising that we were taking a considerable risk in proceeding, I asked Jim if he wanted to go on. With the impetuousness of youth he replied that wild horses would not drag him from this venture.

AW gives Harter Fell a good write up in *The Southern Fells* going so far as to say it is one of the few Lakeland fells that can be described as beautiful, especially so when viewed from Eskdale. The lower slopes, as we could see, climb steeply from the tree-lined curves of the River Esk and, according to AW, have a wide belt of heather above their luxurious covering of bracken. Already thrusting our way upwards, I was praying the light would hold so that we could see our way over the ramparts of rock that lay beyond the heather. These obstacles guarded the shapely pyramid on its summit. What would AW have thought of our foolhardy climb in semi-darkness? Always advocating caution, he would have thoroughly disapproved of our rushing up Harter Fell on a 'beat the clock' escapade.

Jim seemed unconcerned by the fact that we would have to come down in darkness. AW often recommends spending a night on the fells to appreciate the beauty of a Lakeland dawn; it seemed quite possible that we would have to take him up on his suggestion.

Panting with exertion I tried to keep up the punishing pace set by Jim. I am normally unworried by climbing fells at a sensible rate, but this was far from that. Emerging from the band of heather, we began a semi-rock climb up the rugged bastions guarding the summit. As I took a breather, I was treated to the sight of a wonderful sunset developing over the fells separating us from Wastwater. I could see into the heart of Hardnott Pass and the remains of the Roman fort on its lower flank. A host of dark mountain peaks were unfolding in the background as I scrambled from rock to rock, straining to reach the summit. Jim had disappeared above me and may already have reached the top. Despite my struggle it was pleasing to still have some energy left after a hard day's walking, including the ascent of England's highest peak. That first seven-mile walk over Baildon Moor seemed an age away.

As I climbed higher the sun sank lower and, finally clearing the rocks, I made a last dash for that beckoning pyramid where I could at least have a well-earned rest and take some camera shots. Struggling up to join Jim on the pinnacle, I was just in time to experience a spectacular sunset. The lower rim of the sky was transformed into a collage of magnificent red, orange and blue tints which formed a vivid contrast to the darkness above and below. Silhouetted against this rage of colour were the stark outlines of many of the mountains that we had seen earlier in the day. They stood as if lining up for our final inspection, those ever-present giants surrounding the head of Eskdale. Jim and I could only gaze in wonder at this fantastic sight as the sun slowly and inexorably sank below the skyline.

There can be no better point to finish an account of my first Lakeland journeys than at this climax of a superb day's walking. Lakeland had at last revealed its true colours when the weather finally came good.

CHAPTER SEVEN

Coast to Coast Encounters

As another chapter remains, you will guess that I made a successful descent of Harter Fell in darkness with my neck intact. It is not something that I would recommend and I have never repeated such an exercise.

On my return home from that disastrous first Lake District visit that February I got down to choosing my next long-distance challenge. Despite the foul weather I had experienced, I was well and truly bitten.

As AW had been such a reliable guide during my ventures so far, I decided his Coast to Coast walk was definitely the next one to tackle. At the first opportunity I bought a copy of his Pictorial Guide (the original unrevised edition) to take me from St Bees on the Cumbrian coast to Robin Hood's Bay on the North Sea.

I spent an entertaining time reading the wide-ranging introduction to his guide, which I was pleased to see is hand-written in the same style as his *Pennine Way Companion* and Pictorial Guides to The Lakeland Fells. AW stresses that this walk is not an officially designated footpath: 'the point I want to emphasise is that the route herein described is in no sense "an official route" such as the Pennine Way.' His reason for devising it is also explained: 'The walk is one I have long had in mind and in 1972 finally accomplished; and I have committed it to print partly because the growing popularity of the Pennine Way indicates that many people of all ages welcome the challenge of a long-distance walk, and partly because I want to encourage in others the ambition to devise with the aid of maps their own cross-country marathons and not be merely followers of other people's routes.' His route, he wryly observes, is a tidy walk with a definite starting and stopping point: 'You can't walk on water and Robin Hood's Bay is a definite full stop.'

Whilst planning the logistics of the walk I studied his carefully devised route instructions. Once again using his log of the journey, which indicates in detail all the mileages between the towns, villages and landmarks on the walk, as it does in his *Pennine Way Companion*, I selected the most convenient stopping points and immediately set about pre-booking my accommodation. I had not allowed myself much time, for I planned to do the walk early the following June, a mere four months away. Luckily I was able to secure accommodation in a combination of youth hostels and bed and breakfast lodgings. With the subsequent growth in popularity of the walk, following AW's television programme, it is advisable now to book well in advance. The YHA currently operates a booking service with the added facility of experienced guides, and other accommodation publications are available.*

With an apology for repeating myself, may I emphasise that, as in the case of the Pennine Way, some years have passed since I did this walk (1988), and the route has been subsequently revised. The revised edition of Wainwright's *A Coast to Coast Walk* gives details of these revisions.

Optimistically I reckoned that, although my preparation period for this walk was considerably shorter than that for the Pennine Way, my fitness had improved and I did not need to practise parts of the route this time. The total distance is 190 miles, and therefore considerably shorter than the Pennine Way. This is counterbalanced by its variety of scenery, as it passes through three National Parks, each with its own individual character. A fortnight is suggested for the walk, but I planned to take twelve days, based on my Pennine Way Package experience with its two unnecessary rest days. I also decided to walk it from west to east, as recommended by AW, so that the wind and rain would be at my back.

It follows an approximate beeline, but the path necessarily meanders and if one were a bee one could knock four days off the journey. AW's reasons for the deviations are twofold. First, as he says: 'It is never possible to follow a dead straight beeline without trespassing: climbing fences, wading rivers, perhaps swim-

---

* *See* Appendix 5 page 241.

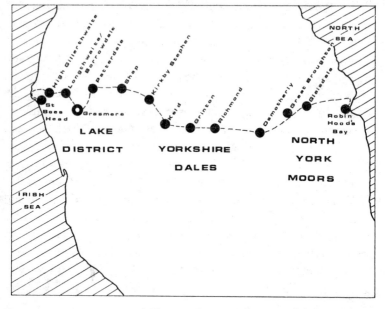

A Coast to Coast Walk

ming sheets of water, and walking through houses and gardens.'
Secondly, it is desirable to visit places of interest which are,
presumably, ones that AW himself liked. An example of this is
his detour to Grasmere en route from Borrowdale to Patterdale. I
think it might have been because he loved Grasmere so much and
couldn't bear to miss it out.

For those interested in mileage and statistics, the route can be
roughly divided into three parts, as it is split by two main arterial
roads. The first section is through AW's beloved Lake District,
terminating at the M6 motorway. It then proceeds over the
Westmorland Plateau and across the Yorkshire Dales following
Swaledale to the A1 motorway at Catterick Bridge. Finally it
crosses the Vale of Mowbray and follows the ancient Lyke Wake
Walk across the North York Moors before descending to Glaisdale
and eventually Robin Hood's Bay. These factors combine to
present an appetising walk which for me would involve re-visiting
both Lakeland and my favourite Yorkshire dale, and culminating

in an exploration of the so far unknown North York Moors.

Although Ben and his finger were once again in fine fettle, he had to decline my invitation to join me in my venture as he had planned another attempt at the Pennine Way at that time. We were, however, able to do some local walks together as part of our preparations.

June soon arrived and it was with less trepidation and more maturity, in walking terms, that I set out from home to the starting point. As it turned out, I nearly did not start, as my journey to St Bees came close to disaster. I travelled by coach from Bradford and unfortunately my connection at Preston was delayed for two hours due to an accident on the M6. After a long and frustrating wait, our coach, destined for Whitehaven, finally appeared. The driver was very apologetic, expressing the hope that we hadn't been too inconvenienced. Some passengers gave him a hard time as though he were responsible for the motorway pile up. Most, like myself, were already resigned to a long day's travelling.

As though stung by the insults thrown at him by the more irate passengers, the driver seemed determined to make amends. The coach sped out of town as though his life depended on making up lost time. Restricted by traffic, his constant acceleration and deceleration tossed us around like straws in the wind. I hoped that the moaners in our midst were satisfied now, having antagonised the innocent driver. Indeed, it served them right if they were feeling sick. Once on the motorway he really opened up and the countryside became a blur as we sped along. Pinned back in our seats, I was half expecting the wail of a siren, but somehow we managed to avoid the police patrol vehicles.

In what seemed no time at all we were heading along the dual carriageway towards Windermere. I peered out of the windows for some views of the approaching mountains but I soon gave up the attempt as, once past the lake, the roads become progressively narrow and more winding. The driver did not appear to notice this fact as his speed remained the same. Feeling like a cork tossing about on a rough sea, I tried to hold down the lunch that I had consumed during my long stint at Preston coach station, and clung to the seat in front of me with my knuckles turning white. Many fellow travellers were muttering dark threats but presumably dared not attempt a risky journey down the aisle to admonish the driver.

As we screeched to a halt in Whitehaven I half expected to see a reception committee waiting to make a presentation to the driver for dedication above and beyond the call of duty. I was convinced that we had just broken the land-speed record from Preston to Whitehaven. Tumbling from the coach passengers lurched in all directions, some even falling to their knees in thanks for their deliverance. Anyone witnessing this exhibition could be forgiven for thinking that we were a coach load of football supporters who had consumed the obligatory thirty crates of Newcastle Brown during our journey. I swear the tyres were smoking.

When my surroundings stopped spinning, I ventured towards the railway station to sample a different form of punishment, as normally meted out by British Rail. To be fair, a train to St Bees was thankfully not long in coming. Blissfully slumped in the seat of a remarkably calm railway carriage I enjoyed a peaceful journey along the coast to my destination.

Unfortunately the introduction to this pleasant town was impaired by the threatening weather. A black sky hung over the dull streets and buildings which I'm sure would normally appear very attractive. I found St Bees to be a quiet but engaging town and agreed with AW that it is a fitting place from which to start a cross-country journey. At its heart lies the Priory Church and Grammar School which date back many centuries, and I'm glad I had time to visit both these fine buildings before finding my way to my night's lodging at Stonehouse Farm where I was made very welcome. The family was adept at catering for walkers.

Day One: St Bees Head – High Gillerthwaite

After a hearty breakfast, I bade farewell to my friendly hosts and, with fingers and toes crossed that the weather during the walk would be kind, I set off to find the start of the path at St Bees Head. The weather was, in fact, cloudy and a gale force wind was howling in from the sea but it wasn't actually raining – yet. I found the path at the sea wall but unfortunately, as AW comments, instead of heading eastwards, it sets off in the opposite direction. At this point, I did as instructed by AW and picked up a pebble from beside the Irish Sea, popping it safely in my pocket. The intention was to carry it with me and deposit it next to the North Sea at journey's end. Life is full of good intentions and unfortunately when I reached Robin Hood's Bay I completely forgot about the pebble and promptly took it home with me.

An initial climb onto the distinctive red sandstone cliffs of St Bees Head revealed a bird's-eye view of the beach which lay under heavy grey skies, spoiling its normally bracing appearance. Between the town and the shore huddled a multitude of caravans and holiday cottages which house the transient community that builds up during the holiday season. White-tipped breakers rolled over the dark expanse of sand, lightening a dull vista that did not augur well for my forthcoming Lakeland crossing. There followed a wind-tossed struggle of three miles along the exposed cliff tops, detouring the jagged indent of Fleswick Bay with its attendant caves which at one time were reputed to be the haunt of smugglers.

The cliff-top path was now heading in a northerly direction and although still not eastwards as desired it was better than walking in the opposite direction to that intended. As I lurched along, battered by the fierce westerly wind I came across a fellow struggling to remain upright: he was peering through a telescope mounted on a tripod that would not keep still. Pausing for a chat I learned that he was a keen bird-watcher and that his telescope was trained on a pair of guillemots bobbing unconcernedly on the surging waves at the base of the cliffs. He allowed me to take a peek at the unsuspecting birds who appeared as though they were only a few feet away. He also recommended that I should visit the display board further along the path. Leaving him fighting the forces of nature, I made my way to the board and read more about the countless seabirds which nested hereabouts. I do admit to being a total ignoramus where birds are concerned, although I have gathered some knowledge of the habits and call sounds of the curlew and lapwing. These wily birds have followed much of my progress over fell and moorland, the latter occasionally dive-bombing, but usually calling to me to get off their patch. I had vowed that I would pay the feathered flocks much more regard on my walk across England than I had done on my walk up England. I did try, but I found I remembered to think about them when it was too late and they were already too far away for close identification.

Grateful that the raging wind was blowing me away from the cliff-edge instead of over it, I battled my way past St Bees Lighthouse, whose piercing light can be seen by shipping twenty-five miles out to sea. This is one of a number of buildings that testify to the shipping hazards in these waters; a coastguard station and several observation huts complement this aid to ships which might otherwise founder on the rocks below. The present sturdy, stone lighthouse replaced a former wooden structure which mysteriously burned down, possibly at the hands of our friends the smugglers.

As the shrouded view of Whitehaven appeared in the distance with the Solway Firth behind it, I was thankful to leave the cliffs and head eastwards at last. Taking a farewell look northwards along the coastline, I could just make out the dim outline of the Galloway Hills beyond the mouth of the Solway Firth. White-haven appeared nearer to hand as a grey, urban sprawl, its buildings indistinct in the gloom.

AW had taken care to avoid towns on his charted route, apart from Kirkby Stephen and Richmond which were perhaps unavoidable. I was pleased to note that he had also left out a visit to the Sellafield Nuclear Power Plant that stood an ominously short distance away along the coast. If this had been included on the itinerary you could at least start the Coast to Coast with a positive glow.

The wind was at my back, and progress along track and road to the village of Sandwith was much easier. Whilst passing a farmyard on the outskirts of the small but pleasant village, I was amused by the sight of the farmer and a helper attempting to force a large sheep into a small trailer hitched to a Land Rover. The unfortunate sheep had concluded that she was being carted away to end up on someone's table complementing the mint sauce and was resisting violently. To complete the scene, there were several goats surrounding the trailer, obviously enjoying the diversion. They were bleating lustily which I interpreted as laughter, or encouragement for the sheep. Does one eat mint sauce with goat?

Walking past a row of delightful red sandstone cottages, I mused on the fact that although I had covered five miles of my journey I was still farther west than when I started. To add insult to injury, St Bees was only two miles away as the crow flies. I consoled myself with the thought that I was at least walking in the right direction and, after all, AW had felt that St Bees Head was well worth the detour. Although enjoying the walk through pleasant countryside, I was hoping that the sun would make an appearance.

Four miles farther on I entered the village of Cleator, now a quiet, unassuming place. In its heyday it was a centre of iron ore mining, but the mines are long gone. AW tempts us with the offer of a bus journey to Egremont for a night's rest, but I planned to cover many more miles before the day was out. I suppose Egremont might be useful for a walker who had not spent the night before in St Bees, but had travelled across Lakeland that morning.

The first stiff climb of the walk took me up Dent Hill. Although only 1131 feet high, it must offer fine views in good weather, but persistent low cloud restricted my visibility. This green and rounded promontory was formerly a deer reserve, but its modest slopes required a considerable amount of exertion on my part. As I stood puffing unhealthily on the summit, I was a bit concerned at my lack of fitness considering the high ranges I had in front of me. I hoped it was just a question of my finding my mountain legs. AW's guide promises a view of the Isle of Man from the top, but this anticipated sight never materialised. That popular island was coyly hiding in a sea mist. I also couldn't comment on AW's suggestion that an old argument can be settled at this point, as to whether the Irish mountains are visible. All I could make out was the village of Cleator and part of the surrounding coastal plain. This was all very sad and not a little frustrating because the great man extols the joys of views that normally stretch to the Solway in the north and encompass most of the Cumbrian coastline to the south.

AW's description of the sparkling view in the opposite direction that rivets attention on a fine selection of Lakeland fells only produced a yearning for what might have been. Partnered by my normal Lake District weather, I was becoming accustomed to seeing the lower sections of mountains protruding from under a veil of cloud. Perhaps I was taking the weather more in my stride after experiencing those unforgettable views around Esk Hause and Eskdale. One consolation was the view of Uldale below, carpeted with a mass of conifers and the sight, as I descended Raven Crag, of the delightful Nannycatch Gate. This oddly-named semi-ravine lay before me, its mixture of rugged contours and wooded slopes giving a great lift to the spirits. Tucked away in this secluded valley it appeared untouched by time and weather. The path took me through this quiet haven and along the valley of the Nannycatch Beck, a deep cleft below a miniature version of the Wasdale Screes. These careered down from the top of Flat Fell, their surface a mass of grey boulders ready to trap any unwary walker who tried to scale them.

If that way inclined, a siesta can be taken in this narrowing valley, according to AW. As the sun was conspicuous by its absence and I still had a good distance to cover that day I did not take up his suggestion. Particularly noting his comment that sleeping walkers were likely to be trampled by herds of pony trekkers, I was careful not to be lured into such excesses.

At the head of the valley the ground opened out and a session of road walking was called for. The interest aroused by the sight of a stone circle by the roadside was tempered by AW's view that it is a bogus one. According to his information the stones had been so placed by a local archaeologist to resemble an authentic prehistoric circle.

Making good progress along the road I could make out some of the buildings around the hamlet of Ennerdale Bridge which AW calls the threshold of Lakeland and a convenient halting place. I still had some way to go and passed through the peaceful hamlet on my way to the next objective, namely Ennerdale Water. Ennerdale Bridge itself stood quiet and unspoiled around the charming stone bridge over the River Ehen. Outlying houses and cottages hid in attractive woodland on either side of the road that led me to another bridge and the pumping station on the shore of the lake.

It was interesting to re-enter Ennerdale from the opposite end, and weather permitting, to see a different view of it. Although actually unaccompanied by heavy rain, it was disappointingly overcast and gloomy. As I stood looking over this fairly remote lake, away from many of the popular Lakeland haunts, I could appreciate AW's love of the area, particularly when he viewed it in beautiful evening sunshine.

On this occasion the waters of Ennerdale Water were inky black as they lapped the rock-strewn base of Bowness Knott and Angler's Crag. I had a four-mile journey to negotiate from my viewpoint on the western end of the lake before my day's walk was complete. The path follows the southern rocky shore and was hard on the ankles, and the spirits, as I found it quite tedious. Perhaps this feeling was due to the poor weather, or the fact that I was eager to reach the Youth Hostel at High Gillerthwaite, which immediately meant that every yard seemed like a yard and a half.

There were, however, some redeeming features of that rugged terrain. At the foot of Angler's Crag stands a small distinctive rock that has been given the name of Robin Hood's Chair. Although unrecognisable as a chair, it forms one of several references to that famous outlaw on this particular walk and I don't expect these are any more authentic than the others. I believe that he spent his outlaw days in Sherwood Forest and not in Yorkshire as some say. There is no denying the references to his chair, grave and finally his bay on the Coast to Coast, but I am convinced that he was not a Yorkshireman. Just as Queen Elizabeth I is reputed to have slept in countless places, Robin Hood has been everywhere.

Leaving the Chair I searched the steep slopes of Angler's Crag for remains of the now defunct Angler's Hotel. When AW published his guide, plans were afoot to raise the water level of Ennerdale and turn it into a reservoir. In order to accomplish this dubious conversion the hotel was demolished. Thus was removed a boon to anglers who were reputed to be able to dangle their fishing rods from the hotel windows direct into the lake. Unfortunately the act of desecration perpetrated on the unfortunate building was in vain. The planners in their wisdom never raised the water level significantly, and thus a popular landmark was needlessly removed.

Although visibility was restricted, I was able once again to make out the general features of the area from AW's wonderful drawings, including Pillar which dominates the skyline at the eastern end of the lake. The sad afforestation of the valley beyond

Gillerthwaite was now plain to see. According to AW, a decision has to be made at this point, as there are three alternative routes into Borrowdale. The soft option was to take the valley route through Ennerdale Forest. I discounted this on three counts: firstly, I did not relish miles of forest walking, there had been plenty of that on the Pennine Way. Secondly, I was familiar with the route on from Black Sail Hut which lay beyond the forests. Thirdly, trusting that the weather would change, I preferred to take one of the two high-level routes and perhaps get some reasonable views. The two alternatives were over Pillar (2926 feet) or High Stile (2644 feet): I chose the latter as that involved a high ridge walk from High Stile to High Crag and Haystacks and this was my reason for pushing on to High Gillerthwaite. AW describes this route as delectable in clear weather, but not for ordinary mortals to attempt. Another reason for choosing it was to visit Haystacks, reputedly AW's favourite mountain.

Reckoning that tomorrow could take care of itself, I made for the hostel sheltering in the valley near the River Liza. It was compact and comfortable, but relatively empty on that evening. It does not lie on any of the tourist routes and caters for the simple needs of walkers and cyclists. Apart from myself there were only three Australians staying. The conversation over the evening meal centred on Australia and I began to feel like a 'Pommie' outsider. Trying to steer the dialogue onto something different, I had the temerity to mention the British. One of the trio, who appeared to be a great traveller, opened up on all cylinders with his knowledge of Britain, America, Canada, Europe and the Far East, hardly pausing for breath. It transpired that he knew everything about any subject under discussion and was never stuck for a tale. I discovered that he had spent the past eight years travelling the world, but I was less successful in finding out how he earned his living. I retired to bed mentally exhausted – and thankful to be me.

Day Two: High Gillerthwaite – Borrowdale

The weather on the following morning looked reasonable. There was no sunshine but the clouds appeared to have lifted and I was at last given a glimpse of the surrounding mountains. Confident that fortune would smile on me, I headed for the slopes of Red Pike (2479 feet) to start the ridge walk which I viewed as my first highlight of the Coast to Coast.

It was a testing climb to the summit but I was rewarded with views over Ennerdale Water to the coast. From my lofty perch on the ridge I looked down on the village of Buttermere in the next valley and the cluster of mountains behind it, with Whiteless Pike the most prominent. My euphoria was unfortunately short lived for, as I traversed the ridge towards High Stile, the cloud descended. By the time I reached its summit I was completely enveloped: I could have sat down and wept. Unable to see more than a few yards, I decided that it would be foolish to stumble blindly along the ridge to Haystacks. Although not in the purist tradition, I deviated from the route and descended the far slopes of High Stile into the Buttermere Valley. The angle of descent was quite alarming and I was very wary of losing my footing and thereby making an impromptu entry into the waters of Buttermere. A few hundred feet of descent thankfully brought me out of the cloud and the sight of Buttermere and Crummock Water opened up beneath me. Following a careful descent to the road, I next had to map a new route into Borrowdale.

Treated to the unexpected close-up view of Buttermere, I walked along its shore weighing up the chances of a new high-level route to Borrowdale. There was the low-level alternative of a valley walk over Honister Pass, but that meant following the road that wound its way through that deep gorge. Ignoring the possibility of the cloud descending once more, I made for Fleetwith Pike (2125 feet) whose sharp, craggy top could be clearly seen. Thus began one of the most strenuous climbs that I had yet undertaken, for the rugged, rock-strewn path ascended at a sharp angle. When roughly two-thirds of the way up, I rested on a rock and was rewarded by a full length view of Buttermere, its neighbour Crummock Water and beyond that the smaller lake of Loweswater. Two fellow walkers were making slow, but deliberate progress below me on the energy-sapping path and, although quite a way up the mountain, they looked minute.

Pleased that I had chosen this route, I headed for the summit, hoping that the notorious clouds would remain at bay. Fortunately they did and the view from the pinnacle was memorable.

In one direction I could look over the deep Honister Pass that had been ravaged by nature and man over thousands of years. The near vertical face of Honister Crag towered above the tiny snake-like road running beneath it. It was pitted with innumerable quarry workings from where the local slate has been extracted for centuries. By turning through ninety degrees, towards Borrowdale, the quarry sheds that I had passed on my earlier visit to Lakeland could just be identified, huddling together high above the village of Seatoller. In the far distance I could just make out the black, sombre outline of the Helvellyn range, the next day's mountains. Swinging round to the south I renewed acquaintance with those now distant central Lakeland fells, seen this time from a new perspective. They were ranged before me, their names now familiar: Scafell, Great Gable, Green Gable, Lingmell and that punishing adversary, Kirk Fell. I was beginning to feel quite proud at being able to recognise many of the Lakeland fells.

Nearer to hand I could see the ridge route that I had been forced to forgo, from High Crag to the summit of Haystacks. Although I could not walk on top of AW's beloved mountain, at least I could see what I had missed. I found it rather strange that AW should select this particular mountain as his favourite when there were far more dramatic ones to choose from. Viewed from this angle, it seemed rather squat against its background of higher peaks. AW obviously disagreed for he loved its appearance, emphasising that it did not admit to any sense of inferiority. In *The Western Fells* he says: 'Haystacks stands unabashed and unashamed in the midst of a circle of much loftier fells, like a shaggy terrier in the company of foxhounds, some of them known internationally, but not one of this distinguished group of mountains around Ennerdale and Buttermere can show a greater variety and a more fascinating arrangement of interesting features.'

It is a well-known fact that AW asked that upon his death his ashes should be deposited on the summit of his best-loved mountain. This request was duly carried out by his family. Displaying his unique brand of humour, AW cautions all walkers to take extreme care when venturing on Haystacks after the scattering of his ashes: if they found a piece of grit in their boot they must treat it with respect as it might be him!

From my unscheduled viewpoint on top of Fleetwith Pike, I could also recognise Brandreth rising behind Haystacks, the remains of its well-known fence crossing its flanks. That fence is suggested by AW as a rendezvous for 'Coast to Coasters'; a meeting place of the ordinary mortals who took the low-level route from Ennerdale and the very strong and experienced fellwalkers who chose the high ridge walk.

Grateful that the cloud had kept away, I vacated my absorbing viewpoint as time demanded that I should head for my night's stopping place in Borrowdale. A much gentler descent down the far side of Fleetwith Pike brought me to those quarry sheds that had looked like miniature models a short time ago. As I dropped down into Seatoller, I was charmed by the village's stone cottages with their gleaming, whitewashed walls. One of the buildings houses the Tourist Information Centre, but I was hesitant about going in as I realised from the notice outside that it was closing time. As I stood pondering on the pavement, the door opened and a very pleasant lady invited me in. She told me to have a look round and that there was no need to hurry. Patiently answering my questions regarding the centre's display of local industry and craft, she also told me about the area and the quarrying that had scarred much of it. When she noticed that the seam of my map case was splitting she kindly repaired it with strong tape.

As I said goodbye to this helpful lady – a model for all information officers – she indicated the riverside route that I should take to the hostel. Consulting AW's guide, I found it was less than a mile of pleasant woodland walking. AW was once more eulogising the Lake District's charms, and Borrowdale's particular appeal. I formed the impression that this section was definitely a highlight of the Coast to Coast walk as far as he was concerned. He mentions that travellers are well catered for in Borrowdale and this was certainly true of my experience in the Tourist Information Centre. He also observes that Borrowdale folk are adept at catering for outsize appetites and tired bodies.

He omits to mention the infamous Borrowdale soup – so he had evidently missed that treat!

I enjoyed the stroll beside the delightful River Derwent during which I watched the sun's reflections dancing on the rippling surface. I soon reached the Longthwaite hostel; nestling between the river and attractive woodland, it occupies an engaging setting. The building has obviously been extended during its lifetime and the earliest section of mellowed red cedarwood resembles an Alpine hut. It certainly lived up to expectations, providing good food and first-rate companionship. An added bonus was the fact that a party of well-behaved schoolchildren was staying at the hostel that night and they served the other hostellers during the meals and did all the washing up.

It was here that I met a rather remarkable young Methodist minister with an exuberant personality and an unconventional attitude to his calling. He told me that he was not averse to sampling the demon drink and the lusts of the flesh since his philosophy was that you couldn't preach about sin until you had experienced it – a somewhat unusual and enlightened approach.

Day Three: Borrowdale – Patterdale

The next section of the route formed AW's 'dog-leg', as the path detours south-eastwards to Grasmere and then heads north-eastwards to the tip of Ullswater at Patterdale. I had decided to ignore AW's advice that two days should be taken to cover this part of the journey; a pretty rash decision since it is a hard twenty-mile walk to cover both sections, which involves two climbs, each of around 2000 feet. I completed the distance without any real problems, but found that all my energy was spent in keeping going and I did not have enough time to take in my surroundings, which I regretted. No one should walk through the beautiful Lake District with their heads permanently down. If I had been a bee, I could have taken a straight line to Patterdale which was only about eight miles due east from the Longthwaite hostel, but the direct route is barred by numerous ridges. AW's book assured me that I would not regret the extra miles.

The day's walk commenced with a journey along the Stonethwaite valley which, according to AW, is a walk in heaven. It did not live up to that high expectation as the weather was having another of its Cumbrian off-days. Borrowdale is said to have the heaviest annual rainfall in England and it certainly lived up to its reputation as I crossed the bridge over the Stonethwaite Beck for a look at the village. This is the reason why the area is so lush and green; and it also provided an attraction for an internationally known tyre company. The inhabitants of one village in the locality were given free sets of wet-weather tyres by the company saying, in their later advertisements, that if the people of Borrowdale could drive on these tyres, then anyone could.

Re-crossing the bridge I continued my journey along the Stonethwaite Beck, which was to lead me out of the valley. A little farther on I could see the sombre dome of Eagle Crag towering above the opposite bank. It has a distinctive outline and its lower reaches signify the entrance to Greenup Gill. Despite the present conditions I imagined that this area would be popular with walkers and picnickers in good weather. Not many about the day I went by.

This particular section of the walk virtually merges with another long-distance path, the Cumbria Way which left my route at Smithymire Island and heads up the Langstrath gully on its way to the Langdale valley. I could imagine that this footpath, which traverses some lovely areas of Cumbria, is a gem of a walk. I had other things to contend with at this point however, the immediate task being the 2000-feet ascent to the watershed that divides Borrowdale from Grasmere.

The rain persisted as I climbed up the testing Greenup Gill. By the time I reached the buttress of Lining Crag I was well and truly drenched. This was probably the low point of my day's walk. Water was trickling down my neck which mingled indelicately with the sweat of my exertions. I had reached the stage that most walkers experience, when they ask themselves why on earth they are torturing their bodies when they could be sitting comfortably at home reading the illustrated edition of *Wainwright's Coast to Coast Walk!*. There must be easier ways of drowning, I thought, but, as ever, the lure of the crest at Greenup Edge spurred me on and I kept climbing steadily. I was assured by AW that the mountain panorama up there was grand and this made me feel ashamed of my defeatist attitude with its attendant thoughts of home comforts. By the time I had finally reached the summit of Greenup Gill, I had all ideas of mutiny firmly under control.

I knew that great care was needed at this point in order to keep on the correct path and not be lured down a side valley. So intent was I on keeping to my route that I omitted to chastise AW for the non-existent views. The cloud was down and I was clinging to the rather indistinct path like a limpet. AW's temptation of a fine-weather, high-level route over Calf Crag, Gibson Knot and Helm Crag sadly had to be ignored as I knew I would see absolutely nothing from up there. The path improved where it entered the valley of Far Easdale and I kept to that direct route down to Grasmere.

After what seemed a long three-and-a-half mile descent, I reached the lovely village of Grasmere with its air of hustle and bustle. It lies in a beautiful setting and is very convenient as a base for the many surrounding walks. Unfortunately it is a victim of its own popularity as it becomes overcrowded at most times but especially at weekends and during the summer. On that particular day it was looking pleasantly attractive, although not at its best due to the cloudy conditions, but at least the rain had abated and I had emerged from the mist halfway down Far Easedale. As time was limited, my stay was shorter than I would have liked. I ate my lunchtime sandwiches on the small green in the centre of the village and watched the ever-present stream of cars passing by.

After being held up in a queue at the post office, where I had gone to buy postcards and stamps, I was impatient to begin the second part of my day's journey which, once out of the village, joined the main Ambleside to Keswick road. After the relative peace, indeed solitude, of the last three-and-a-half days, I did not enjoy the mile-long walk along the roaring highway one little bit; there was compensation, however, for many lovely rhododendron bushes were on display in the gardens alongside.

I was thankful to leave the busy road and head for the hills once more, climbing up Tongue Gill to the eagerly awaited Grisedale Pass and its nearby tarn. Once again AW tempted me with promises of imposing mountain scenery including Helvellyn. Would the weather relent and let me see them in all their glory, I wondered? There was no problem in finding my way to the Grisedale Pass as the path was well trodden by the many walkers who make that popular ascent to Helvellyn. It is Lakeland's most visited mountain and part of its lure must be the dramatic ridge of Striding Edge.

I found the climb up Tongue Gill to be more enjoyable than

that up Greenup Gill, probably because the rain was now no more than fine drizzle. Emerging from the Grisedale Pass, I was not surprised to find an impressive ring of surrounding mountains partially obscured by heavy cloud. Quite a selection of them tower above Grisedale Tarn, with Seat Sandal standing sentinel at the head of the pass. Steep-sided Fairfield sloped away to my right and, across the tarn, I could see that the lower slopes of Dollywaggon Pike were scarred with the snaking gash that forms the badly-eroded footpath to Helvellyn.

It is at this point that AW indicates that a decision must be made regarding the route to Patterdale. The choice is obviously very dependent on the weather and the time but also, according to AW, the state of any blisters. Weather: still poor. Time: not a great deal of same. Blisters: doing very nicely, thank you. In the light of this I decided to forsake the two high-level alternatives of Helvellyn (3118 feet) and St Sunday Crag (2756 feet) and yet again take the valley route, which leads down Grisedale. It was disappointing to have to keep missing out on the mountains but I couldn't see Helvellyn at all and the upper part of St Sunday Crag was shrouded in cloud.

Leaving Grisedale Tarn behind and taking the valley path to the right, at least I had the compensation of seeing, on top of a small group of rocks, a plaque indicating that this was the spot known as the 'Brothers' Parting'. It is supposedly where William Wordsworth said his final goodbye to his brother John prior to the latter's departure to sea. Why they should wish to struggle up 2000 feet to bid farewell is a mystery to me. They could have done it much more easily in Grasmere!

I followed the Grisedale Beck on its downward journey, cursing my bad luck as I went. Looking up at St Sunday Crag I longed to stand on its summit and gaze down upon what I knew was a wonderful view of Ullswater. I knew because AW's book has a drawing of it, but that was not the same as the real thing. At least this time I was heeding AW's advice that if the rain is pouring down, take the direct route and forget the mountains. Being one of the seemingly few people who had never climbed Helvellyn, I found it hard to miss out on it and particularly Striding Edge.

When I did eventually climb Helvellyn, two years later, fate took a hand and nearly prevented me from coming down again.

Luckily I did the ascent with a friend and we set out from the Helvellyn Youth Hostel which stands in the rugged Glenridding valley above Patterdale. Quarrying has scarred the head of this attractive valley and the hostel was originally one of the quarry buildings which huddled in a cleft below the abandoned workings. As we set out that morning, the weather was the norm for my Lakeland mountain assaults, wet and misty. Following a steady climb up the reasonable gradient, following Mires Beck, we made good progress along the steep, well-worn path up to the Hole in the Wall.

Here, where the path divides, we had the choice of following either Swirral Edge or Striding Edge to the summit. As views were non-existent, there was little to choose between the alternative routes but we plumped for the more glamorous Striding Edge – and it was nearly my undoing. Negotiating the famous ridge's rocky pinnacles proved quite alarming; they were *much* more severe than they appeared in photographs. On either side, precariously steep slopes, covered in shale for extra momentum, fell away and disappeared into the thick mist. The lack of visibility was probably a boon, for I was unaware of the drop until, as had happened on Pillar, the mist momentarily parted and I was treated to the unsettling view of Red Tarn lying hundreds of feet below. The heart-stopping thought of plunging down one of those slopes into oblivion was ever-present. This was 'white knuckle' territory without a doubt. Clinging like grim death to those rocky buttresses, I crawled over and round them as access demanded, concentrating purely on overcoming each obstacle in turn. That was, until my progress was suddenly halted by my foot slipping on the wet unyielding rock. I am convinced that I would have careered down that unremitting slope from the ridge had not my rucksack jammed between two jagged clumps of rock. Hanging there like a rag doll with legs flailing and desperately trying to regain a foothold, I yelled at the top of my voice to my friend Tom who, behind me, had seen my predicament. He managed to grab me and help me to get a handhold on a firm piece of rock, before extricating my wedged rucksack. As he hauled me into a safe position, I couldn't thank him enough. What would have happened had he not been there to rescue me I dared not contemplate. I would probably be dangling from those pinnacles until my rucksack straps rotted, or the crows finished me off.

Thankful for my deliverance I cautiously edged my way to the end of the ridge, from where it was a mercifully short distance over fairly level ground to the summit. As we approached the shelter which had finally revealed itself through the all-enveloping mist, the sound of voices tinged with excitement drifted from it. Squeezing inside that stone battlement perched seemingly in the middle of nowhere, we joined a party of young people. Happily shouting to each other, they brought back the memory of sitting on top of that other popular Lakeland peak, listening to the enthusiastic cries of success from walkers of varying abilities who had attained a cherished goal. This group covered the full spectrum from experienced-looking walkers in full walking gear to those who seemed out for a stroll. Amongst the latter, shoes were much in evidence that could have graced the local palais – or, in modern parlance 'disco' – and a few wore hob-nailed boots that would do justice to that dying breed, the coal-miner. Colourful anoraks and soggy jeans were also common. As we talked, I discovered that they had ascended by the less perilous route from Grisedale Tarn, and had not ventured up Striding Edge. Apart from their elation at achieving the summit, they were also celebrating the fact that they had earned a significant sum for charity since they were being sponsored.

As if we were not crowded already, we were joined in the shelter by two sheep. With no sign of vegetation or other means of shelter on top of this frequently inhospitable mountain, who could begrudge these brave scavengers respite from the elements? Like their counterparts at Top Withens they displayed no fear of humans and had obviously latched onto the fact that hundreds of potential meal-providers struggled to this spot almost every day.

Tom and I were hungrily devouring our well-earned sandwiches when they barged in and Tom started to feed one of the intruders. I advised caution, but he continued to throw pieces of sandwich towards the hungry animal. He got his come-uppance when all his food was gone because the still unsatisfied sheep grabbed the sleeve of his walking jacket between its strong teeth. Tom snatched his arm away in fright but, undeterred the animal lunged forward for another bite of Tom's tempting jacket, I couldn't help laughing as he attempted to ward it off. By now he and the sheep were the centre of attention as he retreated from the tenacious animal. Amidst laughter and shouts of encouragement, he admitted defeat by grabbing his rucksack and dashing from the shelter. Grinning broadly I joined him outside, resisting the temptation to say 'I told you so.'

A word of advice, therefore, if you are contemplating a climb up Helvellyn. Take plenty of food with you in case you are set upon by persistent sheep.

My journey along Grisedale on the Coast to Coast Walk was much less eventful and I was glad to see Patterdale emerge under the still glowering skies. As the youth hostel was full that evening, I had booked into a bed-and-breakfast which I had found without undue problems.

Having spoken on the telephone when making my booking to a person with a cultured voice, I expected to be greeted upon my arrival by a youngish, well-to-do gentleman. Imagine my amazement after knocking on the door of this mature, stone-built house to find it opened by an aging hippy sporting the kind of beard that birds would happily nest in, and topped by wild, unkempt hair. Perhaps he was a fellow guest and not my host, I thought. I greeted him in what I hoped was a friendly, relaxed manner, offering my hand. Half expecting to see a grubby hand with dirty fingernails extended to grasp mine, I was pleasantly surprised to see a clean, well-manicured one offered.

'Hello Philip,' I said, ready to be proved wrong in my assumptions. 'Welcome,' came the reply in those cultured tones that I had heard over the telephone. 'Come in and have a cup of tea,' he said invitingly. Having already unlaced my boots, I bent down to remove them. Philip would have none of it and said that I could do that in the hall. This was a different approach from many others who insist that muddy boots are deposited in the driveway, porch, or even the garage before allowing walkers to put a foot through their doorway.

Once in the hall I removed my boots as carefully as possible, not wishing to deposit Cumbrian mud over his carpet. Philip had hastened to the kitchen to organise the tea and was back in no time, ushering me into a comfortable and spacious lounge. He told me to make myself at home and explained that he and his wife had few rules, the main criteria being that guests feel relaxed and have an enjoyable stay.

After a relaxing soak in a deliciously hot bath I was introduced to his wife Irene. She was now the breadwinner, in addition to making a multitude of soft toys during her non-working hours. They were a friendly, open couple, happy to talk about themselves and I learned that Philip, a southerner, had retired early and they had moved up here. His real passion was music and I was entertained that evening with a selection of old songs thumped out by Philip on an upright piano that had seen many years of service. This instrument, he told me, was a poor substitute for the Steinway that he would love to have owned. He confessed that his daily fix was a quick burst on the ivories, without which life would not be worth living. He was also an avid collector of sheet music from the forties and fifties when all the popular songs were sold in that format.

The other guests also enjoyed his entertainment and engaging conversation. Most of them were walkers, but unfortunately none was doing the Coast to Coast. The non-walkers were a family touring the Lake District by car.

Philip's role was now that of host and housewife, and he was responsible for the daily running of the establishment. After cooking and serving breakfast, he told me he would grapple with the cleaning and polishing whilst his CD player thumped out ear-shattering classical music. During his meagre spare time, he would revert to his other love, that of doing tapestry. I discovered that he indulged in the vice of 'skinny-dipping' in the nearby river. To the unwary he would present a startling sight emerging naked from the water like a vengeful prophet. Being an avid reader when time permitted, he had learned much about his adopted Lake District from the many books on the area. Unfortunately, he was too busy actually to explore his surroundings and he seemed to have no great desire to walk the fells.

However, his reading bore fruits as he possessed a wealth of stories, some of which he recounted with his unique brand of humour. It was from him that I learned about the ghosts of Seat Sandal, that legendary mountain at the head of Grisedale Pass. According to Philip there are several ghosts, the principal being Domhnal, the Norse King of Cumberland. He was supposedly killed in battle in AD 945 by Edmund Ironside, King of England and buried under a cairn at the head of the pass, by the foot of the mountain. After his burial, his warriors took his crown and cast it into Grisedale Tarn before slipping away into the mist. Once a year, on the anniversary of the battle, they return, recover the crown from the tarn and take it to their fallen king.

Apparently, these events had a bearing on present-day planning decisions, because the fact that the cairn might be Domhnal's grave led the road planners some centuries ago to leave it untouched and build their road elsewhere. The alternative route chosen is the highway now known as Dunmail Raise, its name being the modern corruption of Domhnal.

The legend goes on to reveal that Domhnal fell in love with and married a beautiful maiden. On snowy winter nights, if you care to venture up there in such weather, you will see the king pursuing her around the summit of the fell.

Another ghostly inhabitant is reputedly John Wordsworth, brother of William, who was drowned shortly after their farewell ceremony at the 'Brothers' Parting' stone by Grisedale Tarn. William was deeply affected by the loss and composed some moving verses of remembrance. In Philip's opinion, William has a lot to answer for because it was his eulogising of the beauties of Lakeland that started the stampede of tourists to this romantic corner of England. William, he said, should have stuck to publicising daffodils.

Day Four: Patterdale–Shap

A sixteen-mile walk was in prospect as I set off through Patterdale the following morning. I hesitate to mention the weather, for fear of boring you, but suffice to say that it was no improvement on the previous day. The attractive village lost its sparkle under a covering of mist and steady rain, even the white-walled buildings could not brighten the gloom.

It was disappointing to miss the delightful views around picturesque Patterdale with, as I imagined, the head of Ullswater particularly impressive in decent weather. The imposing St Sunday Crag and the neighbouring Helvellyn range hid shyly from view. How did I know what I was missing? I carried memories in my head of the wonderful photographs of Derry Brabbs who illustrated AW's large-format book *Wainwright's Coast to Coast Walk*. It was a great pity not to see them as AW loved this aspect of the rugged mountain wall towering above the village. He describes it as a scene of informal but exquisite beauty, not yet overrun with the hoards of tourists that invade Borrowdale – although it can get fairly crowded during the summer.

The ascent to the highest point of my Coast to Coast Walk now awaited me. This was the summit of Kidsty Pike (2560 feet) that stands amidst the High Street fells. Leaving the sombre valley, I was not anticipating any great views from this final barrier of Lakeland. AW kindly informed me that in good weather this stretch of the walk presents little difficulty but should be avoided when the reverse applies. He had obviously reckoned without the stubbornness of walkers like myself, who are used to blundering around in mist. Besides I did not relish taking his low-level alternative route which adds an extra three miles to the day's journey. I did, however, curse my luck as the bad weather continued to dog me.

The path climbed steadily to Boardale Hause where I stopped for a brief rest. Now completely enveloped by the mist, I studied AW's guide intently to ensure that I kept to the correct path amongst the maze of them in this area. A slow and deliberate ascent was then made towards Angletarn Pikes from where there is supposedly a fine view of Brothers Water and the fells surrounding the Kirkstone Pass. All that was visible were the next few yards of path and I concentrated solely on reaching the next objective of Angle Tarn. I nearly leapt out of my skin when, out of the mist, a voice wished me good morning. I had been so intent on the path that I hadn't noticed a figure perched on a rock on the side of the path, map in his hand. Inevitably, we struck up a conversation – and you will never guess what the first subject was: the weather. I discovered next that he was also walking the Coast to Coast and was having the same difficulty in sticking to the correct path. His name was Maurice and he had only started long-distance walking the previous year, also tackling the Pennine Way – just a couple of weeks before me. A further coincidence was that he had a relative living in the next street to me in Baildon and was very familiar with my home village.

When I found out that we were staying at the same locations

for the remainder of the walk, I knew that fate had given me a companion. Like the corny ending of an adventure film, where the two explorers wander out of shot and are never seen again, we headed into the mist together. Angle Tarn, which we passed without a halt, was lying dormant in its natural basin, its grey waters motionless.

I was amused by AW's comment that once Angle Tarn is left the surroundings become dreary. We had no measure of this as there had been next to nothing to see so far that day. AW even tempts anyone finding the approach to The Knott too tedious to take the track branching down to Hartsop and to return to Patterdale for an extended stay in Lakeland. Maurice and I were made of sterner stuff and resisted the temptation to abandon the task of reaching Robin Hood's Bay. Besides, all our accommodation was booked and we weren't going to lose the deposits that we had already paid. Another consideration was that we had just passed the fifty-mile point and only had another 140 miles to go!

In total, Maurice and I enjoyed just two clear and sunlit views during our passage out of Lakeland and the first of them was near the summit of The Knott, a mile or so before Kidsty Pike. Once again the thick cloud did its parting act and a shaft of sunlight lit up the surrounding fells. Out came our cameras, as an opportunity such as this was not to be missed. Speed was of the essence for after a few minutes the sun disappeared and we were once more shrouded in mist. That was the only glimpse we got of the High Street range and it was unfortunately too brief for us to identify the surrounding fells depicted in AW's guide.

Between The Knott and Kidsty Pike, the path we were following is crossed by another which descends from High Street and forms the line of the Roman road from which the fell got its name. We turned onto it and skirted the amusingly named Twopenny Crag which AW points out was obviously named before decimalisation. It was hard to imagine that about two thousand years previously the Roman legions had marched over this high-level route on their way northwards to the fort at Penrith. We certainly did not envy them that exposed journey with the keen Cumbrian wind blowing round their knees which, I seem to recall from the history books, were always bare.

Near the head of Riggindale Beck we left that ancient route, striking out for the summit of Kidsty Pike. When we stood on its summit shortly afterwards visibility was again down to a few yards. Here we were at the highest point of our walk barely able to see each other but, conscious that we should at least record this notable landmark, Maurice and I took photographs of each other, dark shadowy figures enveloped by the gloom. At least I had another example with which to demonstrate the nasty things that mist does for walkers.

A careful descent along a narrow, cairned track led us to an old drove road, one of many examples in Lakeland. Like the Roman soldiers, those drovers had to be hardy folk to endure the harsh conditions whilst driving their charges to market often over very long distances. Their progress was usually limited to ten or fifteen miles per day. Eventually their importance was recognised and during Tudor times they were controlled by statute. This specified that a drover must be at least thirty years old and a married householder. It gave status to the true drovers who not only controlled large-scale movements of livestock but carried important messages and, more significantly, became travelling bankers.

As we skirted the knoll of Kidsty Howes, the sun reappeared and a remarkably clear view of Haweswater opened up below us. I resisted the urge to complain that now we were about to leave Lakeland it had decided to reveal itself in all its splendour. Instead, I took in the sight of picturesque Mardale, sprinkled with woodland and occupied by what is now a reservoir constructed to slake the thirst of Manchester and its surrounding areas. Unlike Ennerdale, the authorities went ahead with their scheme to raise the level of Haweswater. They dammed the lake and submerged several buildings including the Dun Bull Inn, a former resting place for shepherds and fellwalkers. To be charitable, I must say that from our lofty vantage point, the result of their labours was no eyesore, and the drowned inn was replaced with the nearby Haweswater Hotel. Whilst Ennerdale retained its water without change but lost its inn, Mardale lost its lake to the Haweswater reservoir but did gain a hotel. AW bemoans the despoiling of the former charming and secluded Mardale, his guide is illustrated with sketches of what happens when a lake is cannibalised into a reservoir.

Maurice and I were delighted that at least we could see the

whole length of Haweswater in glorious colour. A steep descent brought us to the water's edge for a look along the deep, four-mile-long reservoir. Our cameras were very busy now as we had been starved of good material for so long.

It was a pleasant situation in which to rest for a while and bask in the welcome afternoon sunshine. We sat listening to the lapping of the water and to the enthusiastic birdsong that seemed to accompany the sun. The temptation to remain in those idyllic surroundings was strong, for we lingered longer than was prudent and paid for our sloth at the end of the day. Maurice and I had by now swapped brief life stories and it seemed that we were going to get on well together. We next set about putting the world to rights as walkers are apt to do when invigorated by the fresh air and immune from the pressures of daily life. Maurice had taken early retirement just before setting out on his walk the previous year. Used to facing challenges all his working life, he had taken up a new one because sitting back was not his style. He grew up in the days when opportunities had to be earned and hard work and qualifications were the passport to rising from the shop floor. He had served an engineering apprenticeship, as I did, and had worked his way up to a senior management position. Dedication and long hours had eventually taken their toll and he was obliged to adopt a less strenuous lifestyle. This he did by promptly walking the Pennine Way!

I was soon to discover that he had a fine singing voice and often over the succeeding days we would burst into song. This was only when we were unobserved in the remoter parts of the walk as we did not wish to frighten passers-by.

Time was now pressing and we reluctantly gathered up our packs and set out on our journey along Haweswater. The route along the reservoir's western edge was straightforward and, because of the sunshine we were able to enjoy the sight of several lively becks tumbling down the fellside, across our path and into its waters. Most had a waterfall or even a collection of them to enhance their already sparkling behaviour. The views over the reservoir itself were somewhat restricted by trees lining much of the shoreline, but this was counter-balanced by the sight of many birds flitting amongst their branches – once again I did not linger long enough to identify any of them.

Four miles of reservoir walking, as it were, brought us to the impressive dam that holds back the millions of gallons of water so relied upon by the residents of the Manchester area. The water supply has quite a journey to make before reaching its destination in Manchester. Maurice and I indulged in a little conjecture as to what would happen if the dam broke and released the contents into Haweswater Beck that flows from beneath it. We reckoned we could take a boat over the flooded valley and follow the 'beeline' for Shap. This would certainly have been much quicker than the route which we tried to follow on foot. Although only five miles from the reservoir, Shap could have been twice that distance according to the length of time it took us to reach it.

We set off on this last leg of our day's journey in light-hearted fashion, smiling at AW's remark that if exhaustion were imminent, a night's lodgings could be obtained at nearby Bampton. Not for us, a short day. Our mood soon turned to one of frustration as we searched for non-existent footpaths. AW indicates that this is a confusing section of the walk and that many paths shown on the OS maps have fallen into disuse. How right he is. We managed to get ourselves lost at least twice. Luckily, on the first occasion, I soon sensed that we were walking in the wrong direction but we still had to backtrack quite a distance. Our meanderings, combined with frequent halts to study his guide caused the time to pass with increasing rapidity and dusk began to close in. After what seemed hours of struggle, we finally got our reward. We could just make out the ruined tower of Shap Abbey, its dark mass looming out of the semi-darkness. The sight of the remains of this Premonstratensian Abbey made our spirits soar. We knew that there only remained a mile of road walking to Shap and even we couldn't get lost following a road.

Sadly, very little of Shap Abbey remains intact, apart from some of its tower. It stands in a lovely setting and I didn't realise until I read AW's description that most buildings of that type were built in similar surroundings, the requisites being a sheltered valley, with attendant trees and a nearby river. Then I realised that Bolton Priory in Yorkshire, a place I had visited a number of times, was in just such a setting. During my active working life, abbeys and priories didn't feature much, but do now. Adjacent to Shap Abbey stands a group of buildings, obviously inhabited as a rather incongruous line of washing was on display, somewhat detracting from the atmosphere of the place. On the other hand, the house's inhabitants had to hang out the washing somewhere – and I hoped that they remembered to take it in before it got completely dark.

The road journey, between limestone walls, was accomplished in gathering darkness and we soon arrived in the quiet village of Shap. Traffic that formerly passed through it along the A6, now thunders along the nearby M6. Consequently, Shap has become a tranquil backwater whose buildings, the majority of which line the road, are no longer shaken to their foundations by passing juggernauts. Relieved at not having to spend a night under the stars, Maurice and I parted company to head for our respective lodgings, arranging to meet the following morning.

I was made very welcome by the couple providing my accommodation, who had begun to wonder if I was going to turn up. They had lived in Shap for many years and, after providing a hearty meal, told me about life there before they were by-passed. Due to its altitude – the summit of Shap is at 1400 feet – the old A6 trunk road was often blocked with snow, or congested by accidents which frequently occurred in the mist which rolled in from the surrounding moors. Consequently, there used to be many hotels and guest houses to cater for the needs of such eventualities. Those villagers who didn't work in the hotels or on the railway, toiled at the local quarry or the granite works. Life was never easy at Shap. The volume of traffic in the old days was always considerable because the road was one of the main routes to Scotland, and had been since coaching days. Although now of no interest to the speeding motorist on the nearby motorway, Shap is still an important place – specifically to walkers on the Coast to Coast since it is a vital overnight stop.

Maurice, I heard the next day, had enjoyed an interesting evening as well, meeting a friendly couple who were also walking the Coast to Coast. They apparently had a penchant for mixed bathing, locking themselves in the bathroom for a considerable length of time.

Reading AW's guide that evening, I realised that we had left the Lake District National Park shortly before reaching Shap. Our journey the following day would be across the 1000-feet high, limestone area of the Westmorland Plateau. I was pleased to see that its name had been unaffected by the boundary changes of the seventies, when the old county of Westmorland ceased to exist.

Day Five: Shap–Kirkby Stephen

Tucking in to a substantial breakfast the following morning was some compensation for saying farewell to Lakeland, as we were only to see it for a short time in retrospect that day. AW felt that such farewells are always sad. He knew that walking the Coast to Coast path from west to east means that the best part comes first and the remainder is an anti-climax, but still recommended this direction from the weather's point of view. My feeling is that the great appeal of this long-distance route is in its contrasts. Beautiful Swaledale and the heather-clad North York Moors are just as appealing as the Lake District in different ways and a path that goes continually up and down from mountain to mountain could become slightly repetitive. AW has created a journey of immense variety and I detect an impish 'tongue in cheek' attitude on his part when he bemoans the fact that we must leave his beloved Lakeland. He, nonetheless, certainly extols the virtues of the next section that traverses the Westmorland Plateau.

Maurice and I rejoined forces and headed for the M6 motorway that lay roughly a mile away. It was on the footbridge spanning that mighty sward of tarmac which slices through Cumbria that we took our last backward look at the partially shrouded outline of Lake District mountains. Surprisingly the traffic below our feet was very light and as I took a photograph, the motorway was captured in one of its rare moments of emptiness. Could this be a symbolic observation of two minutes' silence to commemorate the passing of Lakeland?

The crossing of the grassy Westmorland Plateau, in improving but still overcast weather, was a pleasant experience, as limestone walking generally is. It is an area of ancient habitation with evidence of prehistoric settlements, stone circles and tumuli. At one of the tumuli, I took a photograph of Maurice against the backdrop of the distinctive Howgill Fells in the distance. Striking a nonchalant pose he leaned on the stake that marks the ancient burial mound and it must be said that he displayed a superb 'lean'. When looking through the collection of slides and photographs after the walk, I noticed that Maurice was always leaning on anything to hand. His angle was so impressive I was convinced that he could 'lean' for England.

Shortly afterwards we came across evidence of the Roman influence in the area, as we crossed the Roman road that formerly linked the fort at Low Borrowbridge with the camp at Brougham. Another reminder of a famous legend stands in the form of a cairn on Crosby Ravensworth Fell. It supposedly marks the site of Robin Hood's Grave. AW tells us that it is not in fact his grave. I was pleased about that because, according to legend, Robin, when about to breathe his last, shot an arrow into the air and asked to be buried where it landed. I contend that it is an awful long way from Sherwood Forest and even Robin Hood could not fire an arrow over such a distance. How the spot derived its name I cannot explain.

Leaving the plateau, we were forced into a six-mile section of road walking. Apparently this is due to a change of route in 1981 at the request of local farmers who lost patience with the ungentlemanly conduct of some walkers whilst crossing their land. AW makes reference to this by means of an addendum inserted at a later date. He apologises for the fact that an extra two miles must be added to the route to allow for the imposed detour. It is the thoughtless walkers involved who caused damage to walls who should be making the apology.

Around mid-day Maurice and I managed to deviate from the prescribed route by taking the wrong road from Raisebeck. This may have been the result of another 'lean' by Maurice at a road junction where he struck up his usual casual pose by resting an arm on the road sign, thereby, as I contended, moving it to the wrong direction.

Realising our mistake at the fork in the road, we were faced with a dilemma. Should we backtrack for a mile or take a short-cut over the fields to the correct road? I am ashamed to say that we chose the dishonourable course of trespassing over the farm-land. Consumed with guilt and the feeling that if caught by the angry farmers they would further divert 'Coast to Coasters', we commenced our illicit foray across the fields. Oh the ignominy of getting caught! Would we be mentioned by AW in a future addendum to his route as the perpetrators of another diversion?

All went well for a time until we heard the noise of a tractor in the adjoining field. Horror of horrors, we were certain to be discovered. Not daring to peep over the dividing stone wall, we crouched out of sight wondering what to do next. Then a lightning glance over the wall revealed a farmer and two helpers who were apparently unaware of our presence. The best course of action we decided was to creep alongside the low wall that protected us, apart from an open gateway which loomed a little further on. To add to our predicament, an inquisitive herd of deer came up to the wire fence on the other side of the narrow field to see what we were getting up to. As we crept stealthily along the wall with our backs bent double, the deer reasoned that we were playing some kind of game. They followed on the other side of the fence just keeping pace with us. Not wishing to attract attention by having a herd of deer, visible to the farmer, following us we kept stopping to try to 'shoo' them away. Our efforts were in vain as the animals thought it was great fun, stopping every time we did, and then playing 'follow my leader' when we restarted. The worst moment came with the crossing of the open gateway. Maurice and I dashed across in turn, hoping and praying that we would not be noticed. Miraculously the men's backs were turned to us in the next field and we got away with it. We were able to use the remainder of the wall for cover, accompanied by the ever-present deer, until the far end of the field was reached. The stretch of road that we were seeking lay just over the hedge and conveniently there was a gate in our corner of the field. At least we didn't have to go searching for an exit or, worse still, burrow out through the hedge.

I have never been so glad to have the feel of tarmac beneath my feet and we heaved a huge collective sigh of relief at our deliverance. If by any chance the landowner reads this book, then I apologise unreservedly for trespassing – but I would like to know what on earth the herd of deer was doing. When I think of all the times I have been excited to see just one or two deer on the fellside, and here we had a herd to gaze at – and we spent our time trying to drive them away. We gave them a cheery wave before setting off along the now authorised route. Our guilt was such that we vowed never to repeat such a clandestine episode.

At the point where the path left the road linking Raisebeck with Whygill Head, our ears were bombarded by a loud screeching noise that was a little unnerving until we realised it came from hundreds of waterfowl circling around in the distance. Their cries heralded the sight of Sunbiggin Tarn which AW rightly describes as a 'large reedy pond in the middle of a morass'.

For those walkers busily waxing boots and packing rucksacks for an attempt at the Coast to Coast, I am happy to report that AW's 1981 route alteration has since been revised. The official route now avoids the roads that took us through Orton and Raisbeck, although Orton can still be included if required The revised route goes by means of field paths, quiet lanes and finally moorland to Sunbiggin Tarn. There is now no excuse for walkers cutting across unauthorised fields, as we did during our escapade! The elimination of six miles of road walking is tempered by a further route revision of the section from Sunbiggin Tarn to Ewefell Mire, situated below Crosby Garrett Fell. This section must now be covered along roads, a distance of two and a half miles, but don't be disheartened; two and a half miles for six miles is a fair swap.

At the time of our walk Maurice and I were able to skirt round Sunbiggin Tarn by footpath, but this proved to be a dubious privilege. This is an area where watertight boots are required and we squelched our way around its edge, but at least your feet will be drier as you plod along the roads. Although we found the tarn uninspiring, the birds seemed to enjoy it and also the accompanying bird watchers.

A short climb onto Ravenstonedale Moor brought us into another area of limestone and ancient settlements after passing Bents Farm. The path took us through a series of primitive earthworks comprising an ancient complex of three prehistoric villages. If only we had had the use of an aeroplane, we could have followed AW's suggestion that viewing it from the air would be far more dramatic. A little further on we came to the picturesque Smardale Valley with its delightful bridge spanning the beck. It was a shame not to explore such charming scenery but the 'flesh pots' of Kirkby Stephen beckoned from a few miles away. On the way there the path passes under the Settle to Carlisle railway line that I had first encountered during my Three Peaks Walk. It felt like renewing acquaintance with an old friend as I walked beneath it through an underpass.

We had enjoyed a view of the Howgills coming ever closer since they were first seen from the Westmorland Plateau. Distinctive in shape, their dome-like outlines have earned the nick-name of 'Elephant Backs'. Two further fells completed that pleasing skyline, namely Wild Boar Fell and Mallerstang. I have since enjoyed walking the Howgills where picturesque routes in peaceful surroundings are the norm. They appear to be as yet undiscovered by the masses.

Kirkby Stephen, our stopping place for the night, is a pleasant market town. Just as Shap hugs the A6 road, Kirkby Stephen straddles the A685 that runs through that part of the Eden Valley. It stands midway between the northern edge of the Howgill Fells and the Stainmore Gap that is crossed by the Pennine Way.

According to AW it is a good place for licking wounds, a comment which would have been prophetic if Maurice and I had been seen by that farmer and given backsides full of buckshot. In AW's opinion, the town had managed to retain its charm and unspoiled atmosphere. I was certainly impressed by its attractive market square, and my attention was caught by the distinctive and unusually grand archway that marks the entrance to the Parish Church. This brightly decorated, ornate structure had apparently been built at the bequest of John Waller, a purser in his Majesty's Navy. How a person of that position found the money for such an imposing edifice was puzzling. Could it be that he had put a lot of the money he received into his own purse instead of his Majesty's?

Maurice and I had two priorities when we reached the town: finding our accommodation and having a relaxing hot bath. The first task proved no problem as my Youth Hostel and the hotel where Maurice was staying were beside the main road, not far from each other. Kirkby Stephen boasts a hostel with a difference, as it is a converted Methodist chapel. This transformation has been tastefully achieved and the dining room is in the main body of the chapel. The tables are in fact situated between the remaining pews. I was the only person staying that night, but the warden was friendly and obligingly provided a good supper solely for me.

Maurice had invited me to join him later that evening for a drink in his hotel. We had spent a pleasant few hours chatting with some fellow walkers when I realised that it was past eleven o'clock. I hurried back to the hostel to find the door locked and no signs of life. Despite repeated hammering on the door there was no reply. Wondering what to do next, I decided to return to the hotel and try ringing the warden. Back at the hotel, the remaining guests had a laugh at my predicament. At the hostel, a surprised voice at the other end of the telephone said that he thought that I had returned much earlier and gone to bed. He hadn't heard me knocking as his room was in the back of the chapel. I was quite relieved when, a few minutes later, he let me in to go to my lonely bunk.

Day Six: Kirkby Stephen–Keld

The night passed uneventfully, apart from a dreadful dream I had of being pursued by a herd of deer, their antlers clashing in their haste to reach me. Although I was fleeing from them on my hands and knees, they never managed to get close enough to trample me. I was thankful to wake up to the new morning. This was the day that we would enter the Yorkshire Dales National Park and beautiful Swaledale which I was greatly looking forward to.

Although not for us, AW again tempts the timid walker with an alternative bad-weather route by road to Keld. He even dares to suggest that a passing motorist would feel an obligation to offer lifts to seemingly inherently decent walkers struggling bravely against the elements. If that happened he inferred that you would decline, of course. Always prepared to look for the best in people was AW. I wonder how he would have viewed our creep across those fields the previous day. Determined to keep on the straight and narrow from now on, we left Kirkby Stephen by a pleasant footpath which led us to a footbridge over the River Eden. This delightful river rises on wild moorland above Hell

Gill near Mallerstang. Threading its way past the ruined Pendragon Castle it joins forces with the nearby Settle to Carlisle railway and accompanies it through Kirkby Stephen, Appleby and Armathwaite to the historic city of Carlisle. There it spills into the Solway Firth, at which spot a grand stone monument to Edward I stands. This king, known as the 'Hammer of the Scots' died here in 1307 on his way for one last assault on his old enemy. He was the prime instigator of three hundred years of almost continual warfare with Scotland.

The weather was in a reasonable mood as we passed through the village of Hartley resting amongst attractive rural surroundings. An energetic stream glides through its heart passing under a durable stone bridge that has stood the test of time and traffic.

We now faced a climb along the road towards Fell House Farm, the views from which are unfortunately marred by the ravages of nearby quarrying. A large gash in the hillside marks the site of a limeworks and quarry that had at best provided employment for the area. A bridleway then took us a good way towards our next objective, that of Nine Standards Rigg standing proudly at the head of the watershed between the Eden Valley and Swaledale. This is marked by a trig point at 2170 feet. As we left the bridleway for the final climb, we had good views of Wild Boar Fell and Mallerstang as visibility was quite reasonable. Once the boggy summit was reached, the views became panoramic. This was a fine vantage point high above the River Eden, with many fells on view in all directions. Across the valley we were treated to one last look at the Lakeland fells, now shrinking in the far distance. Cross Fell and the upper reaches of Teesdale lay far away to the north. I could not make out the infamous radar station on Great Dun Fell that I had blundered around the previous year. To the south and east, the Pennines stretched as far as the eye could see. It is worth mentioning the nine large cairns nearby which give the spot its name. Their origin is somewhat shrouded in mystery, although it is probable that they were marker stones as the old boundary between Yorkshire and Westmorland passed through them. They now have the appearance of large stone pillars, but like many other cairns they may have been added to by enthusiastic visitors over the years.

(Another pleasing note: a diversion now takes the official route in a more direct line to Nine Standards, which saves a distance of one mile. This saving conveniently cancels out the extra mile added by the diversion along roads from Sunbiggin Tarn to Ewefell Mire. Things are definitely improving!)

Having reached this elevated spot, a quiet celebration would not be out of place according to AW. For the remainder of the walk there would be no higher ground to climb. In fact the highest parts still to come would remain below 2000 feet. Maurice duly obliged with another 'lean' on the trig pillar for the celebratory photograph.

Conditions underfoot on that exposed plateau were glutinous and began to sap Maurice's strength. Shortly after commencing our descent, he had to get some relief from the uncompromising, sticky peat bogs and took a breather on an uncomfortable pile of stones with the rather unimaginative name of 'Pillar of Stones'. From this viewpoint, the greens, greys and purples of the Yorkshire Dales spread themselves into the far distance. Swaledale was beckoning – or would have been, I'm sure, if it had not been hidden from our view by the haze that hung over the lower ground. Being a callous brute, I threatened Maurice with the whip, in order to prize him from his resting place. Muttering mutinous curses he reluctantly left his refuge to carry on the descent over what was now firmer ground.

AW warns against a feeling of entering the home stretch to Robin Hood's Bay at this point and the temptation to think that it is all downhill from here. He insists that we must put such thoughts behind us as we have not yet even reached halfway.

After a short time we came across an inviting shooting hut at Ney Gill which is left permanently open for poor unfortunates who might not make it to their night's destination; I had to drag Maurice past this bolt hole. The next few miles took us gradually downhill as we came off barren, open moorland into typical Dales countryside of green pastures bounded by stone walls and a fair sprinkling of stone barns. Maurice and I certainly agreed with AW's comment that on the outskirts of Keld stands a signpost which indicates the longest quarter-mile in northern England. In fact, all the miles seemed longer in Swaledale, which led Maurice and me to decide that they were measured on the unique 'Swaledale Scale'. The coming day's walk from Reeth to Richmond was supposedly a stroll of eleven miles, but it took nearly the whole day to complete.

That enjoyable descent into Swaledale took us through lovely Whitsundale with its splendid beck bubbling on its way to join the infant River Swale. The charming hamlet of Ravenseat huddles nearby beneath surrounding hills, a welcome collection of stone cottages and farms, so familiar to many outlying areas of the Dales. 'Coast to Coasters' can now enjoy a longer walk through this valley as the new official path misses out the 'Pillar of Stones' and the shooting hut as it heads directly for Whitsundale on its descent from Nine Standards.

We were shortly to be reacquainted with Keld which we had both visited on our respective journeys along the Pennine Way. As we were about to enter the village, AW's faithful mileage indicator showed that we had covered ninety-five miles, exactly half-way to Robin Hood's Bay. In recognition of this achievement we burst into a rendition of 'Keep Right On To The End Of The Road'.

Keld needs no introduction from me, as you will recall my earlier description of this timeless settlement, named by the Norsemen. I will just mention one of its famous characters called Neddy Dick; I had read about him in Mike Harding's *Walking the Dales* and had a good chuckle. He was the inventor of 'rock' music for he discovered that different pieces of stone, when struck, produced different musical notes. Eventually collecting a complete scale, he created a stone xylophone which he played as he travelled round the Dales.

Maurice and I went our separate ways once more. My destination was the Youth Hostel where I had stayed the previous year, whilst Maurice was doing likewise at East Stonesdale Farm on the opposite side of the valley. A reminder here concerning my earlier reference to the watering hole at East Stonesdale Farm where the Coast to Coast path joins forces with the Pennine Way as it passes the farm. Be assured of an entertaining night's stay in the company of Ernest and Doreen Whitehead, for that is what Maurice experienced. The exuberant Mrs Whitehead has compiled a *Coast to Coast Bed and Breakfast Accommodation Guide** and the farm has

* *See* Appendix 5 page 241

become famous in the annals of Pennine Way and Coast to Coast folklore.

It was an interesting experience for me during my second stay at the hostel because I could hear the reactions of the Pennine Way walkers bemoaning their fatigue and blisters. I was happy to report that the Coast to Coast was not such a test of endurance. I couldn't help remembering Ian and his tea bag, as this was one of the places where he had kept up my spirits with his entertainment. I had hoped to meet up with my friend Ben, of dislocated finger fame, at the hostel. He was currently having another crack at the Pennine Way following his disappointment the previous year and was due at Keld around the same time as myself. Apparently he had not made it as yet and I left him a postcard with news of the Coast to Coast. I later received a reply from him with the good news that he had completed his second attempt unscathed.

Day Seven: Keld–Grinton

Maurice and I met up once again on that joint section where the two long-distance footpaths coincide near East Stonesdale Farm. AW recommends a smile of pity for any poor wretches travelling along that section of the Pennine Way for he believes our route to be so much better. And I agree.

The next section of the walk involved a choice between the high- and low-level routes to Reeth. I deferred to Maurice who loved river walking; rather than take the high route over the moors. The main drawback to taking this low-level route, which is not described in his guide, would be missing the extensive remains of the great lead-mining area on the high moors. AW considers this high-level alternative to be of much greater interest, providing the weather is kind; and it is, in fact, his only official route. He refers to the privation and struggles of the lead miners as they scratched a living from the harsh environment and to the appalling working conditions that they had to endure. For further material on that part of Swaledale he recommends the writings of Dr Arthur Raistrick, that great authority on the history of the Yorkshire Dales. The well-respected doctor died recently but he will be long remembered for his vastly informative publications.

I felt slightly uneasy about our unofficial route along the river and vowed to make amends at a later date by returning to walk AW's preferred high-level route. By so doing I could firmly put into place a piece of the jigsaw which was very slightly standing proud of the rest.

Leaving the Pennine Way near the footbridge over the Swale, we joined a wide track that ran along its northern bank. If time permits, do remember to have a look at the forces or waterfalls that I mentioned in the Pennine Way chapter. Do not expect to be alone at any of these spots; they are very popular.

A few hundred yards along the track, perched on a promontory, stood the ruins of Crackpot Hall, occupying a fine vantage point near the head of the Swale Gorge. This once impressive farmhouse had to be abandoned because of mining subsidence and it supposedly got its name because the local people considered the owner to be a 'crackpot' for building it on such a vulnerable site. A more plausible explanation is that its name was derived from the Norse as 'crackpot' meant 'Pothole of the Crows' in their language. Crows are certainly very prevalent in the area.

As we passed the crumbling remains we came upon a party of geology students who were listening intently to their tutor's description of their surroundings. Thinking that we might learn something, we loitered nearby until a meaningful glare from the lecturer indicated that we were not welcome.

Beating a hasty retreat we hurried around the face of the hill to enter the dramatic Swinner Gill. This is a deep cleft that lies beneath Rogan's Seat and forms one of the most impressive views that I had seen whilst following the Pennine Way footpath along the other side of the gorge. Clinging precariously to the sides of this ravine are the remnants of mine workings, long since left to decay. Part of a smelt mill and mine shaft provide examples of a bygone era when the surrounding countryside was ravaged for human gain.

Emerging from this imposing side valley we commenced an enjoyable section of a few miles along the good riverside track and then through multi-coloured meadows to the village of Muker. Now that we were in my beloved Dales, the sun had obligingly made its appearance, highlighting the abundance of spring flowers. For the first couple of miles, where the river passes through the Swale Gorge, the Pennine Way footpath could be seen above the opposite bank, snaking along the side of Kisdon Hill.

Muker, our next port of call, is that busy and popular place which I had visited the previous year. It is situated at a crossing point of the Straw Beck near its junction with the Swale. The main road of the dale passes through and it bends sharply as it approaches and crosses the narrow stone bridge over the beck. This ensures that traffic does not hurtle through the village. The attraction of its tea shop was too much to ignore and we rested tired limbs whilst enjoying a welcome pot of tea. This made a pleasant change from drinking from our flasks, but the temptation was to linger and we had to force ourselves to don rucksacks once more and continue the battle.

When a church was built here, it was no longer necessary to carry the corpses down from Tan Hill to nearby Grinton. The other building of character, previously mentioned, is the Literary Institute with its most attractive gable end. A popular landmark on photographs of the Upper Dales, it is a reminder of the enthusiasm for adult education in Victorian times. In addition to its library, evenings of lectures, discussions and music were held there. It no longer houses a library, but it is currently the venue for Parish Council meetings, local silver band practice and lesisure activities for young people.

Having only our map to guide us now, which served us right for ignoring AW's official route, we rejoined the path along the Swale. The welcome sun beat down on us and life felt good as we walked by the now wider river. As we made for Gunnerside, we passed the splendid Ivelet Bridge, a single-arched structure built for packhorses. According to legend, the spot is haunted by a headless dog, so Maurice and I, being devout cowards, were glad to pass it in daylight.

Gunnerside is one of a number of charming villages to be found in Upper Swaledale. It stands beneath another great cleft, that of Gunnerside Gill, which was at one time the lead-mining centre of the dale. A very popular spot with walkers, it is a place for donning boots on a Sunday morning in order to visit both the upland moors and the sites of extinct lead-mining activity. The small fields adjacent to the village are surviving examples of early sixteenth-century enclosures.

Maurice and I had adopted a leisurely pace, both agreeing that a journey through such pleasant surroundings should not be rushed. Along the path that hugs the river bank, we were accompanied by the sounds of rippling water and the protests of disturbed sheep. This reminded us that we were on the home patch of the distinctive breed of Swaledale sheep that do not take kindly to heavy-booted walkers tramping across their domain.

Perhaps it was the combination of the fine weather, easy going and relaxing countryside that brought on our feeling of contentment and indolence. This walk was too good to be hurried and frequent stops were made. Some entertainment was provided as we passed a farm where sheep dipping was in progress. The reluctant participants were herded into pens to await their ordeal, some of them leaping around and even climbing onto their companions' backs to try and escape. One determined animal prodigiously leapt over the high wall of the pen and bolted for freedom only to be chased by a grinning farmer. It was grabbed and dragged, kicking and bleating, to the dip. Here it was unceremoniously launched into the air to disappear beneath the surface of the evil-looking solution with a resounding splash, which managed to drench the farmer and his assistant, thereby quickly ending their mirth. When the unfortunate sheep re-surfaced I am sure I detected a smile on its face at the thought of the revenge it had wreaked.

We noticed from AW's guide that had we taken his high-level route we would have passed the 100-mile point shortly before Level House Bridge. As we were virtually due south of that point we felt that we qualified for another celebration. The waters of the fast-flowing Swale looked very tempting to these two foot-weary walkers. If we had possessed the courage, or stupidity, we could have succumbed to Philip's penchant for 'skinny dipping'. In the event, we removed our boots and socks for a celebratory paddle. The water was icy cold and the river bed treacherously uneven and slippery as we set out for the middle. With rocks either digging into our frozen feet or moving beneath them, we stumbled back towards the bank. Immediately abandoning our escapade, we staggered back to dry land regretting our foolhardiness. We then indulged in the more sensible and less frenetic pastime of just sitting on the bank and dangling our feet in the water.

By-passing the villages of Low Row, Featham and Healaugh, our destination at Reeth was drawing ever closer. Although seen only from a distance, those villages should not remain forgotten. The first two form one long settlement, which was the home of Thomas Armstrong who wrote the *Crowthers of Bankdam* and *Adam Brunskill*, which brought to life the lead-mining of former times. Healaugh, an unusual name meaning 'forest clearing', was at one time the largest manor in the dale. It became the centre of Quaker worship and the faith lived on here for quite a time after its decline elsewhere.

Despite the long miles of the 'Swaledale Scale', journey's end for Maurice was accomplished at Reeth, the unofficial capital of Upper Swaledale. It was mid-afternoon as we reached the village green and were immediately surrounded by crowds of cheering people. What had we done to deserve this? Apparently we had timed our arrival to coincide with the finish of the Swaledale Marathon, an energy-sapping endurance test around the surrounding fells. One competitor still had enough breath remaining to tell us that he had completed the course in just over six hours. This achievement, apparently, was nothing compared to the winner who had completed the twenty-four miles in the admirable time of three hours. Pleased that our journey that day had not been as frantic as theirs we left the panting and perspiring competitors to recover, and strolled around the village. Maurice took a shot of me standing in front of the village store grinning like a Cheshire cat. This was done at his request because he wished to capture me 'Reethed in smiles'.

The village stands at the junction of the Swale and the Arkle Beck, and was a much more important place than it is today. It possesses a variety of relatively young buildings dating from the eighteenth and nineteenth centuries. Strangely it has no Parish Church, that honour going to its neighbour, Grinton. It does, however, house the Swaledale Folk Museum with its displays of life and crafts in the dale over the centuries.

I was not as fortunate as Maurice, in that I still had some

distance to cover to Grinton Lodge Youth Hostel further along the dale. In fact, the proprietor of the village store gleefully informed me that I had a further two miles to go to my destination and that a stiff climb also awaited me. It is strange how some people thrive on the discomfort of others and I couldn't see anything amusing in this extra burden. At least I was walking part of the following day's route as I had arranged with Maurice that we should meet at the nearby village of Fremington the next morning.

The walk and steep hill to Grinton Lodge was worth the effort as it turned out to be a very impressive building set high on the hillside adjacent to the road running over to Leyburn in Wensley-dale. So impressed was I with the commanding view over the dale that I planned to get up early the following morning for a walk before breakfast. The building itself must be one of the finest that has ever been made into a hostel. Its castellated walls and tower overlook a fine courtyard and its interior is most impressive. At supper I met a fellow hosteller who had attended a function the previous evening at nearby Castle Bolton where he had indulged his passion for Highland dancing. Another visitor, a Dutchman, I found was also keen on dancing but not the Highland variety. Neither of them did any dancing that evening as we retired to the pub in Fremington after our meal. This was not a brilliant idea as we had to re-climb the steep hill that I had toiled up that afternoon, but it was easier to do with companions.

Day Eight: Grinton–Richmond

My pre-breakfast walk the following morning provided some wonderful views in the early sunshine. I could see Reeth in the valley below, nestling beneath Calver Hill which divides Swaledale from Arkengarthdale. The conspicuous ridge of Fremington Edge dominated the far side of the valley. Knowing that this part of Swaledale was rich in prehistoric remains I swept the valley below the distinctive edge for signs of a massive earth embankment which had been built across the dale at that point. Unfortunately my bird's-eye view was too distant to pick out this feature. I thought how the character of the dale must have changed since that earthwork and its neighbour across the river from Reeth were constructed. At that time, the main preoccupation of the people would be hunting the animals in the forests that carpeted the valley, to provide their daily diet. Right up to Norman times and beyond, large parts of Swaledale and Arkengarthdale were reserved as hunting forests and there are records of red deer in the area as late as the seventeenth century.

This thought of food made me hurry back to the hostel for breakfast. I did not hang around thereafter as I knew that Maurice would soon be marching down the road from Reeth, to our rendezvous. He had well over a mile to travel whilst I had an easy journey down the hill.

In Fremington I waited for Maurice to rejoin me for our journey to Richmond, where I was keen to see the impregnable Norman Castle set on a rock above the Swale. Although we were going to need the bulk of the day to cover the distance, I was pleased to see that AW advises against rushing it in half a day. He indicates that sufficient time should be left at the finish to explore the town. We described this as our longest 'short' day because the eleven miles seemed double that amount. A repeated word of warning to those who walk through Swaledale: don't believe the mileage on the signposts.

The first place of interest along the river was Marrick Priory, now mainly ruinous except for its tower. Originally a Benedictine Nunnery founded in 1154, the rule of Marrick was strict, black habits were worn and the entry of novices was strictly controlled. The building suffered during the Dissolution and, although it is now in private hands, a farm and a Field Study Centre now adjoin it. One interesting feature is the nearby flight of steps up to the hamlet of Marrick that are reputed to number 375.

The artist William Turner painted many scenes in the area during his famous tour of Yorkshire to provide illustrations for a projected history of the county. He made a small sketch of Marrick Priory, and later turned it into one of his inimitable atmospheric watercolours. The final version is somewhat exaggerated in size and splendour, a common trait of many of his paintings of buildings and landscapes. He could be described as the country's first 'enlarger'.

Maurice asked to be captured on film at this historic site, but I advised against one of his well-executed 'leans' against the tower for fear of its collapsing. I didn't want to be held responsible for removing one of Yorkshire's landmarks at a stroke. Maurice might inflict more damage in one minute than three hundred years of Scottish plundering.

Our passage through meadows and woodland was very pleasant but the sunshine was soon to desert us. We had rejoined AW's route at the beginning of the day and could follow his guide once more. His route now led us away from the river, up the 375 steps, through the village of Marrick and across walled fields which required the negotiation of several stiles of the 'squeeze through' variety. There are a number of nasty things that beset walkers as I have mentioned, and stiles and fences feature strongly. In my opinion they are only put there to antagonise and injure us. Stiles normally come in two types, those that grip you where it hurts and those that you climb with the aid of oxygen. If you have tried to squeeze through the first type with a heavy rucksack you will have experienced the bitter-sweet tears welling in your eyes as you force parts of your anatomy through the minuscule gap. It is at times like these that you curse yourself for succumbing to that enormous cream cake in the café you just called at. Rigid intentions of fasting and strict diet, common reactions at such times of suffering, usually last until the next meal. The second variety are not to be attempted by walkers with no head for heights because you have to clamber up and over a multitude of energy-sapping steps. There is seldom a way round since the jokey farmers force you over these brutes by fixing copious amounts of barbed wire or other hazards on either side of the stile. Thankfully very few resort to land mines flanking your approach to these wooden monsters. Those of you who have been in the armed forces may be forgiven for thinking that you had finished with assault courses when you took up the gentle pastime of walking.

Fences are usually topped with an obligatory strand of barbed wire to make life interesting for the walker. If required to cross such obstacles, even on the permitted right of way, permanent damage can be wreaked, mainly to those with short legs. With luck, you will end up with only your trousers in tatters, but without them other parts may suffer the same fate. Scottish farmers, obviously a caring breed, recognise this threat to our well-being, or they may possibly have been disturbed by male walkers singing in very high pitched tones as they pass their farms. These helpful Scottish landowners kindly fix rubber strips over the obnoxious strands. This may have been done out of pity or a desire not to be sued for compensation.

Having negotiated this particular section of treacherous stiles, we were treated to a wide-ranging view of the way ahead. Rain-soaked, green pastureland rolled out before us, interspersed with attractive woodland. The river threaded its winding course below us, energetically heading towards the flat Vale of Mowbray. It was maturing now, no longer displaying quite the haste of its infancy. A tall obelisk stood out against the skyline to our right: we discovered this was Hutton's Monument, a memorial to Captain Matthew Hutton who had requested burial at this, his favourite, spot from which he had often admired the splendid view. When we later passed the site, Maurice and I agreed with his choice.

A short distance ahead of us now stood the house of Ellers which has been tastefully converted from a former hostelry, The Old White Horse Inn. Strangely it had no road leading to it, so anyone visiting the inn in times gone by would have travelled on foot or horseback. If it were still in existence, there would be no risk of being breathalysed, apart from those imbibing too freely who could be charged with being drunk in charge of a bicycle. Reading the name of the old inn in AW's guide provided the cue for a song. Maurice and I could not resist a quick rendition of the 'White Horse Inn'. Luckily there was no one around to disturb, but we did receive some disapproving glances from the ever-present sheep. One could feel sympathy for these poor animals, some of which had been recently sheared. They can't have sunny dispositions knowing that at best their woolly coats are removed to end up as someone's carpet. At worst, as lambs, they could be sold on to be fattened as an accompaniment to mint sauce.

Marske lay tucked away in woodland about a mile ahead, a village steeped in history mainly due to the Hutton family. Their home at Marske Hall, an impressive building, was built in the Palladian style of the 1750s with a classical pillared entrance. It stands in sumptuous, well-manicured grounds. The Huttons lived there for several centuries and the family produced two Archbishops of York.

Nearby stands the squat twelfth-century church of St Edmund with its distinctive castellated roof. Although altered over the centuries it still retains some of its original Norman features. The early Norman period was not a good one for this and other parts of Yorkshire. William the Conqueror wreaked a terrible revenge following an uprising in the north of England, embarking on a campaign of death and destruction. The 'Harrying of the North', as it is known, laid this dale and many others to waste. Cloudy and drizzly conditions had now overtaken us which prevented any photographs of Marske's historic buildings. I have been there several times since, but have never once been favoured with decent weather. Obviously Marske is reluctant to have its obvious charms recorded on film.

Making the final push for Richmond, the path runs through some delightful countryside. As it skirts several farms at Applegarth and enters Whitcliffe Wood, it passes two dramatic escarpments. The second of these, Whitcliffe Scar has a monument on its crest commemorating Robert Willance who supposedly fell down the steep slope whilst riding his horse, and consequently the spot is known as 'Willance's Leap'. It has strong associations with Richmond as miraculously Robert survived and he showed his gratitude by presenting a silver chalice to the town. Maurice and I wondered if any exhausted 'Coast to Coasters' had been tempted to throw themselves from that lofty perch. Many may have done if they could have summoned the energy to make the climb.

As the track emerged from the wood, the first view of Richmond was revealed. Even though it was still some distance away, the castle towered above its surroundings. AW tells us to tidy ourselves, as there may still be some 'lasses of Richmond Hill' about. This is a reference to the popular folk song 'Sweet Lass of Richmond Hill', the lass concerned being Frances l'Anson, whose family owned Hill House in Richmond. It was written by her lover Leonard McNally in 1789 and they were secretly married in London a short time later. Sadly she was soon to die during childbirth. Turner put the lass into the foreground of one of his paintings of Richmond during his tour of Yorkshire.

To aid our sightseeing tour around the town, AW provides a sketch map identifying places of interest. One spot near the river is somewhat unusual, being identified as a 'Dogs' Toilet'. We did not actually visit this intriguing place, but AW kindly supplies a sketch of it, a lamp post set in a small square of ground allocated for the dogs' relief. A sign on the lamp post depicting a dog is also provided, presumably so that the dogs know the facility is for them! He does add that toilets for human ladies and gentlemen are also provided in the town.

As much as I love the countryside, it was pleasing to enter a town, especially one so rich with olde worlde charm and historic foundation and, as it was already mid-afternoon, we hurried expectantly along the quaintly named Finkle Street. We then stood in the cobbled market square that is dominated by the castle and its remarkably preserved Norman keep. The place where we were standing was originally the outer bailey, a large open space designed to give attackers the minimum of cover. The castle was built by Alan Rufus, one of William the Conqueror's Norman overlords, who had been granted the honour of Richmond along with hundreds of manors throughout England. This bastion, set in an impregnable position, was one of the first castles to be built of stone. Its curtain walls, strengthened with protective towers, were unique at that time and the keep, or tower, was added in the next century.

A visit to the beckoning castle was a must. As we looked round, Maurice asked to be photographed amidst the historic remains, and actually stood unaided in front of the magnificent Norman keep, forsaking the usual obligatory 'lean'. Perhaps he was overcome with pride at having reached this landmark for he even refused the offer of a stake up his back to enable him to stand erect.

As we climbed the stone steps of the keep, now worn smooth by the friction of centuries of use, we were able to peer through the narrow arrow slits in the walls. Looking over the still active River Swale passing beneath the castle's walls made us realise its impregnability. A sheer rock face rises from the riverside and this is then topped by one of the walls. As there is open ground encircling the castle, I would not have wished to have been a member of an invading army approaching through a cascade of arrows whistling around me. Attaining the top of the keep had the reward of superb views over the market square and for miles beyond. Maurice and I strained our eyes for a glimpse of Robin Hood's Bay but were disappointed.

The remainder of the town, a mixture of old narrow alleyways and wide Georgian streets, is full of character and we could not do it justice in the short time available. We did, however, learn of an old legend that King Arthur and his Knights of the Round Table lie beneath the rock upon which Richmond is built, asleep but ready to rise up should England find herself in peril. Apparently Arthur had many associations with the north and, like our old friend Robin Hood, has been everywhere. He should have been around when the Scots raided Richmond. Not being stupid, they left the well-defended castle alone and were eventually bought off by the burgesses of the town with large sums of money and the canny Scots were happy to have that as their plunder. They proceeded to take it out on Marrick and Ellerton Priory instead.

Richmond has always vigorously guarded its heritage and resisted wholesale changes. By so doing, the town retains a unique presence and atmosphere. AW observes that the centre shows little in the nature of twentieth-century 'improvements', apart from the odd lapses such as Woolworths' shop-front.

Feeling footsore and weary with tramping around the town we headed for Maurice's accommodation. I often think that you can feel more tired walking around shops than doing a twenty-mile walk. Perhaps you are drained psychologically as well as financially by a prolonged bout of shopping.

Maurice could now relax and prepare for the following day's march, but I still had a journey to make to the outskirts of town. Here I was received in a very friendly manner by the owner and his wife. I later discovered that he had at one time worked for the same company as me. We had plenty to talk about but I made sure I went to bed early as I was going to need to be fresh for a difficult next day.

Day Nine: Richmond–Osmotherly

I must confess to a late start the following morning, for whilst waiting for Maurice to rejoin me I came across a colleague from work and stayed chatting for longer than was prudent. This was especially ill-advised because we had a long day ahead of us and it was ten o'clock before we got going. I had twenty-five miles to cover to Osmotherly and Maurice had two miles less as he would be staying at Ingleby Cross. Beginning to regret our dalliance, I was cursing my pre-booking at Osmotherly Youth Hostel; had I bitten off more than I could chew?

As so often happens when you are in a hurry, misfortune strikes and so it was in our case. We foolishly left the market square in the wrong direction and lost more time in getting onto the correct route. Worse was to come.

AW warns us to expect much glorious mud ahead which indicates plenty of field walking, but all went well for a time and nearby Easby Abbey was passed. During a confusing rural section of the journey to Catterick Bridge, the way-markers disappeared and after crossing several fields vainly searching for a path, we ended up in a farmyard. Confronting us was a smirking farmer who sarcastically informed us that we, like hundreds of other walkers on his land, had got lost and he seemed to think this was a huge joke. I do understand that some farmers and landowners must be irritated by the mass of walkers who now follow the Coast to Coast walk but, assuming the route is on a public right of way across their land, then surely a few simple directions would prevent strife on both sides, and stop us and the hundred others from blundering around the fields searching for the correct path?

Maurice and I were so upset by the farmer's unhelpful attitude that we left abruptly and made for the nearest road, having had our fill of pathless fields.

We stuck to roads that took us on an unscheduled journey through the fringes of Catterick Camp, the extensive army garrison. Our mood was still black as we approached the A1; we knew we were getting near by the growing roar of traffic rushing along it, and a few moments later, the huge road thundered over our heads as we walked through the underpass. At least we had the comfort of knowing that we had now completed the first two sections of the walk; just one more to go.

On the other side of the A1, Catterick Racecourse appeared on our right. It was silent that day as there was no race meeting scheduled – and it wasn't a Sunday. We met a woman walking a dog, and she told us that the place is all hustle and bustle on Sunday when a market is held in front of the grandstand. Apparently stalls selling goods of every description provide the highlight of many a local's week.

We next came to Catterick Bridge, the site of the Roman fort of Cataractonium. Crossing the fine sturdy bridge over the Swale recalled the fact that the Romans built many of their forts at strategic river crossings. Rejoining the path below the bridge revealed a captivating part of the Swale, much wider now, as it passes between lush vegetation and woodland on either bank. Time did not permit a halt to admire its charms as we were now well behind schedule. This was a pity as the midday sunshine filtered through the trees at every opportunity, dappling the lively surface of the river. We hurried along the river bank for a mile before leaving it for the last time to head for the attractive village of Bolton-on-Swale. Before we turned our back on the river, however, we made ourselves stop for just a minute to have a last look at the river that had been our companion for so many miles. I know AW would not have forgiven us had we rushed ahead without this courtesy.

We approached Bolton-on-Swale along a series of lanes bounded on either side by cultivated fields of enormous length. The ground had flattened out and we were to meet no hills until the finish of the day's walk. If climbing had been involved, I don't think we would have reached the end of what had now become a strenuous slog. Although we were behind schedule, we were feeling reasonably fresh and made good time towards the village with the sun on our backs.

Bolton-on-Swale was looking at its best as we walked through, pausing every now and then to admire some of the gardens which were displaying a riot of colour. We admired the well-maintained and decorative village pump and then set off down the narrow, tree-lined road to the Parish Church. We were obeying AW's instructions to visit the memorial to Henry Jenkins that stands in the churchyard. This proved to be a distinctive stone edifice which dwarfs the surrounding gravestones. The carved inscription is still visible although it had been erected by public subscription as long ago as 1743. Eager to discover more about this presumably famous local citizen, we entered the attractive stone church of St Mary. Inside is a tablet in memory of this modern Methuselah, who is reputed to have lived to the ripe old age of 169. Born at nearby Ellerton in 1500 he supposedly swam across the Swale when he was a hundred, and often acted as a witness at York Assizes in his latter years. He was able to confirm with his long memory the payment of tithes over a great many years and also that long-established rights of way had existed. A story is told of a lawyer who, seeking Jenkins' advice in a legal case, called at his cottage. On seeing this white-haired old man sitting in the garden, the lawyer began to question him. The man replied, 'You'd better ask my father,' Entering the cottage, the visitor found a very old man bent over the fire. 'You'd better ask my father,' said this old man too, 'he's chopping sticks out at the back.' There indeed in the back garden was Henry Jenkins, then aged 166. A nice story, whether or not it's true.

Bolton-on-Swale was in the news a year or two ago for a very different reason. It was nearby that a woman, who was walking the Coast to Coast unaccompanied, was savagely attacked and beaten. What a sad indictment on our society when it is not possible for anyone to enjoy the countryside on her own, free from molestation.

It was now time to gird our loins once more for, according to AW, there is no escape from the forthcoming trek across the low-lying Vale of Mowbray. The area is little walked and though, in theory, it can be crossed by means of footpaths and bridleways, in practice they are rarely used and many have disappeared. Another factor in favour of the roads and lanes is that there is a long way still to go and there really would not be time to recover from getting lost in the poorly-marked fields. AW tells us that we must 'tramp, tramp, tramp' along the tarmac to get this section of the walk over as soon as possible. He tells us that if we look for any contours on his accompanying series of maps, there aren't any because of the dead flat terrain. As you plod mechanically along, he continues, you may think nostalgically of Lakeland and the Yorkshire Dales. In fact, he warns you may feel lonelier here than on the mountains as people are few and far between. Danby Wiske, the only village that we would meet on our level traverse, is in his opinion the lowest part of the walk both literally, as it is only 110 feet above sea level, and psychologically because it creates a yearning for high places.

So it was that Maurice and I embarked on the yomp, with our eyes firmly set on our destination and no inclination for anything else. We set a sharp pace and made good time across the fertile plain until a long diversion round a farm cost us a considerable loss of time. We found a recently constructed fence blocking our approach and a terse notice informing us that the footpath had been diverted away from the farm. Our frustration increased as we were forced farther and farther across the field boundaries and it seemed an age before we were returned to the original route. AW warns of the local disregard for rights of way and said that footpaths may be blocked by obstructions which at worst might include bulls – which, thankfully, we didn't have to tangle with. Our misery was compounded by the mud we encountered which had better adhesive qualities than superglue. Not only did we have to make a wide detour, but we had to carry a large amount of the farmer's fields with us. This did our legs no good at all and probably contributed to our later fatigue.

On reaching Danby Wiske Maurice and I hurried through the village, pausing only to look at the road sign which indicated that we were four miles from Northallerton. Time was now of the essence and we could not dally a single moment. Our feet were becoming increasingly hot as we pounded along. However, we did have time to notice a sign proclaiming the site of the Battle of the Standard which was fought between the English and the Scots in 1138. AW makes the wry comment – one of my favourites in the guide – that before the building of Hampden Park they fought their battles wherever they happened to meet, and 'the English, playing at home, won this match', thus depriving many poor serfs from getting the requisite number of draws on the Treble Chance.

I was very grateful for Maurice's company during that route march. It was a boon to have a companion matching you stride for stride and exchanging light-hearted banter to help the miles along.

As we passed Brompton Moor Farm we caught our first real glimpse of the dark grey mass of the Cleveland Hills which were still several miles away. It raised our spirits to see the North York

Moors appearing at last. Inevitably our hot pace was beginning to tell. Our tramp, tramp, tramp was gradually deteriorating into tra-mp, tr-a-mp, tr-a-a-mp. Muscles began to protest in abused legs and our walking boots were transformed into miniature ovens. Maurice was clearly suffering badly and his bright conversation had faded into occasional short bursts. Sweat poured down his face and his breathing became laboured. I began to feel concern for him as he struggled on, never once complaining. Wondering how best to help him, I was hesitant about stopping, for grim determination was written across his face. I felt that if we did stop he would find it difficult to get going again.

Eventually he solved the problem for me by declaring that he could go no further and that I should leave him. I now realised why he had pushed himself to the limit. He didn't want to hold me back as he knew I still had a good few miles to walk. Also he was concerned that I would not reach the hostel in time for my evening meal. Insisting that I go on without him he slumped down beside a waymarker. This made me realise how bad his condition was for he evidently hadn't even the strength to lean on it. Despite my protestations he told me to be on my way and that he would be able to reach his destination at the Blue Bell Inn at Ingleby Cross. As the village was less than two miles away I reluctantly agreed and arranged to meet him the following morning on Beacon Hill, at the start of the Lyke Wake Walk section.

Trudging along on my own, I crossed a footbridge over the sluggish River Wiske that we had not even noticed on our hurried passage through Danby Wiske. Its meandering course had brought it back across the path. AW comments that it is wandering aimlessly, searching for one of those non-existent contours.

My conscience was troubling me now that I had left Maurice to his own devices. I felt guilty at leaving him slumped by the sign. What a fine friend I had turned out to be, not even sparing the time to accompany him and ensure his safe arrival at the Blue Bell Inn. Surely my meal at the hostel was not that important. Could it be meanness on my part, not wanting to lose a meal that I had paid for in advance? These thoughts ensured a disturbing journey to my next obstacle, the busy dual carriageway of the A19. Hindsight is a wonderful thing and as I listened to the roar of the traffic ahead, I suddenly realised that a meal with Maurice at the pub would have been the ideal solution; I could have walked with him there and gone on to the hostel later. Cursing my selfishness I approached the race-track across my path.

Maurice was temporarily forgotten as I stood waiting for a seemingly non-existent gap in the traffic. Taking my life into my hands I scuttled across each carriageway in turn, realising how a hedgehog must feel just prior to being flattened. The hurtling vehicles seemed intent on a game of 'Hit the Walker'. Reaching the far side unscathed, I heaved a sigh of relief and headed down the road for Ingleby Cross a short distance away.

I felt exceedingly uncomfortable as I walked past the attractive village green, in the middle of which stands the distinctive stone cross that gives the village its name. Just beyond the green I could see the Blue Bell Inn, and in an attempt to ease my conscience I hurried past it as quickly as my tired legs would permit. The village lies at the foot of the Cleveland Hills and some contours were at last returning to AW's drawings. The drawback, of course, was that I now had to start climbing at the end of an already tiring day. In different circumstances it would have been a very pleasant ascent past Arncliffe Hall with its accompanying church and through the wooded slopes beyond.

In quiet seclusion by the steepening road stands Arncliffe Hall and the church in a lovely tree-lined setting. I wished that I had time to stop and admire those charming buildings properly, but had to be content with a quick photograph. Time was pressing and I still had two miles to cover to Osmotherly. Straining up the one-mile climb through Arncliffe Wood, I was rapidly running out of steam. The ancient Mount Grace Priory situated in the wood near to the path had to be given a miss as I could not afford to lose any more time. It was with great relief that I eventually emerged from the wood because it meant the end of the laborious climb. From there it was a gentle descent to the hostel. With as much strength as I could muster I rushed down the sloping path, not bothering to take in the view of the Vale of Mowbray that lay below, its fields and hedges stretching as far as the eye could see. AW would not have approved of this headlong rush, with no time spent in looking at the surroundings.

I finally reached my objective and, panting with exertion, I ripped off my boots and hurried into the dining-room with a couple of minutes to spare. The warden enquired the reason for my haste and when I said I hadn't been sure that he would have kept a meal for me had I been late, he said that he wouldn't have, so it was just as well I galloped the last mile. As I hungrily ate my meal, my mind again returned to Maurice. I hoped that by now he was relaxing in a well-earned bath that would hopefully revive him.

Trusting that my unkempt and sweat-soaked appearance did not put off my dining companions, I struck up a conversation with some of them. Walkers, I soon discovered, were in the minority. The hostel was full of cyclists, and many of them were welcoming, particularly a married couple who had cycled together for many years and toured numerous countries. Their view of walkers was somewhat coloured by an advertisement they had read in a national paper. It was for the ultimate in walking holidays at a hotel in the north of England. Amongst the unlimited comforts and services offered in its purple prose was a chauffeur-driven car to take participants daily to their starting point and return them on completion of their day's walk. Picnic lunches of smoked salmon, caviar and champagne were provided to ease the rigour of their exertions. Walking boots would be cleaned and polished overnight and routes provided that avoided such tiresome things as steep slopes and bogs. I couldn't believe that such pampering actually existed. The only thing that would not be relaxing on such a holiday would be the price. Resolving to tell Maurice about it the following day, I assured the couple that ninety-nine per cent of walking falls far below that standard.

Day Ten: Osmotherly – Great Broughton

The following morning I hurried back along the path from Osmotherly that would return me to Arncliffe Wood. Rejoining the main track along its upper edge I climbed past the unusual looking television booster station sprouting its gigantic metal towers and dishes. It looked incongruous in such a rural setting, but is obviously vital to the viewing public. As far back as Roman times the spot had been used as a signal station, for it offers a fine vantage point from the western fringe of the Cleveland Hills.

The summit of Beacon Hill (928 feet) lay a short distance away and I was immensely relieved to find Maurice waiting for me. He appeared to be his normal cheerful self and happily recovered from the strain of the previous day; he had walked comfortably from Ingleby Cross to meet me. I told Maurice how glad I was to see him in fine fettle and that the day's walk should be much less strenuous. The mileage was considerably less and there would be no distractions. I myself felt much happier now, with Maurice fit and well and a good day in prospect. The weather was dry and reasonably clear, although a haze hung over the farthest reaches of the plain below.

A stiff wind was getting up and Maurice donned his colourful woolly hat that matched the bright red socks that he was wearing. This I thought was a clever ruse on his behalf to enable me to keep him in sight at all times. He must have found some hidden reserves of energy for throughout the day he would often surge ahead of me, particularly when I was dawdling with my camera. His fine singing voice appeared once more and we encompassed a wide repertoire of songs.

With the cares of the previous day now behind us, we set off with jaunty steps along the Lyke Wake Walk, so named because it followed an ancient corpse road used for carrying coffins for burial at Ravenscar, a small village on the coast. We joked that there would, we hoped, be no corpses on this occasion, particularly ours.

The next twenty-eight miles to Glaisdale, where the Cleveland Hills end, AW classes as the finest section of the walk outside Lakeland. I called it our 'up and down' period because the initial two-thirds of the distance was spent ascending and descending the escarpment overlooking the flat plain of Teeside. It was reminiscent of walking the testing Hadrian's Wall section on the Pennine Way. We didn't reckon there would be any great problems with route-finding as the first sixteen miles follow the Lyke Wake Walk which AW tells us has a path that is almost as wide as a road, with signs at the few doubtful points. In his opinion only a genius could go astray; we wondered if this was to be the only time that Maurice or I would be classed as a genius for we were not immune to losing our way. It was easy to define the first part of our walk for the eroded ribbon of land denoting the footpath which stretched beneath us snaked along the top of the escarpment for all to see. We agreed that we were in with a chance.

The day was spent on the 'Big Dipper' of a path crossing heather-clad summits having a variety of unusual names such as Near Moor, Holey Moor, Live Moor and Cold Moor. Our undulating progress was embellished with some landmarks, such as the stone seat on Cringle End accompanied by a view indicator on a stone pillar. This illustrates the many fells that can be seen from that lofty viewpoint, but we were not fortunate enough to have a clear view of them. The seat was apparently erected in memory of Alec Falconer who championed the cause of walking. His grateful devotees had probably erected this unusual memorial on his favourite spot. The seat stands within one mile of the 150-mile point that indicated we had covered more than three-quarters of the walk. Maurice and I leapt around in celebration, although not as violently as my Highland fling near Hadrian's Wall on the Pennine Way. With only forty miles to go to Robin Hood's Bay we weren't taking any chances on falling down the escarpment.

Other notable features of the area are the numerous marker stones and tumuli. Like the Westmorland Plateau, these moors have their reminders of ancient habitation and old trackways. The buttresses of the Wainstones on top of Hasty Bank stand like sentinels from a bygone age above Broughton Plantations, one of the many forests found on the escarpment. Above all, the distinctive abundance of heather gives the North York Moors its own character, although AW remarks that you do need relief from it occasionally.

It proved an interesting day filled with the delight of new surroundings and several unexpected characters whom we met along the way. I had a pleasant surprise when, amongst a party of walkers stomping towards us with heads lowered, I recognised someone whom I had hostelled with one night on the Pennine Way. He nearly passed unobserved as everyone was hiding beneath their tightly drawn hoods, sheltering from the boisterous wind and a heavy shower that had overtaken us. Following a friendly greeting, I learned that he had decided to follow up the previous year's walk with an east to west crossing of the Coast to Coast. I certainly did not envy him and his companions because the prevailing wind was at our backs and they were fighting their way through the teeth of it. AW had been proved correct in his recommendation of the west to east route. Wishing each other luck and a safe completion, we parted with a promise to keep in touch. We didn't

Maurice was having a much better day, despite the mixed weather. He admitted that he had approached the previous day's walk across the Vale of Mowbray with great trepidation, almost admitting defeat before he had started out. The sun appeared and I was just on the point of explaining where I had met my Pennine Way companion when we came across a lone walker, leaning into the wind. This fellow, we discovered, had set himself an unusual target for a long-distance walker. He had apparently taken up our masochistic hobby in his mid-twenties in an attempt to get his inactive body into shape and hit upon the idea of annually walking as many miles in a day as his age in years. This was fine, Maurice and I reckoned, when he was young but it would be progressively more difficult the older he became. Explaining that this challenge would counter the aging process, he alleged that contrary to popular belief he would be capable of greater distances the older he became. He was currently aged forty, hence his journey along the Lyke Wake Walk that covered the same number of miles. We wished him well in his strange enterprise but privately expressed doubts about his continuing to be successful when he reached pensionable age. I also feel that AW would have frowned upon such gallops.

As the descent of Hasty Bank was accomplished we reached the end of our official day's journey along the path. We bade farewell to the undulations here as the following day would entail a flatter course across the moors. As AW points out, accommodation is sparse in the area and we had to make a two-and-a-half-mile road walk to Great Broughton for our night's rest. We were staying in different bed and breakfast accommodation and Maurice, I discovered later, spent a convivial evening in the company of other Coast to Coast walkers. By contrast I was the only guest and on my arrival I was immediately put in my place by the taciturn lady of the house who didn't mince words. I was told sternly to go into the garage, remove my boots and leave them there out of the way of their car. The ambience of the place did thankfully improve and the food was particularly good.

Day Eleven: Great Broughton—Glaisdale

After a tremendous breakfast I became one of the participants in the service offered by what I refer to as the 'Carriers of Clay Bank'. These are the people who feed and shelter weary 'Coast to Coasters' in Broughton. In the morning, for a fee, they return walkers to Clay Bank car park which is near the footpath. The young lady acting as my chauffeur was in a hurry that morning, obviously running late for work. She was so keen to depart that I barely had time to dash to the garage to retrieve my boots and leap into the car without putting them on. The journey was covered in record time and her vehicle screeched to a halt in the middle of the car park, tyres practically smoking. I was immediately propelled from the car, followed quickly by my rucksack and left standing in my stockinged feet as she hurtled away in a cloud of dust. I hadn't even had time to pull on the boots that I was still clutching in my hands as I did not wish to dirty her car by donning them whilst travelling. To add insult to injury, when Maurice arrived, having travelled at a more sedate speed, I found that my lift to the car park had cost me *six* times more than his.

Shrugging off such mercenary thoughts, I looked forward to an enjoyable day's walking. It proved to be just that, as the weather was fine and there was plenty of interest en route. We enjoyed better visibility than the previous day and some of the views were superb, particularly over Rosedale and the oddly named Great Fryup Dale. Although another day of heather-clad terrain, it was rich in variety. On the few occasions when the path became indistinct, we had a springy carpet beneath our feet.

We were joined on part of the day's journey by Maurice's colleagues whom he had met at Broughton and I found them to be extremely approachable and talkative. One of them told me that he had written to AW with an enquiry regarding one of his walks and received a very friendly letter in reply.

The first section of the day crossed Urra Moor where the going was easy. We followed what was formerly a road but was now only a track and passed numerous marker stones, cairns and tumuli. A distinctive stone, called the Hand Stone standing by the side of the wide track, forms one of a line of way-markers stretching over the moor. It was easy to follow the track which still has some of the original stone pavings visible. Botton Head, the summit of Urra Moor, is the highest point (1491 feet) on the Cleveland Hills and from this point, there were extensive views over Farndale toward Rosedale with its distant scar indicating the decline of its old railway. In fact, this part of the North York Moors must have been well served by railways when mining was in full swing. As the path dropped gradually from Urra Moor we met up with the line of the former railway that ran across Farndale Moor to join Rosedale near the Lion Inn at Blakey. The 'Coast to Coast' path follows its line for six miles along the surviving embankment. It makes an excellent stretch of easy walking, but its original use was to serve the ironstone mines around Rosedale. Iron ore had been mined in the area for centuries and this intriguing line was built in 1861 to carry the high-grade ore to the steelworks of Teeside and Durham. Making good time along this convenient elevated path, we crossed the head of Farndale where A W says that speeds of up to five miles per hour would be reached.

Although marching along this high-level highway at a smart pace, we could not aspire to such a rate, but we did come across a discarded walking boot just visible amongst the heather. It looked in decent condition with a new-looking red lace. I suggested that Maurice should take the lace and then find one to match it, thereby complementing the other red parts of his outfit, but he smilingly declined. One could only guess at how the boot came to be left there – possibly through exhaustion and subsequently being carried to the nearest habitation, carelessly minus one boot. Maurice added that we should keep a look out for a walker hopping along the path, or one using a crutch and bearing a parrot on his shoulder.

Despite maintaining a reasonable speed we were overtaken by an enthusiastic group of walkers near the point where the Lyke Wake Walk path leaves the Coast to Coast for a while. Judging by their parched expressions and dangling tongues they were hell bent on reaching the Lion Inn at Blakey by opening time. That oasis amidst a desert of ling and heather is the only watering hole for miles around, acting as a magnet for thirsty, battle-scarred walkers. It stands a tantalising two miles farther along the path in a prime position overlooking the charms of Rosedale. The head of the dale can be reached along the unfenced road that passes the inn, a popular route for sightseeing motorists. Dating back to the sixteenth century, the isolated inn formerly quenched the thirst of coal miners and iron workers. Maurice and I did not succumb to its lure, feeling that we could become so comfortable inside that the rest of the day's walk would be abandoned.

The next section of route after the inn follows the road that climbs the dale before branching off to rejoin the Lyke Wake Walk. We soon had to say goodbye to the tarmacadam and hello again to the peat and heather as we left the road at a stone boundary post known as Margery Bradley. This is a good area for unusual names because close by stand three distinctive ancient stone crosses each with an intriguing name. Side by side farther up the road that we had just left stand two conventional tall crosses called Old Ralph and Young Ralph. Presumably father and son, Maurice and I reckoned. Closer to our path was a dumpy stone with what resembles a head on it. Not looking much like a cross, it bears the unflattering name of Fat Betty. Anyone walking the Coast to Coast by the name of Betty would have cause to feel insulted at this point.

The terrain was rather difficult now for we were alternately squelching through slime or goose-stepping through the heather like Hitler's storm troopers. There was the compensation of a magnificent view along the whole extent of Rosedale. We skirted its head and admired its colourful heather-clad upper reaches that eventually changed to the contrasting vivid greenery of the valley floor. A mile farther on we finally parted company with the Lyke Wake Walk near a signpost bearing the name 'Fryup', a name guaranteed to give us an appetite. We were consequently soon enjoying our break, sitting on Great Fryup Head with its extensive view over the equally lovely Great Fryup Dale. Basking in the afternoon sunshine, we could make out the North Sea shimmering in the distance.

Excitement welled up inside us as our goal beckoned. There was even foolish talk of forsaking our night's stop at Glaisdale and heading straight for the coast, but prudence prevailed; there were twenty-five miles remaining to Robin Hood's Bay and we had to concede that we couldn't cover such a distance by nightfall. How impatient we had become when victory was within our grasp.

Abandoning thoughts of a quick finish to our walk, we were seduced by the hot sun into a long rest. Consequently we felt lethargic as we crossed Glaisdale Moor, joining a wide track known as Whitby Road, which was once a well-used highway. In front of us lay Glaisdale Rigg with the Esk valley partially visible beyond. We later found this charming secluded valley, which we were to follow for several miles the next day, to be a real gem.

Walking was easy now and in what seemed no time at all we were standing on the lower edge of the declining ridge of Glaisdale Rigg, looking down on our destination, the village of Glaisdale. The tree-lined valley sides obscured many of its buildings but we could make out the church and the nearby railway. Beyond this idyllic setting, the winding valley ran its course towards the fertile coastal plain.

As we followed an easy descent to the outskirts of the village, Maurice and I agreed that we had enjoyed a day of variety and contrasting beauty that would be difficult to repeat. We were not to know it then, but our last day's walk would be equally rewarding. Still having a certain amount of strength and time remaining, we walked through the village to examine two of its landmarks. The first was the railway station which, although quite small, has an impressive stone, castellated frontage. Just down the road stands Glaisdale's claim to fame, its well-known Beggar's Bridge which spans the River Esk. A fine, high-arched stone packhorse bridge, it has stood at that spot since the seventeenth century and there is a local legend attached to it. Apparently a young man from a very poor family fell in love with a girl who lived across the river, before the convenience of a bridge. It was extremely difficult to cross the swift-flowing river to meet his girl friend so he vowed to the girl that would leave the village to seek his fortune, and that when this was accomplished he would return, build a bridge so he could meet her regularly and eventually marry her. He did all that he had promised, built what became known as Beggar's Bridge, married his girl and, true to all good legends, lived happily ever after.

Maurice could not resist requesting I take a photograph of him on the bridge, displaying once more his subtle art of 'leaning' on the parapet. If he had been around in the early days of the bridge he wouldn't have been able to strike such a pose because the parapets were not added until later.

Maurice and I were conveniently staying at the same place for the first time that evening, which turned out to be a revelation. The three-storey house was beautiful both inside and out, and the owners were most hospitable. It was very nicely decorated, its walls lined with paintings and old photographs. Everywhere was Victoriana, period furniture, stuffed birds and animals; they showed us two stuffed buzzards and an owl which had been knocked down and killed near the house. The centrepiece of the dining room was a magnificent mahogany table that could seat twelve guests. Its legs were beautifully carved, as were the accompanying chairs. As we ate our supper Maurice and I emulated the imaginary lord and lady of the baronial mansion sitting at each end of the massive table and sliding such things as salt and pepper pots to each other down the great expanse of mahogany.

Another unusual feature was the numerous poems, rhymes and cryptic quotes adorning the bathroom and toilet walls. One that particularly caught my eye read, 'Lord give me patience – but please hurry!' A sumptuous sleep in ultra-soft beds guaranteed total satisfaction and we agreed the next day that our stay was one of the most memorable that we had ever experienced.

Day Twelve: Glaisdale – Robin Hood's Bay

The time had now arrived to start our final day's journey on the Coast to Coast Walk. This, according to AW, has a wide variety of scenery. So it proved, as we enjoyed a mixture of river bank, moorland and cliff-top walking. Although the path is far from straight and includes a five-mile detour through Hawsker it was a fitting end to our twelve-day traverse of the country.

AW warns against excessive haste to reach Robin Hood's Bay as the surrounding are too good to be rushed. True to his word we were surrounded by pleasant pastoral views as we passed through the village of Egton Bridge which stands in an attractive wooded riverside setting. Egton Manor, amidst its luxurious and impressive grounds, would make many a weary walker envious of its abundant charms. We were glad that we had forsaken our spontaneous and idiotic idea to dash to the coast on the previous afternoon.

The sparkling, tree-lined River Esk took us to the outskirts of Grosmont, a small village astride the North York Moors Railway. As we arrived at its old-fashioned station, reminiscent of a bygone age, a steam locomotive conveniently pulled in. Such engines take passengers along the Whitby to Pickering line, and the section from Grosmont to Goathland is operated privately by enthusiasts of the North York Moors Railway Society. Our brief visit to the station took me back to my childhood when I loved to travel in the steam trains, or just to hear their distinctive chuff. The village itself has an engaging charm, being set in a valley surrounded by tranquil, rolling hills. It is certainly a place for tourists, flocking to admire its station and spending their money in the adjacent souvenir shop.

A short, sharp climb up the road took us out of Grosmont and onto open moorland once more. We were now amongst the familiar mixture of heather, stones and tumuli again. After crossing Sleights Moor, we negotiated the busy Whitby to Pickering road with care. We weren't used to such traffic and it would have been a great pity to be flattened by a speeding vehicle so near to the finish. This performance was to be repeated a few miles further on when the Robin Hood's Bay to Guisborough road appeared across our path.

Dropping down from the moor we entered the hamlet of Littlebeck, tucked away in a deep valley, reminiscent of Egton Bridge. It stands in similar surroundings, on the banks of the Little Beck, and is enveloped in more of the very attractive woodland. The refurbished Old Mill, whose power was formerly provided by the beck, stands quietly and tastefully amongst the trees. A walk along the beck brought us to a massive stone which has been hollowed out and furnished with seats. It bears the name of 'The Hermitage' and its exterior is covered with numerous initials and inscriptions which have been carved over the centuries. One prominent inscription above the entrance indicates the date of 1790.

A little further on, a resplendent waterfall known as Falling Foss cascades over rocks at the side of the path. It formed a fitting conclusion to our waterside walks, for we were soon to climb to the final stretch of moorland before the coast was reached. Parts of this moor are quite boggy, but AW tells us not to worry about wet feet with only a few miles to accomplish. As we skirted the Whitby to Scarborough road a tantalising road sign beckoned, indicating that Robin Hood's Bay was a mere two miles away. AW advised against the temptation to take this short cut via a side road, but recommends that we stick to our guns and press on across country to Hawsker. This we did, but our impatience was gathering momentum.

Our pace definitely quickened as our journey's end drew near but it was here that we were slightly held up by some angry lapwings as we walked across their territory. Obviously intent on steering us away from their nearby nests, they circled above us, their screeching calls emulating the sound of rusty, swinging gates. One particularly aggressive bird started a dive-bombing act, swooping low over our heads. Maurice and I were not going to be distracted with victory so close, or be lured from our path. A few loud curses ensured that the offending bird kept its distance. As we left the open countryside to join the lane that would lead us to Hawsker the birds flew away, their mission accomplished.

The two miles to the last village before Robin Hood's Bay were soon covered in our haste to reach the coast. Standing at the crossroads in the centre of Hawsker, we couldn't imagine that some walkers chose to stay the night here, so close to their goal, despite AW's explanation as to why people might want to stay there. Our anticipation was now so great we would have been incapable of delaying completion of our walk for a further night.

In his introduction to the final day, AW reminds the walker to think back to when he last saw the Irish Sea, and to give thanks that he didn't succumb to the temptation in Patterdale of staying in the Lake District. He agrees that, although the beauty of Lakeland cannot be surpassed, the cross-England route will have shown the walker much that is new and interesting. And we agreed entirely; in fact, we had a little sing-song to celebrate.

Hurrying from Hawsker, the lure of the North Sea becoming

stronger by the minute, we hardly paused to take in our surroundings. Only caravan sites stood between us and our target; to gaze at last over the North Sea, our goal for so long. A further ten minutes of brisk walking brought us to the cliff top with a great expanse of surprisingly blue water glistening before us in the afternoon sunshine. It was not time for the last celebration yet, however, as there is a final sting in the tail of the Coast to Coast. We still had a three-mile walk along the cliff top path to our final objective. To record my impatience, I asked Maurice to take a photograph of me complaining about this final burden.

Despite a certain feeling of frustration Maurice and I quite enjoyed the elevated walk along the promontory of Ness Point since the coastal scenery was so different from the moors. After all we were, according to AW, now on the royal road to Robin Hood's Bay. It is amazing how energy courses through the body when your destination is almost within your grasp. With our pace hotting up even more, we strode along those bracing cliff tops. We even began to make plans to walk together the following year which did come to fruition when we spent a splendid fortnight walking in Scotland. However, that is another story.

Eventually as we rounded Ness Point itself, Robin Hood's Bay could be seen below us, huddling in its narrow cove. Lush meadowland rolled down to the sea, forming a patchwork around the village of green fields criss-crossed by sturdy hedges. The North Sea rolled energetically over the shore and several small boats were bobbing around amongst its waves. Descending the narrow streets to our meeting with the eagerly anticipated sea was like taking a journey into the past. The old village has retained its character and charm, access to the shore thankfully being denied to cars. Brightly-painted buildings pulsating with character lined our route, as did the inevitable souvenir shops and pleasant cafés. Aching legs and troublesome blisters forgotten, we scuttled down the steep hill to the sea which was beckoning us at the bottom.

Immediately I reached the water's edge, I dipped the toe of my boot into the sea, as instructed by AW. Maurice did the same and this symbolic act effectively completed our walk from the Irish Sea to the North Sea, from one side of England to the other, with 190 miles in between. 'One hundred and ninety beautiful miles,' I shouted, and gave my faithful walking companion a hug, and we both let out a rather undignified whoop of unconcealed joy. 'We have made it!'

Several locals leaning on the rails outside the Bay Hotel looked on impassively. They were undoubtedly used to observing periodic invasions by parties of bedraggled people bearing large packs on their backs and wearing size ten boots. The performance of dashing to the water's edge followed by great hilarity and back slapping was to them commonplace. Not wanting to disappoint them Maurice and I performed the ritual hand-pumping and back-thumping routine.

A short time later, sitting on the stone steps by the beach, we relaxed, took stock and examined our blisters. As AW says, we had reached the end of the road and could now rest upon our laurels. He suggests a celebratory pint in the Bay Hotel, but stresses that this would be at our own expense. It is no use charging it to him, as we had done at the end of the Pennine Way. The backdrop of Robin Hood's Bay and the view over the North Sea provided a fitting climax to AW's Coast to Coast Walk. I know of no better way to end my tribute to the remarkable man than by completing his own long-distance walk.

Thank you, AW! You are sorely missed.

Finale

I hope that you have enjoyed this venture in the footsteps of Britain's best loved fellwalker. My book will have achieved its purpose if you have been entertained by my struggle to graduate from a weekend stroller to an accomplished long-distance walker. If you are not yet a walker, I hope you have been encouraged to get out there and have a go. The world of walking is a friendly and rewarding one. It is not imperative to walk great distances or climb the most arduous of peaks. What is important is that you enjoy yourself whatever your limitations. There is a world of fascinating countryside – some of the best in the world – waiting to be explored.

You cannot have a better teacher than I had in AW. The legacy that he has left is the conversion of countless people who would otherwise never have sampled the sights and sounds of the fells and open spaces. AW teaches us far more than how to put one foot in front of the other; attributes such as sticking to the task whatever the difficulties will be learned, and not being afraid of walking in silence for miles on end. Challenge and adversity bring out the best in people, and true companionship can be experienced at such times. AW is an inspiration to us all and his books do not end with describing the fells, or the walks; they also teach us about life.

Three Peaks Walk

Information

The following literature can be obtained from: The Penyghent Café, Horton-in-Ribblesdale, Near Settle, North Yorkshire, BD24 0HE

'Yorkshire's Three Peaks' leaflet issued by the Yorkshire and Humberside Tourist Board. Information includes:

- Booking-out and booking-in procedure
- Safety instructions
- Safety equipment checklist
- Availability of the monitoring service – i.e. every day *except* Tuesday and Friday

'Three Peaks footpath map and guide' compiled by Arthur Gemmell

Other reference material

OS Map 1:25,000 Outdoor Leisure – Map 2 Yorkshire Dales – Western Area

Walks in Limestone Country by A. Wainwright (published by Michael Joseph Ltd)

Wainwright in the Limestone Dales by A. Wainwright (published by Michael Joseph Ltd)

APPENDIX 2
The Fellsman Hike

Information

Entry forms and information leaflet from: The Fellsman Hike, PO Box 30, Keighley, West Yorkshire, BD21 3EP (Please include a stamped addressed envelope)

Information leaflet includes:
- The objective
- Trophies (team/individual) awarded for specific categories
- Rules of entry
- Safety rules i.e. Boots
  Clothing
  Equipment to be carried
- Disqualification or retirement rules
- Entry system
- Accommodation prior to and after the hike

Hike Route

It must be stressed that the route is negotiated annually as it does not necessarily follow public rights of way. Permission is sought each year for access from the farmers and landowners concerned.

Pennine Way

Accommodation/Information

YOUTH HOSTELS ASSOCIATION

General information on YHA and accommodation: YHA National Office, Trevelyan House, St Albans, Hertfordshire AL1 2DY; Tel. (01727) 855215
YHA Northern Region, PO Box 11, Matlock, Derbyshire DE4 2XA; Tel. (01426) 939215

Accommodation enquiries and application for leaflet and booking form: Laurie and Ann Rhodes, YHA Pennine Way Bureau, Mearbeck, Bridge End Mill, Settle, North Yorkshire BD24 9JS; Tel. & Fax (01729) 823844

PENNINE WAY ASSOCIATION

The Pennine Way Accommodation and Camping Guide (current price 90p): John Needham, 23 Woodland Crescent, Prestwich, Manchester M25 9WQ

THE RAMBLERS' ASSOCIATION

General walking information and accommodation: The Ramblers' Year Book and Accommodation Guide, The Ramblers' Association, 1/5 Wandsworth Road, London SW8 2XX; Tel. 0171 582 6878

Other Reference Material

OS MAPS

Outdoor Leisure Series: 1:25,000
  Map 1 – The Peak District Dark Peak Area
  Map 21 – South Pennines
  Map 10 – Yorkshire Dales – Southern Area
  Map 2 – Yorkshire Dales – Western Area
  Map 30 – Yorkshire Dales – Northern and Central Areas
  Map 31 – Teesdale

Landranger Series 1:50,000
  Sheet 110 – Sheffield and Huddersfield
  Sheet 109 – Manchester
  Sheet 103 – Blackburn and Burnley
  Sheet 98 – Wensleydale
  Sheet 92 – Barnard Castle
  Sheet 91 – Appleby
  Sheet 86 – Haltwhistle
  Sheet 80 – Cheviot Hills
  Sheet 74 – Kelso

COUNTRYSIDE COMMISSION

Information regarding revised route (Free Leaflet CCP 366):
Countryside Commission Postal Sales, PO Box 124, Walgrave,
Northampton NN6 9TL; Tel. (01604) 781848

GUIDE BOOKS

Pennine Way Companion by A. Wainwright, Revised Edition 1994
  (published by Michael Joseph Ltd)
National Trail Guide (CCG05): *Pennine Way South* by Tony
  Hopkins
National Trail Guide (CCG06): *Pennine Way North* by Tony
  Hopkins

The last two are available from: Countryside Commission Postal
Sales, address and telephone number as above. Please ring and
check price before sending payment with your order.

APPENDIX 4
Lake District

Reference Material

GUIDE BOOKS

Wainwright's Pictorial Guides to the Lakeland Fells (all published by Michael Joseph Ltd):

    Book One: The Eastern Fells
    Book Two: The Far Eastern Fells
    Book Three: The Central Fells
    Book Four: The Southern Fells
    Book Five: The Northern Fells
    Book Six: The North Western Fells
    Book Seven: The Western Fells
    The Outlying Fells of Lakeland

LARGE FORMAT BOOKS

All published by Michael Joseph Ltd:

    Fellwalking with Wainwright
    Wainwright On The Lakeland Mountain Passes
    Wainwright's Favourite Lakeland Mountains
    Wainwright In The Valleys Of Lakeland
    Wainwright's Tour in the Lake District

OS MAPS

Outdoor Leisure Series 1:25,000

    Map 4 – The English Lakes – North Western Area
    Map 5 – The English Lakes – North Eastern Area
    Map 6 – The English Lakes – South Western Area
    Map 7 – The English Lakes – South Eastern Area

Coast to Coast Walk

Accommodation/Information

YOUTH HOSTELS ASSOCIATION

General information on YHA and accommodation: *see* page 238

Accommodation enquiries and application for leaflets and booking forms: YHA Coast to Coast Bureau, PO Box 11, Matlock, Derbyshire DE4 2XA

Leaflets include:
Coast to Coast Accommodation Package for Independent Walkers
YHA Guided Walking Holiday Across England

THE RAMBLERS' ASSOCIATION: *see* page 238.

INSTEP LINEAR WALKING HOLIDAYS

Coast to Coast Walk Information Service (Self-guided walk accommodation/transport and luggage service): 35 Cokeham Road, Lancing, West Sussex BN15 0AE; Tel. & Fax (01903) 766475

THE COAST TO COAST PACKHORSE

Accommodation package, luggage and passenger transport including daily minibus service and car parking: Mr and Mrs J Bowman, West View, Hartley, Kirkby Stephen, Cumbria CA17 4JH; Tel. (017683) 71680

Coast to Coast Bed and Breakfast Accommodation Guide: Mrs Doreen Whitehead, East Stonesdale Farm, Keld, Richmond, North Yorkshire DL11 6LJ; Tel (01748) 886374 (Please send a stamped addressed envelope and £2)

Other Reference Material

OS MAPS (IN CONJUNCTION WITH MICHAEL JOSEPH LTD)

Outdoor Leisure Series 1:25.000
    Map 33 – Coast to Coast Walk – St Bees to Keld
    Map 34 – Coast to Coast Walk – Keld to Robin Hood's Bay

GUIDE BOOKS

A Coast To Coast Walk by A. Wainwright, Revised Edition 1994
    (published by Michael Joseph Ltd)

LARGE FORMAT BOOKS

Wainwright's Coast to Coast Walk (published by Michael Joseph
    Ltd)

Index